Paper Cuts

Paper Cuts

How I Destroyed the British Music Press and Other Misadventures

Ted Kessler

WHITE
RABBIT

First published in Great Britain in 2022 by White Rabbit,
an imprint of The Orion Publishing Group Ltd
Carmelite House, 50 Victoria Embankment
London EC4Y 0DZ

An Hachette UK Company

10 9 8 7 6 5 4 3 2 1

A CIP catalogue record for this book is
available from the British Library.

ISBN (Hardback) 978 1 4746 2553 1
ISBN (eBook) 978 1 4746 2555 5
ISBN (Audio) 978 1 4746 2556 2

Typeset by Input Data Services Ltd, Somerset

Printed in Great Britain by Clays Ltd, Elcograf S.p.A.

www.whiterabbitbooks.co.uk
www.orionbooks.co.uk

Contents

Part Four: Post-Millennium Tension

The Content Abyss

For a long while, there was a joke in the office at *Q*, the monthly music magazine where I worked as editor, about the Content Abyss.

All paid-for print media was being sucked into that pit, we'd say, as we gloomily scrolled through thousands of new album reviews and interviews with musicians online, prospecting for golden nuggets in amongst all the tat tossed liberally down the tube. Publishers both highbrow and low chucked everything into it, but very few charged for their work. It was all there, for free. What was the business model? Who knows. Eyeballs on the content was all that mattered, even though advertising was in an even worse shape on the Internet than in the physical realm. Quality control was minimal, hobbled by a lack of attributed resources, so quantity was king. I'm writing in the past tense because this particular story is old. But it goes on. Just chuck it down there, as much and as often as possible. Anything will do.

For our part, the company who published *Q*, Bauer, provided a big clue about where they believed the future of Internet publishing lay when they made our website editor, Paul Stokes, redundant in 2015. For a while he'd hung on to his job by doubling his workload and maintaining both *Q* and our fellow Bauer music magazine *Mojo*'s online presence. Then Bauer did some sums and the Internet came up short. We were print propositions. We lived within our means as dictated by the balance sheet. Profit, no loss. The era of online financial speculation had been squandered long before I was elevated to editor in 2017.

The Content Abyss

And yet, despite our lofty ideals about being a premium print product, we were unable to pull ourselves clear from the malign power of the Content Abyss. The sheer volume of free gear being bunged down it impinged noticeably upon *Q*. On one hand, we hated that there was so much undeserving nonsense covered online. But on the other, we increasingly found ourselves being gazumped for exclusives with big (and sometimes not so big) artists. We'd plead our case to press agents, explaining that a physical magazine that plots ten luxuriously designed pages for a profile, with commissioned photography and seasoned editors proofing everything, ensured much deeper engagement from the public with an artist bleating about their creative toil, drug addiction or love life. People read print. Online, readers roll through a story without digesting any nuance or detail, in a rush to be the first to post about it on social media. Yes, the earthly representative would reply, but Bumfluff.com get a million eyeballs a week. *Q* sells 30,000 copies a month now. It's what the label and artist want. They like the numbers.

Making the case became increasingly, fruitlessly hopeless, and boring to argue. The pull of the Content Abyss was inexorable. Everything went in.

Friday is generally the day of the week new music is released, and that was also the day our increasing impotence became most apparent. My deputy Niall Doherty would sit next to me, flicking from site to site, reading out what was up on the broadsheet newspaper music pages. Instead of charging directly, several broadsheets offered the opportunity to salve your conscience by stumping up for that 300-word Bonnie 'Prince' Billy album review or 2,000-word Carly Rae Jepsen profile *after* digestion, not before ('we've noticed you've visited this site 695 times in the last year, please consider a small donation if you can, reader'). When we had finished wiping that gruel from our lips, we'd turn to the music blogs that had hoovered up the week's remaining flotsam and jetsam for their analysis and interrogation. This, in particular, was hazardous research that felt as if with each line ingested it damaged the ability to write our own coherent sentences. 'Oh well,' we'd laugh darkly, as we considered our quaint model of providing physical goods in fair exchange for money. 'More meat for the Content Abyss.'

Then, one sunny summer's day in 2020, *Q* was also sucked into the chasm.

An email arrived from our publisher early on Monday, 18 May inviting the five permanent *Q* staff members to an online Microsoft Teams meeting with her at 9.30 a.m. The meeting was titled 'Publishing Update'.

'This looks ominous,' texted Niall.

It did. We'd been sent home to work in mid-March as Covid-19 sunk its claws into London, and we had produced two and a half issues of *Q* from our respective bedrooms and kitchen tables. It hadn't been easy, it had been stressful, but the imposed limits of not being able to gather stories for the magazine in our normal fashion had produced some of the best issues we'd worked on. Necessity being the mother of invention and all that jazz. We had some good ideas up our sleeve for the next few months as well. Despite this, *Q* magazine did not appear to be selling well. We had been in lockdown, prior to which the news-stand had accounted for over half our sales. Non-essential shops were closed and there were new hurdles involved with getting the magazines delivered to the few stores that were open anyway. People were only meant to leave their homes for essential supplies and exercise. Did buying a music magazine qualify as either? Seemingly not.

I was sent the sales stats of the magazine and those of our rivals on a weekly basis and, to be honest, I struggled to read the jumble of numbers at the best of times. Like many subjects, maths is not a strong point. But even I could see that sales looked depressingly like we were at least 50 per cent under the budgeted sales. That surely couldn't be right. The subscription numbers were up, and we were selling a load directly online too. That news-stand sales had to be wrong. I asked the question. Should I be worried about that number?

'No, don't be. It's in line with where we thought we'd be once we recalibrated due to the pandemic.'

That was the message I received on Thursday. Yet, here was the email inviting me to a 'Publishing Update' on Monday.

I joined the meeting. Five square boxes, some clear, some buffering. I knew all these faces so well. They belonged to my comrades, my friends. We'd all worked together for at least ten years. One colleague, the production editor Simon McEwen, had joined a month before I had in 2004, sixteen years earlier, back when the Internet still seemed like an opportunity, not an assassin. Chris Catchpole, the reviews editor, had been the teenage work-experience tea ninja then. I instantly recognised the pale, clenched-teeth tension in them all. Outside, the sky was the deepest, we're-all-going-on-a-summer-holiday-no-more-worries-for-a-week-or-two blue. Even the nearby A12 had fallen into locked-down silence. I could hear birdsong. It was glorious.

A sixth box appeared. *Good morning, everyone. There's no easy way to begin this meeting, so let's just start . . .*

The news was indeed bad. Due to the devastation to our profit margin since the start of the pandemic, the *Q* brand would now be made available for sale. If it was not bought within a month, we'd be closed down. In the meantime, our roles were all placed into consultation. There was some very mild protestation, but, really, what could we say? We logged off and awaited the invitations to our first online consultation meeting with human resources the next morning.

I was shocked, but not surprised. I had been made well aware of the delicate ecosystem I was overseeing upon being appointed editor. We'd been through one drastic round of redundancies in 2015, reducing the workforce by half. Each year, the freelance words and photo budget was punishingly reduced – quickly it became clear that unless the staff wrote the bulk of the magazine each month we would never meet budgetary expectations. I was also tasked every twelve months with discovering new revenue streams, whatever that meant. My view then and now, however, is that you work with what you have as best you can, that imagining and then collaboratively producing your own contemporary music magazine each month without corporate interference is the very pinnacle of human existence. All my employers wanted me to do was make a really good monthly music magazine that didn't lose money. I loved that job. It was what I'd spent thirty years inching my way towards.

Before the pandemic struck, all the *Q* plates were spinning just as they should. Budgets were on target. We'd agreed media partnerships with festivals which created satisfactory additional revenue streams. The magazine was singing – though let me not kid you into believing that our demise was entirely due to a perfect storm of the Content Abyss and Covid-19. There had also been serious, brutally stupid editorial missteps that had amputated readers over previous decades. I'd witnessed all that. Been part of it, too. In March I was nevertheless awarded an extra month's wages as a bonus for hitting targets. By May, the worm had turned so violently that the title was either going to be divested or I would be made redundant.

Locked in our homes to keep Covid-19 at bay, the disease had nevertheless found a way inside. We admitted defeat.

We wondered who would really want to take ownership of a fragile print magazine on life support at the height of a pandemic. Quite a few people, it turned out. That old red *Q* logo meant something. It had valuable brand recognition. We were told that Bauer would need to extend our consultation period another month to continue negotiations with several bidders. This would require us to produce a second final issue of *Q*, too – though it may not be the *final* issue, so please don't be too explicit about it being (another) final issue. I ignored that directive.

I knew that one of the bidders was a large multinational entertainment company who had no interest in print but probably could've done some damage with a well-loved music brand name, because they'd asked me for the Bauer contact details. I never found out who the others were, but they must have been serious as we ended that second month still unsure of the future. We were asked to hang on for another couple of weeks, then we'd know either way. In the end, there was no sale. People wanted *Q*, but – and this is just idle speculation – our 15,000 subscribers were probably too valuable to just sell on. As soon as we closed, the subscribers were transferred (with an opt-out option, of course) to lucky old *Mojo* magazine.

When I joined, *Q* comfortably outsold Bauer's heritage music monthly *Mojo* by nearly two to one. *Q*'s remit was to cover the big music stars of the current era; *Mojo* looked in the rear-view at yesterday's gold. Both magazines were promoted each month with cover-mounted CDs and gifts. Then, in 2007, in an experiment to see how the market would take to a music magazine that withdrew from the covermount arms race, *Q*'s then-editor and its publisher (who was also *Mojo*'s publisher) removed six of its twelve annual covermount CDs. Within a year or so, *Q* was down to one CD per year. *Mojo* did not remove any of its CDs. By 2010, *Mojo* had overtaken *Q* in sales. When it closed, *Q* was producing thirteen issues per year to generate the required revenue, none of which were promoted with a covermount gift of any description. *Mojo*, meanwhile, still had a CD every month, but only needed to print twelve issues because it was also now outselling *Q* by nearly two to one. That, I think, concludes the experiment. Our final penalty for this foolish survey was to gift *Mojo* all of *Q*'s subscribers, too. Boo-hoo.

In the last week of July, we agreed to return to the office in Camden to clear out our lockers, remove old shoes from under desks and rummage through postbags for anything worth selling. We needed to hand over IT and door passes, too.

Niall drove by my home in Wanstead in his family wagon, then we picked up Chris in Walthamstow and nosed the vehicle towards Camden. As we drove, my phone rang. I looked at the name: Ted Cummings, an avuncular old-school press officer who had been PR-ing musicians for even longer than I'd been interviewing them. He'd called several times the previous week, but I'd blanked him, along with all my music business contacts. I wasn't ready to accept condolences. I'd turned down all press invitations to muse over the end of *Q*, too. I didn't want to talk to a stranger about the death of my industry and my subsequent unemployment. Leave me to soak in it alone, please.

Ted kept ringing though. Fuck it.

'Ted, hello,' he said. 'It's Ted.'

'Hello, Ted.'

He had something important to run by me, he explained. Paul Heaton, the singer and songwriter famous for fronting the Housemartins in the 1980s, the Beautiful South in the 1990s and subsequently as a solo artist alongside Jacqui Abbott, wanted to pass a message on.

'Oh. That's nice,' I thought.

Earlier in the year, before the arrival of the pandemic, we had started work on the annual Q Awards, which we'd booked to take place in October as usual, at the Roundhouse in Camden. To make the whole caboodle work financially, so that we didn't have to charge artists to enter, which is a typical awards racket, we instead planned two gigs for which fans bought tickets. One gig was to be the night before the awards and the other directly after the awards. We had done that in previous years, too. It meant we broke even. This year, Paul Heaton was going to play one night. His was also the only award we knew for sure we'd be handing out. He'd told Simon Goddard during a recent *Q* interview that he'd never won an award, despite having a knack for selling huge numbers of good records. He'd scored number one singles and albums. He sold out arenas and stadiums. His music had been repeatedly subversive, yet also massively popular. In the Housemartins, he'd fused a typical 1980s jangle-pop guitar sound with atypical soul vocals that preached strident socialism. Even the name of his mainstream pop act the Beautiful South was sarcastic, a radio-friendly vehicle he used to taunt the monarchy and Christians, amongst others. When the Beautiful South split, they'd sold 15 million albums of this provocative yet middle-of-the-road music. No prizes, though. Just money and adoration, not industry or peer recognition. It was unusual in a business prone to back-slapping. Unfair, too, I thought. A few years earlier, he'd even had to hand over a prestigious songwriting award to his former Housemartins colleague Norman Cook, a.k.a. Fatboy Slim. Cook made an embarrassed acceptance speech saying it was all the wrong way round. He was right. It was. So we were going to get Norman Cook to hand over a Classic Songwriter Q Award to Paul Heaton. But then coronavirus rained on our smart-arse parade. I assumed this was why Ted Cummings had called.

'I'm so sorry about the awards,' I told Ted, as we drove through Finsbury Park. 'I wish we could still put Paul's gig on and give him that award.'

'No, it's not that,' replied Ted, sharply. 'Paul Heaton wants to make a donation to you to thank you for all that *Q* has done for him over the years.'

'I'm sorry, what?'

'He says that *Q* was there for him when he needed support and now he wants to be there for you when you need it, too. He wants to give you £1,000 for each of *Q*'s years. £35,000. He wants to give you £35,000 to do what you see fit with it.'

'£35,000!?'

'Yes.'

'I can't accept that, obviously.'

'You have to! Really. Paul won't take no as an answer.'

'He might have to.'

'He's not like anyone else I've ever met. He asked me to make it really clear that he wants you to have this money. You should take it. You don't know what's around the corner. Please think about it.'

I looked at Niall, who was trying to navigate London's traffic while also shooting me side-eyes and mouthing 'what?'.

'OK, Ted,' I said. 'I'll think about it.'

When *Q* first moved to Academic House, the Bauer offices in Camden, from our more luxurious Shaftesbury Avenue address during the early summer of 2017, we were placated by the promise of more space in our new, specially designated, third-floor room. We could close the doors and play music loudly, without complaint from *Closer*, *Heat* or *Take a Break* magazines. We could decorate the space. We could even write on the walls as they were wipe-clean. I took this literally and scrawled the dates for that year's Q Awards, alongside various forthcoming events, covers and so forth on the wall in bold, black Sharpie. I was the new editor and I was going to do things differently. I was going to make my mark.

We stood in the office on this final warm July morning, packing away our possessions into holdalls and duffel bags. The building was otherwise silently empty. What did I tangibly have to show for my sixteen years at *Q*? A few old magazines, a compilation of articles I'd edited for an anthology, a tankard from an American trip with my surname on it that a photographer had found in his shed. A couple of box sets. I unplugged the Bluetooth speaker we'd blagged and stuffed it into my bag as a bonus. Then I swept everything else into a bin bag and suggested we head to the Lansdowne for some very heavy afternoon drinking. There was nothing else for it. We'd been asked to 'eat out to help out' by the government and, bank accounts swollen with redundancy, we were ready to oblige.

The Content Abyss

'What do you want to do with the wall planner?' asked the always-effervescent building manager, Dublin Jean.

I looked at the giant issue flatplan we'd created specially to fill the wall. Every month, we printed out the finished pages as they were designed and then affixed them to the flatplan so that I could make sure the design flowed from article to article. I was always fucking about with the order and micro-managing our poor art editor Dan Knight, but I'd managed to convince myself and the rest of the team that it helped the magazine's continuity each month.

It also provided a vital service in the longer run: it covered up all the award dates, artist names and forthcoming events I'd written in massive Sharpie letters on the wall in 2017. You cannot wipe away Sharpie pens, only dry-wipe pens, as I discovered shortly after the Q Awards in 2017. Now just a couple of excerpts crept out from beneath the flatplan. The name 'Anna Calvi' was scrawled in my daft hand next to a date, 16 September, as was the legend 'Awards Noms Party 17' in big black letters. I'd left my mark on Q all right. No, I told Jean, we'd leave the planner here.

'No problem,' she replied. 'We'll take it down when you've gone.'

Perfect.

We left our room for one last time, dropping by the lift doors bin bags full of gear we'd always imagined we needed but, in fact, did not. Within all our lifetimes, there had been a dozen magazines devoted to contemporary mainstream music, selling hundreds of thousands of copies to devotees like us each month. Q had been the largest, clearing a quarter of a million copies each month in its early 1990s pomp. The door clicked behind us. Now there were none.

We stepped out of Academic House into the perfectly blue afternoon and strolled alongside the dappled canal towards Primrose Hill where, at a wooden pub table beneath an awning outside the Lansdowne, we toasted the death of our careers. It was the end of music magazine publishing as we knew it, but, sipping ice-cold Peronis in tall pint glasses, we felt fine.

A few hours later, I sat midway up Primrose Hill slurping at an ice-cream cone. In moments of workplace fury over the decades, I'd often thought to myself that I would be able to write my way to revenge over the blowhards and dilettantes who'd fouled the path to my publishing success with their repeated, unconnected flights of idiocy. I no longer felt that way. Now, I felt blessed, amazed that an unqualified, delinquent doofus such as I had lasted this long in the trade in the first place.

I wrote my way to survival because I was otherwise unemployable. Not just because I was a good-for-nothing no-hoper, though I am that, but because I'd once rendered myself impossible to employ. Through a series of very bad choices, I'd been left without alternatives other than self-sufficiency through writing work. Or perhaps those choices had intuitively led me to the only thing I could succeed at? Maybe, subconsciously, that had always been the plan. I'd never before allowed myself to look in the rearview long enough, lest it catch up with me. I had time to reflect now. I was floating, adrift in the abyss. I could trace the journey here, to the last stop aboard music magazine publishing, to this final bite of a 99 Flake, up on Primrose Hill.

I pressed the Uber icon, strolled down the hill, ducked inside a Prius and rolled silently through the streets of Camden, heading back towards the beginning.

Part One
Lost in France

1.

School's Out

It was the end of a difficult first year in France. Nobody wanted to be there, nobody felt at home. And yet, there we were, in late June, in the sun, intact and through the worst of it.

We decided to celebrate.

Jane had brought cigarettes. Chloe had Coca-Cola, Pete: rum. I brought my own sweet self. We pulled back the wire and squeezed through the fence into the woods behind the school. I was twelve years old.

When my mother had told me that we were moving to Paris, I was in the bath in our flat in Paddington. I thought she must be joking. She was not joking. We were moving to Paris. You have got to be fucking joking. I cried. Worse news followed. We were not moving to Paris as advertised. We were moving to a new-build estate above a small village surrounded by fields and eventually forest, about a forty-minute drive from Paris. There was a newsagent, a hairdresser, a doctor's surgery, a bar-tabac, an ice-cream parlour, a bakery, a football pitch, two tennis courts, a municipal pool, a primary school and an hourly bus between the hours of 07:00 and 19:00 to the SNCF station five miles away. It was not Paris.

I wasn't a strong candidate for semi-rural French life. I loved QPR, the Jam, square London paving stones and a girl called Tracy who lived in Swiss Cottage, but my dad, an American journalist who'd lived for all of my life in London as a foreign correspondent, had scored a promotion to Paris. So one gloomy day in August 1980 we packed the flat up and closed the front door upon that massive spider in the kitchen sink for one last time.

In years to come, it would become apparent that the reason he'd deposited us in a new-build house in the furthest possible suburb from the city was because he had a second secret family on the left bank of Paris itself, but back then we just wondered where he was all the time, what we were meant to do with ourselves and why they had overdubbed the theme tune for *Starsky & Hutch* with a French soft rock song. The Internet was yet to be invented, so our only contact with the English-speaking world was a crackling World Service broadcast, an occasional letter from the Jam fan club and a ten-mile Sunday morning drive to Parly 2 shopping centre where yesterday's English newspapers were sold. It was not a happy home.

My younger brothers started at the village primary school and I climbed aboard a forty-five-minute school bus ride to the Lycée International in Saint-Germain-en-Laye. The Lycée was daunting in every respect. An enormous state school that catered for students between nursery age and eighteen, its campus was the size of the village we'd just moved into and it contained around 5,000 students, all of whom, apart from me, were bilingual at the very least. Students received six hours a week in their native tongue and the rest of the time were taught as per their age group in the French state system. New kids like me were given one year to learn French – taught in French, in our Français Spécial class – before being assimilated into the mainstream school system in September. I was hopelessly out of my depth from the start. I had two tracks in my mind and they were occupied by music and football. How was I going to fit French in there, too? Never mind geography or history, in French. My mother bought me the second Cure album for my birthday soon after arrival, which I put the needle to and then attached to my veins, soaking in the sparse grief and turmoil. Lost in a forest, all alone.

I was culture-shocked into a state of permanent daydream. While the Danish, Dutch, German, Portuguese and Italian kids in my class racked up the verb conjugation and vocabulary passes, I scored my wins by following the dubbed storyline in *Dallas* on TV. I will say, though, that the school lunches were consistently, outrageously delicious (four courses, including a cheese plate; the teachers drank from carafes of red wine). Otherwise, I felt as if I was in a war of attrition with France and that France was definitely on top for the first seven months or so.

Remember the happy times. It snowed heavily in January and for four days the school bus was unable to make it up the road to our village. Later that month I caught tonsillitis and missed another week. During a school medical, an old lady tapped my penis three times with a small wooden hammer. And, of course, there was Jane, who I liked very much.

My father never really took to London. A New Yorker, he'd lived with my mother and a crazy half-Siamese cat called Benji in a small apartment on Leroy Street in the heart of Greenwich Village throughout the 1960s, until he knocked her up with me and was immediately but coincidentally given a posting to the London bureau of his newspaper. Weeks before leaving I was born and, shortly after that, they married.

Once, he'd been a Jewish refugee from Nazi Austria, arriving on Ellis Island in February 1939 as a five-year-old with his parents, sister, suitcase and not a word of English. Unlike me, he feared neither change nor challenge, as both were hard-wired into him. Through desperate, sharp-witted necessity he'd mastered English with such skill that he became a news reporter, prized by long-forgotten US newspapers until the *Wall Street Journal* nabbed him and sent him to dreary old London, where he investigated local mobsters and politicians with a nous that prompted the *WSJ* to demand he cover the Middle East too. He wasn't around much, which suited him, as the power cuts and dismal food of 1970s

Britain set within the claustrophobia of a two-bedroom, fifth-floor flat inhabited by three pent-up kids and his wife depressed him.

My mother became a housewife in London, a destination she'd determinedly sought to avoid when she had left England as a nineteen-year-old for a new life in New York a decade earlier, escaping with nothing more than the phone numbers of two acquaintances. She'd taken those numbers to a phone booth upon landing and used them to engineer a new life, working as a secretary, gloriously alive under the bright lights of the sleepless city, happy after a childhood of lonely desperation. She was the only child of Anglo-Irish army parents, sent to boarding school in Brighton and imbued with wanderlust early on. After leaving school, she went hitchhiking across Europe with a boyfriend for a time, then, having tasted life in London, decided her future lay across the Atlantic, where she met my dad upon the leather banquettes of Chumley's bar on Bedford Street, all dark-haired New York charm and cheek. They shacked up together, no plans on the horizon for several years, until I arrived and made plans for them.

When they left London, they left for good. When I left, however, I left only for a short while. We had competing agendas.

As they had quit London for ever, they'd enrolled me in the American section of the Lycée for my six hours of 'home' study per week. The US was clearly my father's intended final destination. These classes may have been in my native tongue, but they were as alien to me as French. Aimed in their familiarity to anchor expats, they further disorientated me. I had no idea what they were talking about. They had a weekend baseball game that I was expected to join, in order to socialise with my fellow countryfolk, a feat that was considerably harder for me than playing football for the school football team, where I could at least communicate in fouls and the international language of goals. What was 'stealing first base'? I refused all future participation after the first weekend of corn dogs on bleachers. I wasn't ready to become American any more than I planned on becoming French.

Soon, though, I noticed a fair-skinned, full-figured girl called Jane in the American class. Her mousy, flicked hair caught the sun while she blew bubblegum at the back of the room, rolling her eyes extravagantly throughout lessons. Her sarcasm was out of step with everything else in the room; though she had a softly southern American accent, her cynicism was cultivated in London. Her dad worked in computer science and she'd done time in England before being billeted across the US, most recently and happily in Florida. Like so many jet-trash kids blown repeatedly across the globe from new city to strange school, her rootless anonymity formed a shield of weary cynicism that she used to deflect enquiring eyes. As I would discover too, there was no point in making friends when those new friends would just as quickly become nostalgia.

We were pals, though. She kissed me in an empty classroom one lunch break, my first kiss, and I imagined that I was in love. Neither of us felt as if we belonged anywhere on campus so we huddled together on our own outpost.

Joining us on our island was a kid called Pete from Palo Alto, California, who had a Swiss father, no mother that he ever mentioned and some deep-rooted authority issues. He rocked terrible jumbo cords and a glossy hairdo that made him look a bit like Officer Poncherello from the American TV cop show *CHiPs*, but he also had *Emmanuelle* on VCR and a packet of Camels that he taught me how to smoke so I felt we were very much in business together. We'd bunk school and go shoplifting around Saint-Germain, loading our pockets with cassettes from the music shop, as well as non-essential items, before climbing aboard our school buses at the day's end. I wanted to be caught. I wanted to be expelled, but they weren't alive to the mischief. It wasn't that kind of school. We upped the ante.

Lost in France

A few weeks before the end of that first school year, I was told to my surprise that I would be accepted into the main French stream the following year. *Really?* I wondered. It couldn't have escaped anybody's attention in the room that I wasn't fluent in French yet, far from it. I could follow a conversation, I could tell someone to fuck off, I could recite a few verbs, but could I lead a conversation? Not really. Could I write a paragraph off the top of my head? No way.

The meeting took place in a ground-floor administrative room in the school. I was sitting on a chair adrift in the middle of the room, while a full crescent of desks faced me, behind which sat a dozen or so teachers and heads of department, with *le directeur* at its centre. My mum was on another chair at the back of the room, forbidden to speak. In the hall outside the room the entire *5ème* year group lurked in strict silence with one guardian each, awaiting their fate. It was intimidating.

I didn't want to pass into the mainstream French system because I knew it would be beyond me, but, at the same time, what twelve-year-old wants to fail in front of so many people, one of whom is their mother?

I repeated, 'I've passed?'

'Oui, mais . . .'

Ah, oui . . . *mais*. I had passed but I would have to repeat the year so that I'd have a chance of going up the following year, fluent and fantastic. I looked at all the blank faces staring at me. I thanked them and rose.

'And of course,' said *le directeur* as I moved to leave, 'this will allow you to continue playing for the junior football team.'

In other words, you can't speak French, lad, but you can hit a moving ball. In a school of dweebs, they needed kids to play competitive sports. I was one such kid.

Over the coming days, school started to wind down. The pupils' grades were out and that meant the stress was over. The end of the school year is momentous in France because the summer holidays are luxuriously long, and a soft, anticipatory delirium set in. Some children wore costumes for the last day, others brought flour bombs. There'd be tears, too, as some jet trash would be blown to a new city soon, but the last day nevertheless promised a relaxed atmosphere.

'We should go and get wasted in that wood behind the school,' suggested Pete. I agreed. I'd never been wasted. How hard could it be?

Jane joined us with her goofy, posh new English friend Chloe Pope who'd joined the school for the final term after her dad landed a job locally. She would be full-time in Français Spécial next year, but today she brought an energetic enthusiasm for rum and coke, a drink none of us had ever tasted before.

Two 1.5-litre bottles of Coke, half emptied and refilled with a bottle of dark rum in each. That's about the measure, right? A little shake, watch out for froth and take a gulp. Go on, take another, and another . . .

We were whirling around in circles between the trees, a few hundred feet from the school but at that moment on another planet, small children hideously drunk on mid-morning empty stomachs.

Jane lay down, saying she wanted a little sleep, and started to remove her clothing. Embarrassed at the sight of her midriff, I stopped her in this task. I rolled her on her side, just in case. Suddenly I didn't feel very drunk at all. When I turned around, Chloe was also on her back, flat out, and Pete was on his knees, retching. We'd been at it around an hour but the booze was done. Pete's dream had come true. He was wasted. I surveyed the scene and made the decision to seek help.

Squeezing back into the bottom exercise yard through the fence, I spotted one of the sports teachers and appraised him of the basic facts without incriminating myself. Then I headed up towards the food van parked outside the gates. I ordered a hot dog and, as I drunkenly scoffed it, listened to the sirens from a series of ambulances approaching the road to the school gates. Then the gates parted and the sirens rolled down towards the woods.

The school rang two weeks later, on one of those rare days that my dad was at home. Unlucky for me, unlucky for him.

We drove the Datsun in silence to the school, where *le directeur* and his lieutenants awaited us in that same ground-floor school meeting room. The conversation was short and pointed.

My three friends had all been admitted to hospital, where three stomachs had had to be pumped. They were all now discharged, both from medical care and the school. They would not be returning to Le Lycée International. As for you, Monsieur Kessler . . .

They were unsure of the role I'd played in events, as was I, really. I was therefore issued with a suspended expulsion. One more misstep and it would be curtains. See you in September.

It was high summer. The sun scorched the earth. Ahead lay the Autoroute du Soleil, right down to a rented house on the bustling Côte d'Azur for August. The conflicting mixture of relief and dread I'd felt after learning my fate in that meeting room sank to the back of my mind as I became aware of a few of the undeniable benefits living in France provides, namely its incredible geography that includes some of Europe's most glorious beaches, filled with naked people watching pancake-flat seas.

A marker pen aimed at full force and from some distance towards my head during the first week back at school in September snapped the world into focus. Not only was I obviously not capable enough in French to read Émile Zola aloud, nor describe *Nana* in essay form, I was also, according to the teacher who'd launched the missile at me, a stupid American. I determined to get out.

I feigned a sinus illness for months on end, choosing throat swabs and elderly French nurses injecting antibiotics into my arse every week over school for as long as I could. When, eventually, I was forced back to school I bunked it, getting off the bus at the gates, walking down to the RER station and heading into Paris to spend my days chewing up pavement throughout the city, aching with metropolitan love. I felt a pull. My mum agreed to remove me when the brown-enveloped letters in French started to stack up from the school. My dad was missing in action, so she decided the English School of Paris was the best place for me. I strongly agreed.

The head teacher was, like me, new to the ESP and was back and forth to England attending to late domestic arrangements when I applied, so I was interviewed by the deputy head instead. He was glad to admit me after the Easter holidays, 1982.

On my first day at the new school, I was invited to meet the incoming head teacher in his office on the second floor of the grand main house, one of the few quiet rooms in any of the buildings. The place was a nuthouse. At least half of the students were children of IBM employees who came from that company's UK headquarters, in Portsmouth. They were generally on secondment for a couple of years before going home, and the kids, many of whom knew of each other from rival comprehensives along the south coast, treated their time in Paris as an unexpected beano designed purely to enliven their teens. An acute 'Brits abroad' mindset reigned. Big weekend rave-ups. Lots of shagging. Gangs of local kids hanging around outside because they knew it was one school where they'd be guaranteed a fight. The new head was public school and had been brought in to change the mindset, to upgrade the place considerably so that they could charge proper fees. I'm sure he managed it eventually, but for the next couple of years at least he'd be engaged in an arduous guerrilla battle with his own pupils.

'So, Teddy,' the new headmaster began, stiffly. Wire-wool hair, steel-rimmed spectacles, tightly knotted green tie with a Latin-encrusted crest upon its tongue. Features: pinched. 'I understand that you were at the Lycée International previously. How did you find it?'

'I found it difficult, sir. My French just wasn't quite good enough.'

'Hmm,' he considered, fiddling with his lapels. A little brush of his shirt. Nostrils flare. 'My daughter was there, at the Lycée, for a short time last year. But she's back in England now.' He looked to the window for a moment, then faced back to me, locking eyes.

'Perhaps you knew her? Similar age group. She's called Chloe. Chloe Pope?'

'No, sir,' I replied. 'I'm afraid I never came across her.'

2.
Adventures on the Metro

Charles de Gaulle–Étoile to
Saint-Nom-la-Bretèche–Forêt de Marly

There once was a bar just behind Avenue des Champs-Élysées in Paris, on Rue de Ponthieu, called Roscoe's. It may not have actually been named Roscoe's, but that is what it was most widely known as amongst expat drunks and their parents.

A thin drinking hole next to an aromatic underground car park that became painfully cramped when the dozen or so booths were full, Roscoe's was nevertheless where all the British and some American school kids in Paris went to drink on Fridays. It was the one joint that always served us without ID and that fact demanded loyalty. It was where I learned all about the majesty and treachery of the Kir.

A Kir is a cheap French cocktail, one part crème de cassis and nine parts white wine. It's normally an aperitif, a hit of something strong served before eating to get the juices going. That wasn't how I enjoyed it.

I had failed pretty conclusively in my early experiments with lager. I just didn't like the flavour of it as a fourteen-year-old, nor did I have the patience to acquire the taste. Kir, on the other hand, tastes like Ribena and as I was still a child anything that tasted like Ribena was OK by me. I sucked those little glasses of sickly-sweet red hooch down.

Roscoe's was also the venue where, one Friday night in the autumn of 1983, my friend Teifion told me he'd smuggled four tabs of acid over in a book from his summer in England. He'd arrived into our school, the newly renamed British School of Paris, from Bognor Regis the previous term alongside his siblings, twins Morgan and Katie, who were in my year. Teifion was in the year above: Welsh of heritage, Bognor by design, anarchist through instinct. They were part of a fresh intake that would make the seasons 1982–83 through 1984–85 extremely testing for our adversaries both inside and outside of the school gates. Battle was joined with his arrival.

Teifion hadn't brushed his teeth in a year or so, wore his hair in a shaved flat-top and had a self-administered Joy Division tattoo writ large upon his wrist. He brought with him tales of following horrible punk-rockabillies the Meteors on tour through his school holidays, an amazing post-punk 7-inch record collection and an advanced taste for hedonism. A strong alliance was formed. We took a look at all that adolescence in a strange city had to offer, all that potential experimentation and reckless adventure, and sank completely into its overwhelming newness. Most kids there did, in one way or the other. The school was far from everyone's ancestral home – suburban Paris was culturally remote from suburban Britain – but nobody expected to be there longer than a couple of years, so kids bent the environment to fit them rather than attempting to fit in. It was the reverse of my experience at the Lycée. The BSP kids imposed their tastes and habits on to Paris – an imposition that often proved violently provocative. I swung both ways. I was wholly invested in British youth culture, its music and personal presentation, but my eighteen months at the Lycée meant I spoke street-level French. I'd consequently made friends with a handful of near-minded kids in my village, bored wannabe outsiders who liked the Stray Cats, showing off to girls, mindless acts of petty vandalism and driving motor vehicles at suicidal velocity.

Teifion was my high priest, though, my guru, and I tuned in when he made a lifestyle suggestion, be it listening to Josef K's new single or carrying a bent fork in my coat pocket for protection when travelling through the city. Did I want to try one of these tabs of acid he'd brought with him? I placed one upon my tongue.

As the picture started to change, I sought refuge from the storm. I took a detour on the way to the toilets and spent several hours, or minutes, hanging on to the fire escape at the back of Roscoe's watching the animations of lions blowing fire upon the walls of the car park below. Tamsin, a smart, music-mad girl from Kent I thought I might love and had decided to impress by taking LSD and drinking white wine cocktails, occasionally came to check on me. I don't recall our conversations but eventually she left me behind. The lights of the bar were aggressively turned up. I was patiently led out.

I stood in the middle of Rue de Ponthieu gazing at the lights cast twinkling into the sky by the nearby Arc de Triomphe, cars honking in chorus around me, until a kind girl from the year above at school called Susan guided me back on to the pavement. Susan, from Greenock in Scotland, another IBM hub, lived in my village of Chavenay and was now heading home via the Métro and SNCF overground line with her friend. Maybe I'd like to catch the last trains with them?

'That's a very good idea, you know.' I put one arm around each shoulder. 'Come on.'

Thanks to Susan, we caught the last Métro. Then we managed to scramble on the SNCF at La Défense towards its final destination, Saint-Nom-la-Bretèche–Forêt de Marly, our stop. I rested my head against the window and sleep swallowed me instantly.

Susan and her friend shook me awake at the end of the line.

'We're here, Teddy,' Susan said. 'My parents are picking us up. We can drive you home.'

They knew that the alternative was that I would walk the four miles home through the forest, the nearby town of Saint-Nom and finally around the wide-open fields towards Chavenay. It was a walk I did many Friday nights alone. The first mile via an unlit, heavily forested road in the midst of the Forêt de Marly could be terrifying, the night only cracked ajar by the yellow beam of an occasional speeding car. Otherwise, black woody silence, which is no kind of silence; rustling, howling, crunching. Wild boar lived in these woods. Sometimes, there would be one other figure on the road, either just ahead, out of reach, making you consider the wisdom of overtaking, or just behind on the shoulder, slowly gaining with each step as you attempted to speed up too, reaching for that bent fork in your coat pocket . . .

Bonsoir; bonsoir . . .

There was no bus from the station at night and, for me, no alternative solution. I was fourteen years old and left entirely to my own devices by my mother, my dad having quit home a few months after arrival. My father had made his girlfriend pregnant shortly before we arrived in France. His girlfriend lived in Paris, they were in love – where they remain – and he was in deep, deep trouble. My mother did not know that then and would not know it for another decade or so, until my father introduced his OG family to his lovely daughter, my sister. Then, in Saint-Nom, my mother only knew that she had been ditched in a remote home in a foreign country and was having her own, long introspection about that break-up. I became more like a confidant than a son, the pal she caught up with when we were both in town together. Alone in a strange land, in the prison of her break-up, she needed someone to talk to over lunch and a glass of wine. I was only thirteen when offered that position, but I could be that guy for her. I was the nearest thing to an adult friend she had within reach.

Once we'd established that level footing, she was a liberal mother. Anything went. Other parents and schoolteachers declaimed her as an accomplice to delinquency – but the little kids understood.

My friends welcomed the smoky refuge she provided without inquisition. She would survey the yearly wreckage of my school report and ask me if I knew what I was doing. I'd say yes, I was going to become someone who listened to music professionally. Incredibly, she believed me, she didn't mock me, didn't dissuade, she encouraged me to immerse myself even more fully in music and all associated youth culture because she could recognise my zealotry. I wasn't rebelling, I had nothing to kick against. Thanks to her benevolence, however, I was also discovering early on the disappointment that lurks at the limits of personal freedom. One of those many let-downs is that after a night out in Paris, I'd have to take a long, frightening walk home in the dark on my own through a forest.

But not tonight.

'You have to get up if you're coming,' insisted Susan, tugging me from the train seat. 'My parents are waiting.'

We walked down the platform, an arm under each of my elbows, before Susan spoke through the window of the car to her father. She nodded happily at me, opening the door. Her friend was already in the other window seat. I was in the middle seat, as Susan climbed in next to me.

'Hello, Mr Collins, hello, Mrs Collins,' I said. Or words to that effect.

We set off.

'How are you, Teddy, all OK?' asked Mrs Collins, warily, as if enquiring about someone's surgery.

'I'm very well,' I told her.

But I was not very well. I was not well.

I felt the vomit rushing from my toes upwards as soon as we turned out of the forest on to the main road. The car was so warm. I was too far from a window.

Where could I put this sick so that nobody noticed? I raised my hand and ushered it down each sleeve of my prized donkey jacket, filling both arms very quickly. Too quickly, perhaps, as the car suddenly halted and the rest of my vomit flew forwards between the front seats all across the gearstick and both the pilot and his co-pilot. Then I stopped.

A few screams.

'I'm sorry everybody,' I managed.

Silence. The car started. We drove on for the remaining few miles with the wind rushing through all four open windows, into picturesque Saint-Nom-la-Bretèche, down through the fields and to the edge of Chavenay where the car stopped abruptly in the main Centre Commercial. A door opened and Susan leapt from the car. I climbed out after and sank to my knees on the grass verge.

'Fuck's sake, Ted,' she muttered, and got back in.

The Collins' car pinged off at a lick. I lay on my back and let the lukewarm vomit inside my coat squelch all over me, gazing up at the stars. It was a clear, bright night. The sky glistened with thousands of frogs, millions of Kermits, waving back at me. I laughed out loud at its majesty.

Gare Saint-Lazare to Saint-Nom-la-Bretèche–Forêt de Marly

Bleached hair, grown out so that the roots are visible midway into a two-inch flat-top. Shaved bald at the sides and the back. Three earrings in the left earlobe. Green button-down shirt, short-sleeved beneath a cream 1960s sports jacket. Sta-Prest, black. Six-hole Dr Martens boots, black, rested upon the seat of the chair opposite, heading in a westerly direction after a day's stomping around the city with Omar, Charlie and Teifion, leafing through record, comic and clothes shops, perhaps a little shoplifting, trying to avoid skinheads and the bored CRS police cooped up all day in vans. The typical Saturday afternoon after the Friday night before. I'd stayed at Teifion's and I needed a wash.

At Puteaux a couple of likely lads catch my eye as the train flashes down the platform. They climb aboard and make their way down the carriage, sitting in the four-seater next to me. One is casual in tracksuit top and jeans. The other has a moddish skin vibe. He looks quite sharp, but I can't really ignore the fact that he's staring intensely at me.

'Ça va?' I ask, blankly, turning to face him. The kid smiles. He's a couple of years older than me. I'd say around seventeen.

'Ça va bien. Toi?'

I'm OK too, I tell him. He gives me a cheery thumbs-up.

Well, this is nice. I have been chased all over Paris and its many suburbs over the previous year or so. I've had a policeman smack me in the mouth for no reason other than walking into his tear gas in the Métro as the CRS attempted to disperse Maghrebi kids in Les Halles. I've had a gang of black rockabillies – the notorious if unimaginatively named Black Cats – put me up against a wall in Clichy and frisk me at knifepoint, removing my wallet from my back pocket and, with some hilarity, the bent fork from my jacket. I even had a skinhead kick me from behind down a moving escalator at Oberkampf, before another then ripped the Harrington from my back. At a fairground in Saint-Germain-en-Laye some squaddies had followed us and then kung-fu kicked us in the car park until they realised that, despite our provocative hair, they were beating up children and wandered off, unsatisfied.

Nobody asked me how I was first.

'Where are you from?' asks one.

'London,' I say, 'but I live here.'

'Ah, OK,' says the mod-skin. He sizes me up. 'Is that where you get those Docs from?'

'Yes.'

'They're great,' he replies. 'You can't get them here easily.'

'They're cheap in England,' I tell him. 'Work boots. Everyone has them.'

'Hmm,' he says. 'What size are you?'

'43.'

'Let's swap.'

I look at his feet. He has massive old canvas army boots on, covered in stains. They look terrible.

'No thanks.'

'Come on,' he insists. 'French army boots, vintage. Very cool. It's a cultural exchange!' He starts unlacing his shoes. Meanwhile, his pal slides across seats and sits next to me. He punches me on the arm about as hard as you can when you're friends with someone, maybe even a little harder. He nods at me. 'It's a good exchange. Fair. Take off your boots.'

I turn around, gazing down the carriage. There are a few people further down, in singles, looking out of windows or reading. There is no cavalry. I unlace my boots.

'Merci mon pote!' my new pal says, grabbing my Docs, then shaking my hand. His mate gives my head a massive congratulatory shove and stands up. We are pulling in at La Celle-Saint-Cloud.

'You know what,' says Mod-skin, 'as you don't really like my army boots, I'm going to keep them. OK?'

I shrug.

'Salut!' they shout as, laughing, they jump from the train. They walk by the window, waving my boots at me. I put my feet back on the seat.

At Saint-Nom I walk down the platform in my socks and step into the phone box to call home.

'Mum,' I say. 'Could you please come and pick me up from the station? I won't be able to walk home.'

Châtelet–Les Halles to Le Vésinet–Le Pecq

Early March 1984, and in a brightly lit bar near République a couple of dozen skinheads were singing a jolly song about fucking the English up the arse. This was a commemorative hymn, as three days earlier the English had come to Paris and, figuratively speaking, the French did fuck them up the arse.

I turned to my friend Omar.

'Don't worry,' he said. 'There're more of us here and these guys weren't even there on Wednesday.'

Omar was my guardian angel and, as far as I could tell, one of the greatest things about Paris. He deserved his own plaque. We'd bumped into him one Saturday walking around Les Halles, looking into shop windows. Spotting our personal stylings, this Anglophile had come to introduce himself. Omar, the son of Algerian immigrants from the northern suburbs, was two or three years older, at least eighteen, but he had the street intelligence and intuition of a superhero, a gift that if the French police had any wits about them – which they didn't – they'd have paid him royally to share. Like many second-generation Maghrebi kids in Paris, he was adrift from both the land his parents had fled to and the one they had left behind. The racism he experienced from the French, at school, as he went about his daily business, from the authorities, was routine and harsh, yet he was French, not Algerian. Born in Paris. He'd never even been to North Africa. Like us, his religion was music, alternative culture, clothes and art. He loved comics. He cut his hair into a flat-top, pulled on a bomber jacket, steel toe caps, a Cramps T-shirt. He wasn't French, he wasn't Algerian. His tribe were made up of the rockabillies, the punks, the skins (in small, particular doses) and other outsiders he collected on his long marches through Paris. He was the rolling stone that gathered moss.

He was a pass key to a Paris that would've remained unknown to me otherwise, and we arranged to meet him in town every Saturday for his grand tours of the hidden city. He never caught public transport, he only ever walked. Meeting in Les Halles, he'd announce he needed to go to see someone in a comic shop by Porte de Clignancourt, up in the north, stopping at the flea market on the way. So we'd set off marching through the city, talking about records, the adventures of the week, the near misses, the frustrations, reciting the names of enemies we had better avoid, oh hang on, is that one there, quick, step in this bar . . . When cornered, though, there were very few situations he couldn't talk himself out of. Then, when we'd finished whatever affair he needed to take care of, we'd turn tail and walk back down to the other end of the city, down to somewhere near Place d'Italie where he'd arranged to meet his best friend Charlie as Charlie knew how to get into a gig later nearby . . .

Charlie was another Maghrebi from the suburbs who had dramatically rejected both the uniformity of French culture and that of his immigrant parents. He was a showstopper. Five-foot-six, if that, in massive brothel-creeper shoes, he added another seven inches to his height with an enormous bleached quiff. His fingernails, which he claimed to have only filed but not cut for years, curled from his fingers like filthy superhero weapons. Not only did he rock full-sleeve tattoos on both arms and legs, he also had the word 'Zorch' inked on the inside of his lip, which he'd curl down as a deadpan gag in moments of boredom or ennui. On my fifteenth birthday he took me to get a tattoo on my shoulder of a skull entwined with a snake – for free, because the tattooist, he said, 'owed me a tattoo'. The guy happily obliged for his old pal Charlie, telling me that he could tattoo under the influence of any drug other than cocaine. It had gone badly whenever he tried it. Heroin, on the other hand, he found a great aid in his profession. Nevertheless, I returned a few weeks later with an advert torn from the *NME* of the Meteors' logo for their 'Mutant Rock' single – a snarling green face, Frankenstein's monster in bowel distress – to be inscribed on my arm, even though I didn't really like the song much. I was just an idiot.

Charlie was the most well-connected kid on the streets of Paris, seemingly on good terms with every hood on any corner, able to turn a screwface into a grin every time. He was also naturally melancholic and profoundly introspective.

'I wish,' he once said, 'I knew what I know now about life, about people, when I was young.'

'How old are you?' I asked.

'I'm twenty-one. It's too late for me now. In a way, it's always been too late for me.'

Lip. Zorch.

Charlie had brought us this evening to a large bar near the Gibus Club as he had an in with the person doing the door there later. It was an alternative night at the club, some long-forgotten French bands were booked, and loads of punks, skins and psychobillies had gathered before opening. The French paid such attention to the minute detail of British subculture in the eighties and every stitch had to have perfect provenance. They were always disappointed by the more haphazard real thing. So it had proven that week.

On Wednesday, the England football team had played France at Parc des Princes. It had been a date ringed in the diary of every tough-guy idiot in France for months, a chance to pit themselves against the fabled English hooligans. Domestic rivalries were paused as French dumb-bells arrived in town from Lyon, Marseille and Lille especially for the occasion. The English had not taken the supposed battle quite as seriously. Dozens of English fans were arrested soon after alighting the ferry in Calais, having drunkenly smashed up that town instead. Those that arrived in Paris were just oiks dressed in hoodies and trainers. The meticulous French skins, punks and mods felt disillusioned by what they'd come up against: fat casuals, drunks from Bedford and Rotherham.

The French TV news after England's 2–0 defeat covered the fighting inside the ground during the match, but the real story, we were told repeatedly during our march around Paris on Saturday, was that of English fans being ambushed on the Métro, in bars, to and from the stadium. They had, as the skinhead chorus repeated loudly while standing upon the pub's tables, been fucked up the arse.

Teifion disagreed. He was involved in what he no doubt believed was good-natured banter with some of the skins about the disorder. Teifion's French was rudimentary so perhaps he didn't pick up on the needle in the French skins as they argued with him about events. Omar and I did.

'He's just messing about,' Omar told them, reassuringly. 'Don't worry about him, he's a kid.'

'It's all good,' replied the skin, throwing his arm around Teifion's shoulder. 'We'll have a drink. Do you like brandy, Calvados?' he asked Teifion.

Teifion admitted that he might.

'You know the best way to have a shot of Calvados? Inject it.' He mimed jacking up into his arm.

Omar jumped in. 'Non, mais arrête!'

Teifion raised a hand. He was a sixteen-year-old anarchist who would not back down from such a dare. 'Let's go, come on.'

A few minutes later, he emerged from the toilet and staggered across the room with the skinhead holding him up. The Calvados had hit his bloodstream instantly and he could barely stand, collapsing across the table as soon as he made it back to us. The skins cheered and the room burst into song one more time. They had more material for their number about the English.

Omar turned to me. Time to go. We pulled Teifion up and with our other English friend from school, Sean, dragged him down the road to the Métro at Strasbourg–Saint-Denis, where we said goodbye to Omar. From there we headed to the RER overground at Châtelet–Les Halles for the ride back to Teifion's home.

We threw him into a seat and sat down laughing at our lucky escape. It was one of the last trains of the night and the carriage was mercifully empty. We put our feet up on the seats, settling in.

At Charles de Gaulle a trio of rangy-looking Maghrebi guys in sports gear jumped on at the other end of the carriage and immediately started to kick the windows in. One of them pulled the train doors apart as we sped underground into La Défense and hung out between them, shouting 'I want to die!' at the walls of the tunnel. Sean and I sank a little lower into our seats, as Teifion dozed on oblivious.

As soon as the train pulled into La Défense one of the group ran from the carriage and launched himself at an advertising hoarding on the platform with a kick, and another, and another, knocking the Plexiglas out, before running back to the train and diving in between the closing doors on the final peep. They collapsed in laughter, but as they gathered themselves the trio noticed us. Bleached hair, earrings, partially unconscious. We were conspicuous.

The train pulled in at Nanterre, the sprawling high-rise town at the north-western gates of Paris, and as it did one of the group sprinted down the carriage. Arriving at our bank of four seats, he pulled his hand up and aimed a small canister at my face.

From a couple of inches away he sprayed.

'Pour toi!' he shouted as he fired the CS canister at each of us in turn, before punching me in the head and arm a couple of times and sprinting back through the closing doors, on to the platform.

As the train left the station they booted the doors, but we were lost in mucus, struggling for breath. Coughing and gobbing, our faces on fire. Tear gas. We tried to pull Teifion away from the fumes, but he was a dead weight, half-boy, half-brandy, lost in Calvados dreams. So we sat with our shirts over our faces, spluttering and wheezing through the poisoned air, all the way back to Le Vésinet–Le Pecq, six stops down the line.

In the morning, Teifion awoke on his bed, fully dressed. Coughing and loudly hoiking up phlegm even more dramatically than usual, he walked down his stairs into the kitchen, where we were at his table, relaying the night's tale once more to his guffawing brother and sister.

He eyed us up, suspiciously.

Lost in France

'I don't know what you did to me last night,' he said by way of greeting, flicking the kettle on, removing a mug from the cupboard. He sniffed the same button-down he was wearing the night before, inhaling those rusty CS gas aromas. 'But you've ruined this shirt.'

3.
The Last of the Mohicans

Like a hair-shirted, middle-England Mafioso, Mr Pope slowly picked off my friends one by one. He didn't like them, the way they behaved. The smoking, the earrings, the extravagant haircuts, the constant, unrepentant bunking off. Sta-Prest trousers and monkey boots. Mopeds. As head teacher, he expected better. So he expelled a couple of our group and sought assurances from the remainder's parents that they'd be returning to England for good later in that summer of 1984. Coldly, he served his revenge.

He also inked in an appointment to see me with my mother for a similar conversation in April, just after the Easter holidays. By a stroke of luck, though, I managed to give myself glandular fever piercing my ears during a lesson with a much-shared stud earring and had to miss a month's school after the break, prone and swollen on the sofa, watching well-worn VHS copies of *Scum*, *The Godfather*, *Being There* and various episodes of *The Tube*, transmitted in black and white because they were technologically mismatched with our French video player.

When I returned for the summer term, the expulsion storm had not only passed but, in my absence, an English essay I'd written for homework on the theme of 'the countryside' had been read out in assembly as an example of an English essay that was good enough to be read out in assembly. In fifteen long years alive, it was my first academic achievement – also the last.

Mr Pope soon invited me to a meeting in his office. I expected the worst. Immediately after my sick leave I'd been accused of dealing speed to other kids by a teacher, Mr Agnew, who'd received a tip-off from another student (the dirty rat). It was an outrageous allegation. I wasn't selling speed. I was giving it away for free.

Unlike in England, anybody could buy ephedrine – an amphetamine – in French chemists, sold as small, round pink pills bottled and stored behind the counter, if you knew to ask. A kid from our village had hipped me to them. That year I always had a vial somewhere, particularly at parties where I'd gladly hand them out to all comers.

When nabbed with a bottle in my bag having been ordered to empty all my pockets in a classroom, I told Agnew that they were prescribed for my recovery from glandular fever – something to give me a little va-va-voom – and he appeared to buy it. This invitation to see the headmaster undercut that assumption.

I knocked on the door.

'Come!'

I stepped inside the headmaster's lair.

'Ah, Teddy, take a seat please.'

I sat. I loved the peace of his room. The deranged screaming of the kids on break in the yard below sounded like chicks softly clucking up here.

'How are you feeling now? Fully recovered?'

'I am, thanks.'

'Good. Now, you may not know this yet, but while you were away, we decided it was time to launch an annual school magazine, edited by students and overseen by the English department.' He paused to fiddle with some paper clips on his desk, raising his eyes to mine to address me. 'You were volunteered to work on it, after your essay was read by Mrs Kennet in assembly.'

'I was?'

'You were. How do you feel about it?'

'All right, I suppose. Yeah, I'm happy to do that.'

'Glad to hear it because you were nominated by Mrs Kennet to edit it, too. You were then voted unanimously by everyone involved to be this year's school magazine editor.'

'Shit! Sorry, sir. But, really?' (I was clearly nominated editor because I was absent at the time of nominations.)

'Really, yes. Do you want to do it? I hardly need tell you that this has saved your career at this school, as you were on the same knife edge as Chris, Teifion and your other friends.'

'Yes, sir. Understood.'

'Mrs Kennet spoke very highly of your English, of your essays. She said you were among the best English students she's had here at this school. She convinced me of your promise.' He didn't look very convinced. 'Don't let us down.'

'No, sir.'

'She'll be in touch about the start date. OK, you may leave now.'

'Thank you, sir.'

I walked to the door, pausing as I placed my weight on the handle. For a moment I considered turning around and telling him the truth, that I'd copied much of my prize-winning essay from an Alan Sillitoe short story I'd been reading at the time. Instead, I stepped through the door and carried on downstairs to lunch break.

A couple of months earlier, I'd bleached my suedehead hair as white as I could get it. Now the dark brown roots were as long as the inch of blond above. I could cut it all short, leave a little blond quiff. I'd done that before. Girls liked that, I thought. Or I could bleach it again.

'Or I could shave it into a Mohican if you like?' suggested an older kid, a sixth-former called Adrian, who claimed to have trained in a relative's hairdressers in the school holidays. That Friday I took the bus to Adrian's parents' flat. He sat me down in his kitchen and shaved the sides of my head smoothly bald with a razor. A couple of nicks. Basically all right. A two-inch high, four-inch wide, nothing-on-the-sides Mohican haircut. I didn't stick it up or any of that nonsense, it just flapped down, like a dead ferret upon my bald dome. In lieu of a helmet, I stuck a colander on top of it and accepted a lift home on the back of a scooter as night fell.

The next day, Saturday, was the school fête. Another exciting new event in the school's march to respectability. Upon seeing my hairdo once I'd emerged from bed, my mum gasped, laughed, then gave me a lift to the station, sad-proud eyes checking me out in the rear-view, ahead of a train ride of significant sotto voce whispers towards Croissy, where the school sat on the banks of the Seine.

Entering the arena beneath the low-hanging willow trees by the main gates, my hair became a flute and I was its piper. Children of all ages flocked towards me as I strolled in along the dusty path by the prefabs, into the sunlight below the grand main building. Everyone wanted a closer look at the idiot with the new bleached Mohican haircut.

One pair of eyes in particular burrowed into me, lasered from the highest step of the whitewashed house as I stood in my polo shirt and jeans, a dead white stoat upon my head, pretending to inspect the fairy cakes for sale on a trestle table. I raised my eyes to the house and met Mr Pope's stare, narrow and hard, a bullet to the noggin. I'd overestimated the good-natured banter of this new hairdo.

At nine on the nose, the ringing of our home phone cut through the dead weight of Sunday morning. I could hear my mum answer it, suspicion and irritation in her voice.

'Allo?!'

I raised myself to my knees and opened the window behind my bed, pulling out the smokes from my jeans on the floor and leaning into the chill of the morn with a puff. I knew exactly what the call was about.

Mr Pope was on the line, telling Mum that my haircut was unacceptable, that it was one transgression too far, that I would be expelled from the school . . .

A quick knock and the bedroom door opened.

'That was your stuck-up headmaster on the phone.'

'I know.'

'He's not happy with you!'

'I know.'

She shrunk a little before me, head to one side, pulling her dressing gown tight. Big sigh. 'He's suspending you from school.'

Suspension?

'I know,' she said, sympathetically. 'He says you can return in a week or so, once your hair grows back a bit. You can't have that hair at school, Ted. Not a full Mohican. You'll have to cut it off.'

'I thought I was being kicked out, Mum.'

'Well . . . what did he say? His instinct is that you deserve a final chance. He said that as you have been announced school magazine editor it's up to you to demonstrate you can rise to the challenge.'

I laughed at the irony. My plagiarism had saved me from the more minor transgression of my appearance.

My mother lingered in the doorway. 'Just get through this school year, yes?' she asked, softly. 'Next year, knuckle down please.'

My friend Michelle shaved off the back of my hair, leaving an island of blond adrift on the top of my head, fenced in by baldness. Over the next ten days my roots grew back as I considered the best way to both knuckle down and rise to the challenge. I decided to use this moment of reflection wisely. I sat at the kitchen table and began to write my first article for the school magazine. It was the story of my suspension from school for having a ridiculous bleached Mohican, an unabridged version of which you are now reading. It was the first piece I wrote for the British School of Paris magazine, published in the summer term of 1985, but the last one I submitted, slipped in right on deadline, unseen by any teacher. My final farewell gift to Mr Pope.

Part Two
London Calling

4.

Our Favourite Shop

'Then I saw a new heaven and a new earth, for the first heaven and the first earth had passed away, and the sea was no more.'

– Revelation 21:1–2

The conversation with my mother in our kitchen in France in the early spring of 1985 was quickly resolved. She told me that now the divorce from my dad was coming, we would be moving to Washington DC that summer. She'd found a job working as an assistant at NBC News and had friends in the city from when she'd lived in Manhattan in the sixties. My dad had already moved to New York. I would have no family in Europe. The die was cast.

'I'm sorry, Mum,' I told her. 'I can't come.'

She looked at me, radiating doubt. 'You're still at school,' she replied, with exasperation. 'You're sixteen, a child. I can't leave you here.'

There we were, together, Mum and I, standing amongst the orange and brown flowered wallpaper of our rented kitchen in Chavenay, both aware that we were also at the central crossroads of my short life. Two paths lay ahead. In one direction, I'd be moving to the US to start at a Maryland high school with my brothers in time for my seventeenth birthday. In the other, London, my new girlfriend who was also returning to England, accelerated maturity and the freedom to make my own catastrophically silly decisions. I'd spent nearly five years acclimatising to France, but now I yearned so badly for those square paving stones and inner-city blues. There was an escape route for me. I had to chase it.

'I can't move to another continent,' I told her. 'I just can't. It doesn't mean I don't love you, but I was English, then I had to pretend to be French. I'm not going to be American.'

She chewed her lip. It was a fraught enough move for her already. She was a single mum of three children and limited means, starting a new job 6,000 miles away. Was it worth dragging me against my will?

'Let me phone Su and see if we can make something work,' she said.

That was all I needed to hear.

My mum's best friend from school, Su Strettell, lived in Hammersmith with her husband James and three children, Jo, Polly and David. The kids were between two and seven years older than me and every now and then the sisters would look after my brothers and me when we still lived in London. Both girls joined us on holiday sometimes, so that my folks would be able to find a bar to argue in without us. They felt more like family than most of the real thing, though that revelation would have no doubt surprised them.

The Strettell kids were worldly and funny, champion socialisers, at ease in their space. Open to all. We idolised them. They always seemed hip, as older kids often can – but the Strettells substantiated that impression. Later, Jo would go to Saint Martins alongside her friend Sade, and became integral to Spandau Ballet, Steve Strange and the early eighties London club scene that coalesced around the Blitz and then the Wag, before growing to become one of the top make-up artists in the UK, eventually the world.

She and her siblings would invite all of their mischievous friends over to the family Sunday dinner, Strettell Soup, which involved the gently formidable and partially deaf patriarch James emptying every savoury ingredient he'd saved up from the week's previous meals into a large pot – cuts of roast chicken, leftover curry, tin of salmon, a leek – pouring in a couple of pots of cream, milk and parsley, whisking. It could be rich. But it was an unmissable event of great jollity in the weekly calendar. Huge goblets of fighter-jet-strength gin and tonic (even for children, if desired; otherwise Red Stripe), a guest list that included a mix of people you recognised from early issues of *The Face*, alongside Su and James's ribald pals that they knew from the stall Su had selling antiques in Covent Garden market, or from the dusty corners of sixties London bohemia that remained posh no matter how cash-poor they might actually be. All squeezed around the wooden table in the compact, smoky kitchen, heads back, roaring with scandal and gossip. It was the perfect design for dining: low on pomp, intimate volume set high. The stories of where-are-they-now pop-culture nobility I heard. The indigestion I knew.

The Strettells rented a room to a friendly student every year. I could be that friendly student, surely, fifteen quid a week, very, very reasonable indeed.

'You have to finish school, though,' said my mum, warily. 'You have to. It's not worth the aggro from your dad otherwise.'

'Of course.'

'And I won't have enough money to pay for your everyday needs. You'll have to get a weekend job and work in the holidays. Are you up to that?'

I promised her that I was.

So, in July 1985, aged sixteen, I caught the ferry back to England and unpacked my two suitcases in the basement of the Strettells' terraced house in Tabor Road, Hammersmith, ready to start my new life as an A-Level student at Richmond Sixth Form College in Twickenham. I was distantly aware that I had to negotiate the fact that my place there was dependent upon a minimum of five O-Level passes and I only had one, but I was confident in my powers of dishonesty. First, though, I took the train to Bognor and spent three weeks shoplifting and shivering on comedowns with Teifion and his merry band of teenage junkies.

When I returned to Tabor Road in August I shared the bedroom, and the bed, with David Strettell for a few weeks. He was moving to New York that autumn, staying with his sister Jo in her apartment. In some ways it was a mirror of my mother's emigration in the early sixties. He had a couple of phone numbers, a bed, and not much else to go on but he was determined that, at eighteen, his life would be lived in New York. He never returned. Thirty-eight years later, he is the owner of the renowned Dashwood Books store and imprint in NoHo.

Then, though, in 1985, without realising it, David had his work cut out designing my immediate future. His taste and personal style were impeccable, light years ahead of my own confused psychedelic-rockabilly stylings.

This look had already been semi-dismantled early in my time back in London, after I'd stepped into the basement of the Clarendon on Hammersmith Broadway one evening in August to witness Kent garage-mods the Prisoners for the first time. The brutal melodic groove of their Hammond organ allied to the crunch and fury of the songs, exploding in that tiny room to a few dozen dancing, devout teenagers like myself, immediately gave me something to believe in. I was lonely in London. I knew nobody, other than the Strettells and my girlfriend Jo, who had returned to Egham, Surrey from Paris, and was currently interrailing in Eastern Europe. I needed something to believe in and the Prisoners gave me so much: four sarcastic Medway wags in smart suits, Breton tops and polo necks, only a few years older than me, gulping down plastic pint pots, simultaneously taking the piss out of and encouraging their audience, all of whom were regulars at every one of their many London pub dates around their lo-fi masterpiece, *The Last Fourfathers*. I didn't miss a gig for six months. Soon enough, other audience members started talking to me, swapping numbers, meeting before shows, offering a social lifeline. I briefly (and regrettably) took to wearing Chelsea boots.

David, meanwhile, was shedding the bits of his life he couldn't bring to New York in his one suitcase and I was greedily accepting whatever came my way. An exquisite red V-neck cashmere sweater, battered black brogues and vintage Levis. Thank you. John Handy's *Hard Work* and Herbie Hancock's *Head Hunters*: landmark jazz-funk albums, amongst many other records of his that I knew nothing of previously but that became cornerstones for me. A heavy-plated book of saucy Helmut Newton photography. The video of *Koyaanisqatsi* that we'd sat down to at the end of Superman-tab acid trips, threading the images of collapsing Western society through our melted brain mush. *The Sensitive Sound of Dionne Warwick* and the 7-inch of 'Love Don't Live Here Anymore' by Rose Royce. Several handsome button-downs and white tees. An original sixties mac and checked suit jacket: fits perfectly. Copies of dub testament *Scientist Wins the World Cup* and Sly and the Family Stone's *There's A Riot Goin' On*, two albums that remain fixtures in my all-time top ten . . .

It was like the greatest ever episode of the conveyor belt in the *Generation Game*. Much of what he left to me became my own style and my own musical ground zero. But there was one final gift in particular that opened doors to new worlds, and changed the course of everything for ever.

Their modest patio garden was surrounded by spare bedding. The previous spring David had planted some marijuana seeds in the vague hope that he might grow a couple of small plants from it, to while away his time before he left for NYC. Instead, through a mixture of a very wet spring, unusually sunny summer and natural green fingers, he'd produced five enormous, six-foot bushes. After he harvested them in early August, hung them upside down in the kitchen and then plucked them clear of twig and seed, they delivered four supermarket carrier bags full of homegrown.

We smoked it for a few weeks. It was light, but it was very good for something grown in an inner-London back yard. You could puff it pure and go for a fun-filled wander through Ravenscourt Park or Shepherd's Bush Market, giddy enough, but low on paranoia. It was gentle.

'You might as well have it,' he said, gesturing to the remaining three and three-quarter carrier bags full. 'I bet they won't let me bring it into America.'

I gladly accepted the donation.

Soon after, I caught the 267 bus out west towards Twickenham, and an appointment with the college secretary who cheerfully accepted the lie that the certificates of my delayed exam passes were on their way from France still. She inked my name into A-Level English, French and Politics.

A few days later I returned for my first day at Richmond College, armed with several bunches from David's weed bush decanted into plastic coin bags: essential tools in making new friends quickly. The means, too, to avoid the necessity of that weekend job for the time being.

Within two years I was working on the third floor of a well-known high-street retailer's buying office in Fulham, in the fast-moving consumer goods department, as a clerk assisting a buyer. It was not exhilarating work, nor was I a gifted clerical administrator. I'd followed my carefree path to its natural conclusion.

In January 1986 I had walked out of Richmond College for the last time, promising to return when ready to pick up my A-Levels again. The weed had run out, however, and so had my income. So I applied for a job at Fred. Olsen Cruise Lines off Regent Street as a reservations clerk, booking travellers on to the wrong ferry at the wrong time from the wrong port, either from Harwich or Hull to Bergen in Norway. I made a lot of customers very unhappy for £100 a week until, five months in, I resigned, walked downstairs to the sister agency and secured a staff-discounted open-return flight to Rhodes.

When I got back a month later I signed up with a temporary agency. There was a fortnight microfiche copying at the Kodak Factory on Lillie Road, pressing a green button from eight-thirty until five with a bunch of stoners blasting out *Dark Side of the Moon* over the factory speakers. Sign on. Two days lugging postbags up and down the ICL tower on a brutal speed comedown, until I was sent home. Sign on. Some filing at an estate agent for a week. Sign on. Office furniture removal for a fortnight. Sign on. Stint in a stockroom. Sign on . . .

Then, I got six weeks temporary work clearing a building, dumping the rubbish, and carrying the serviceable office furniture across to the adjacent building, that well-known high-street retailer's buying office. They'd hired a rum crew of the agency's Hammersmith regulars for this longer-than-usual job. They knew we'd turn up for the duration. What else had we going on? There was a guy whose main gig was organising medieval banquets and jousts at the weekend, but business was slow. There were a couple of students on gap years, saving up for big summers. There was a doctor who'd been struck off for something that nobody could bring themselves to ask about, but who was very keen to share his medical knowledge. There was a murderer out on licence. There was a guy who lived so hard for clubbing that he didn't have mental space for a full-time job. A couple of actors in loud, perpetual, passive-aggressive competition. And there were the terminally unemployed, me and an old soak who claimed to have been retired and wealthy but wanted the flexibility, as he described it, of temporary work. We moved tables and swivel chairs, scooped up polystyrene and ceiling mesh, and tipped it down a chute.

I enjoyed it. There was a building manager only vaguely interested in what we achieved, so just so long as the office was clear and the tables were in the opposite building in four weeks we were our own masters. We took a lot of tea breaks. At lunch we'd buy trays of subsidised pies, lasagne and chips, crumble, and lounge around on the sofas in the suits' top-deck canteen in our dusty jeans and stinking T-shirts arguing forcefully about Maggie Thatcher and unions and jazz-funk and the IRA and drug laws and the Smiths and capital punishment and why the market for medieval jousting was never going to be there in 1987, the actors boring on at full whack, darling, until the building manager would roll up, shushing us and tapping his wrist. We turned up late. We skipped out early on Friday. At the end of it, they asked if I fancied a fortnight in the post room. You bet.

Towards the close of that stint, one of the women who worked in the offices started chatting to me about the book I was reading on my break (*Money*, by Martin Amis: living the eighties). The next day the agency said she'd requested I do some work helping her out next week on the buying desk for cameras and films.

I was a young man working with fifty or sixty women and a handful of lecherous old men in charge of the fast-moving consumer goods division. I brought the maternal urge out in some colleagues, so they overlooked the woeful attention to detail I brought to the task. At the end of the temp period they offered me the role of buyer's assistant. £7,800 per annum, starting in April 1987. Where do I sign?

The thrill wore off very quickly. Mainly, I dealt with customer complaints. Boilerplate apology, routine replacement and a couple of free films as a 'gesture of goodwill' no matter how ludicrous the claim. Always complain. I spent a good while redirecting stock between branches. Every now and then, I was also given a list of goods needed for our own model shop floor on the adjacent wing of the building. It was a full-scale fast-moving consumer goods department built to scale in order to experiment with signage, racking, display – all the good stuff. This model shop was the domain of a lad called Paddy. Paddy was a similar age to me, around nineteen, twenty, from a family of East End butchers. Sturdy. Reliable. Felt the heat, not the cold. Prone to sweat.

Silk Cut in his top pocket, frizzy barnet, a bit of a waddle. Tony Blackburn playing soul on Radio London in the morning; his Depeche Mode and U2 compilations in the afternoon. He could build the displays himself, but every now and then he needed someone to help lug them around the empty shop.

'Fancy a Uri?' he asked one afternoon after we'd carried some units back and forth.

'A what?'

'A Uri Geller,' he replied, as if addressing a toddler. 'Stella. The liquid mindbender.'

Two pints in, he asked if I was happy with my wages, if I was interested in earning a bit more. Of course I was.

'I know a bloke in Whitechapel who'll buy those Kodak films for a pound a pop, sell them on his stall. If you order in an extra slab, we can go 50p each on them.'

I had so many 35mm films already in my drawers and stacked next to my desk I could just put a slab of fifty straight in my bag. The office was awash with films, cameras and all associated paraphernalia. I was posting 35mm film in envelopes to disappointed customers unchecked all day. There was no accountability. Getting film stock in was not a problem. I ordered all the films in for the office anyway, hundreds every week. Carrying them out of the building was the risk, as the front-desk security did random bag searches. Where am I going with these 250 Kodak 400s? That's a very good question. Fuck it. We did it once in a sweat and never thought twice about it again.

There was a limit to how many 35mm films Paddy's pal wanted passed under the table in a Bethnal Green pub every month, so there was a natural, necessary brake on our ambitions. How many times? Not many. Every time, I put half of the payout into my body and the other half into an envelope hidden inside a Thee Mighty Caesars album sleeve in my rack because I knew that nobody in the flat I shared would ever take that record off the shelf. I dropped ecstasy for the first time at a rare groove night at the Electric Ballroom in Camden one Saturday and had a revelatory journey on the upper deck of a night bus back to West London. I decided I'd saved enough inside that album sleeve. It was time to change the channel.

In May 1988 I walked into my boss's office and handed her a note saying I was leaving in a month. She understood. She wasn't sad to see me go.

'How will you pay for your posh shoes without a job?' asked Carole, my colleague who sat opposite me, a little bitterly. She had a son my age and treated me with concern and care throughout our fifteen months together – even though she despaired of my fondness for clothes and records. She thought I should instead be saving to buy a flat in Sutton, near her. She looked down at my new Bass Weejun loafers. 'I bet you regret those now.'

A month later, I stood on the verge of the A20 with my girlfriend, watching the traffic scoot down the ramp. I had a rucksack on my back, a two-man tent packed on top. It was late June. We were headed down to the Côte d'Azur to work on the beaches for the summer selling doughnuts, camping on a site behind the dunes for ten weeks. By the time of our return in mid-September, we'd have made enough money to buy flights to New York City, where, in a small Midtown apartment, my father would introduce me to my new, hitherto unknown seven-year-old sister, Gaby, before we headed down to DC to see my mum and brothers. That grand bonus I'd awarded myself remained largely uncashed as traveller's cheques in my waistband until we reached the States.

I stuck out my thumb. Soon, an articulated lorry pulled over. The driver, nose flattened, leaned over and opened his passenger door.

'Where are you going?' he shouted down.

'South of France?'

He laughed. 'Paris do you?'

We climbed in.

5.
Doughnuts

The police marched sideways across the sand, kicking up menace from their boots, wide-bottomed trousers flapping, resisting the breeze. As they passed down the incline towards the sea, greased-up sunbathers rose topless to watch the procession from their mats and towels, hands raised to protect their gaze from the glare. It was hot. The coppers' ties were tucked into their shirts.

'Come here,' said one, irritably, bored, offering his hand out, ushering me up the bank of the beach from the edge of the ocean with a flick of his fingers. I shrugged. I knew the drill.

Every few weeks the local gendarmerie would send down a van of police to pull over sellers on the beach, confiscate their goods, take their names and send them on their way. It was a half-hearted administrative gesture to appease local bureaucrats, nothing more. They knew the dozens of doughnut, caramelised peanut and drink sellers pounding the five kilometres of sand between Cavalaire and La Croix-Valmer were a necessary cog in the local economy, even if we looked like walking health hazards.

The first time it had happened to me I joined the queue of sellers outside the lifeguard hut where the police had set up base to reprimand us. I signed my name on a sheet attached to a clipboard, writing Dennis Watts down just below Mike Baldwin, Bet Lynch, Arthur Scargill and John Noakes. Then I handed my doughnuts to them and walked back along the beach with the tray slung over my shoulder, letting the surf lap my ankles.

When I got back to the rendezvous that evening in La Croix's car park, I told our doughnut boss Cha-Cha what had happened. He laughed.

'You gave them your doughnuts? You should've said you worked for Cha-Cha. That's why I pay the police!'

I explained I'd only sold ten or so before being stopped.

'You keep the money then,' he replied, generously. We went fifty-fifty on all two-franc sales normally. The more we sold, the more we were allowed to take out the next day. My girlfriend regularly sold over a hundred. Typically, I sold seventy or so.

'But next time,' he said seriously, 'tell them you're with Cha-Cha. They're only after the dirty English with all the drinks who get bussed here. Those drinks fuck the beach bars.' He coughed up a huge ball of phlegm and gobbed it across the pebbles. 'I know all the cops. They're cool with me.'

Cha-Cha believed he ran a superior operation and, it was true, his apple doughnuts were delicious. They were baked freshly every morning, and we picked them up at midday from his van before our afternoon shift ended at six in the car park. We were allowed to eat any we hadn't sold, and we did, but we weren't allowed to sell anything else other than his apple doughnuts. After an enterprising employee was caught by Cha-Cha's spotters selling yesterday's wares one morning, we were banned from taking leftovers away after a shift. The seller's tent quietly disappeared from the site overnight. He wasn't seen again.

Cha-Cha was a small, wiry Vietnamese guy with flappy hair who chain-smoked Gitanes and had the gnarled teeth of pre-dentistry man. He ran a big baked goods operation along the Côte d'Azur, scooting to three or four beach car parks along this stretch of coast every day in his transit van with his stoic, book-keeping teenage daughter by his side, all the while dressed in just the snuggest budgie smugglers, a pair of flip-flops, wire-framed sunglasses and a bumbag stuffed full of money. On the dashboard of his van he had a baseball bat on view. In the back, he kept a sword and CS gas canister hidden. Every now and then he'd grab the sword after someone had returned with a bad sales total and jokingly pull it from its sheath, shouting, 'Don't make me use it!'

Cha-Cha had an ongoing 1,000-franc bet with his sellers that none of them could eat one of the small chillies he kept in his money pouch without regurgitating it. He would put a big stack of banded notes down on an upturned doughnut tray next to the tiniest green chilli and offer up the cash to whoever dared while we waited for the rest of the crew to arrive. Every week a new recruit would end up bent double, crying and vomiting as Cha-Cha laughed at them until he wept too. Then he scooped up the cash and put it back in his belt, firing off a volley of insults about Western digestive systems. He derived sadistic joy from the wager. His daughter silently maintained a poker face throughout, unconcernedly marking down the sales totals in her pad. She had no doubt seen worse.

Despite this, each of his sellers defrauded him once. If you had a really good day, selling 120 doughnuts or so, it was worth chucking any remaining doughnuts into the bushes behind the quietest stretch of beach, telling him that you'd been arrested early on and keeping all the profits. We figured that he probably knew this happened and gave you licence to do it once as there never appeared to be any serious discipline afterwards. He just reached for his sword, laughing. What made him more angry was a poor day's sale. He'd want a full debrief on your route, whether you were hungover, on drugs, all that. Generally, these were the reasons he avoided English sellers, he said. 'All drunks, junkies,' he said. 'Hooligans.' I was OK, though, as I spoke French with him and came as one of a pair with the beach's top saleswoman.

I followed the cops up the dune towards the lifeguard's hut.

'Keep going,' said the policeman, as I stopped to look inside. 'We're going to the road.'

Well, hmm. All right. Now seemed like a good moment to employ my magic safe words. 'I work for Cha-Cha,' I told them confidently.

'And?' said the cop. 'I couldn't give a fuck. Go up to the road.' The cop gave me a little nudge to keep walking.

On the roadside there were two parked police vans with their blue lights silently flashing. Beside them on the verge were thirty neatly packed red doughnut trays and several blue cool boxes. I was told to add my wares, which were packed in Cha-Cha's brown tray, to the pile and climb in the second van. I placed my hand on the open door and peered in. It was full of despondent-looking Brits in shorts and beach shoes. Bleached hair. Dennis the Menace and Cockney Reds tattoos. Orange fingers. Baked eyes. Sweat. They shuffled up and I sat down.

'English?' asked one. I said yes. 'Did they take your money?'

'Er, no. Did they take yours?'

'Yeah, cunts. They picked us up on Pampelonne and we've been sitting here waiting for ages. Got any fags?'

I chucked a packet over. Pampelonne beach was fifteen kilometres away. What were the police from over there doing sweeping these beaches too?

A copper walked around to the doors and with an '*allez-y*' slammed them shut on us. The engine chuntered on and we pulled into the road with a jolt. We rode wordlessly for half an hour or so, swerving left and right repeatedly, the nose of the vehicle seemingly on an incline upwards throughout.

The van came to a halt and the doors were yanked open with another '*allez-y!*'. Two cops stood before us, a gang of another half a dozen lined up behind them staring at us. 'On y va! Let's go!' shouted the one holding the doors open. 'All shoes in the bag, stand there!'

The glare from the afternoon had subsided. One of the coppers had a sack open, like a mailbag, and he shook it as we climbed down into the twilight. Each seller placed their flip-flops or sliders inside the bag and hobbled barefoot over the rocky verge to a row of large roadside boulders that had been placed to prevent speeding cars flying over the edge of the cliff we were parked upon. When we were all lined up with the cliff behind us and the vans blocking the view in front, one policeman walked in front of the vans.

'Pampelonne,' he shouted, pointing to his left. 'Twenty-five kilometres, là-bas.' Pointing down to his right, he shouted 'Cavalaire, quinze kilometres.' He rubbed his hands together. 'Bonne chance.' He called over to his colleagues. 'Allons-y les mec.'

The cops walked by us and up into the vans, smirking at us as they passed. The engines started. The lead copper leant out of the window. He pointed to me. 'Toi, viens-voir!' he shouted.

I tiptoed over the rubble and pebbles to his window. 'Oui?'

'When you get home tonight . . . or maybe tomorrow,' he said in French, with a chuckle, 'tell all your little Cha-Cha friends that every time one of you says they've met us and they in truth haven't, we'll bring one of you up here, to see how we treat the English. And maybe we won't be as gentle, you know?' He whacked the side of the door as he hung from the window. The van started to roll forwards and he yelled at me over the engine: 'Cha-Cha knows *everything*, always!'

In two enveloping plumes of dust, the vans drove away.

On a clear day, when the Mistral wind blows in off the sea and clears the haze from the horizon, fanning the flames of not-so-distant wildfires, you can look up from Cavalaire beach and see the top of the hills high beyond the pine forests. That's where we stood now, admiring the view of the trees below, the sunset glow of the towns and the distant depths of the Mediterranean. Then we gingerly stepped on to the gravel road in our bare feet and began the long trek south through the woods, one callused foot at a time.

'What did that copper want from you?' asked one of my new walking companions.

'Oh, nothing really,' I replied. 'He was just answering a question I'd been wondering about, wishing us luck.'

'Got any more fags?'

I told him I was out.

We marched on silently into the pines, bare feet pressed upon pebble and needle.

6.

Early Retirement

'The Lord's Prayer is less than fifty words long, and six of those words are devoted to asking God not to lead us into temptation.'

– Aldous Huxley, *The Doors of Perception*

I stole regularly from the till at work. There's no reasonable excuse for that, of course. It's shameful, selfish, sociopathic behaviour. The wages, however, were terrible, barely more than the unemployment and housing benefits I'd been on previously. I was desperate.

On the other hand, it was a record shop. There was music all day long. You could indulge in whichever sleeve caught your eye from the long, labelled racks that fanned from the counter towards the doors, and if you couldn't find what you wanted to hear in the store you could just order it in. Soon, a girl started there whose boyfriend was a low-key drug dealer and she had at her disposal over a thousand tabs of acid, which she distributed freely. There was a lot going for the job. But the money was terrible.

So, I stole. First, I took records. I know others did that, I saw it happen enough. A busy Saturday afternoon and you spot a familiar face approach the counter. After they hand over the sleeves that they need filling with vinyl, you return to them a bag full of albums you'd stored earlier, then ring in the price of a 12-inch single, take the cash and away they go. I presume there was harm done, to the shop and possibly to the label, the artist, but I didn't care. Music was the only constant in my life. So if I wanted it, I took it. What can I say? My morals are low.

When applying for a job in the record shop, you had to first pass a music quiz to be considered for a position. There was a section about the charts of the moment, another around back catalogue, as well as a picture-based multiple choice where you matched sleeves to artist names. Unprepared for this test, I failed it. Three months later I reapplied, spending thirty minutes in WHSmith reading *Music Week* and *Smash Hits* beforehand so that I'd have my chart blanks filled. This time I passed and was given a post in the Richmond branch, where West London merged with genteel Surrey at the end of the District Line.

That first test failure had confirmed that while I knew what I liked, perhaps I didn't know as much as I thought I did from simply reading *NME*, digging through friends' record collections or those of their parents, or from dancing in discos. Starting work in a record shop shone a light brightly upon my ignorance. I knew the contemporary indie and post-punk canon as well as I wanted to. I could quote any Orange Juice or Pale Fountains lyric instantly. My *Mastermind* subject was the recorded work of the Fall, 1980–87. That covered it, right? I felt like I had contemporary guitar music logged with these artists, along with the Smiths, New Order, REM. Mid-eighties rock appeared otherwise moribund to me. I had albums by the Byrds, the Velvet Underground, Love. What more could the 1980s teach me about guitars that these hadn't?

I wondered if I was, in fact, growing out of guitar music. I listened to a lot of seventies and eighties dub reggae because everyone I knew religiously smoked dope and those were the hymns we prayed to. I went to On-U Sound, Jah Shaka and Manasseh sound system nights, swinging through the dry ice and smoke belches in dusty halls in amongst the occasionally heavy manners. And I loved dancing, the abandon of whizzing off your chops with pals on a dance floor, under disco soft lights or beneath bare bulbs in a chilly warehouse. So my antennae were also tuned into soul and electro, rare groove and funk. We made giddy pilgrimages to see Curtis Mayfield and Gil Scott-Heron play at the Town and Country Club. When I finally snuck by Philip Sallon on the door of the Mud Club at Busby's on Charing Cross Road, making it on to the floor to hear Eric B & Rakim's 'Paid in Full' remixed live by Coldcut for what seemed like an entire session, weaving seamlessly into Joyce Sims's 'Come into My Life' as if the two were some repeated motif for the night, I knew a musical portal had been cranked open. It was the dawning of a new era. Decks controlled the immediate future. Maybe guitars were done for?

So I regarded myself, incorrectly, as an expert in particular strains of popular music. I had all the good stuff covered. But as the first job interview test proved, my fields of expertise were too narrow. More knowledge was required to work behind the counter of a high-street record shop in 1988. It turned out that the best place to learn was on the job.

Pulling up the hatch and stepping behind the counter for the first time, you were faced with thousands of alphabetised white-sleeved albums, walls of singles. Most of them were unknown to me, but there they were, just waiting to be discovered. It was like entering a university for music nuts. The lecturers were my peers, the other oddball kids who'd wound up behind the counter, all with their habitual foibles, personality kinks and particular areas of musical insight to impress upon me, and at times to infuriate me with. We all took our turn on the shop stereo.

'Should we listen to my namesake?' asked Neil, a tall, long-haired fellow in slightly flared blue cords, white shirt and a waistcoat one day. 'What's your favourite Neil Young album?'

I liked Neil, my co-worker, a gentle giant who'd dropped out of a science degree in Manchester the year before and was trying to find his feet again back with his parents at home. I didn't like Neil Young, though, because I'd never heard him. I didn't want to say it aloud, but I was too much of an idiotic snob to listen to music made by someone called Neil.

'I don't have one,' I replied to Neil, making a pained expression. 'Not my thing.'

Neil sized me up. 'You've never heard any Neil Young, have you?'

I didn't reply.

'Right,' said Neil, marching over to the filings marked with a Y. He slipped a record on the deck, carefully moving the needle above the vinyl before dropping it towards its end. Slow, cyclical dual guitar riffs started to flow from the deserted shop's speakers. The reliable stillness that denotes life-changing musical sounds settled upon the room. *Be on my side, I'll be on your side.* Neil pulled out a sleeve from the rack and placed it in the 'Now Playing' holder on the counter: *Everybody Knows This Is Nowhere,* by Neil Young.

'If you say you don't like Neil Young after this,' he shouted across the floor to me as Young harmonised 'Down by the River' above the magnificent swirl, 'then fair play. I'll change my rota to someone else!'

I took the Neil Young compilation *Decade* from the rack and deposited it in my pile of newly discovered old gold that I was hiding for later retrieval. Perhaps guitars still had more to teach me, after all.

I needed my ears about me. New musical fronts were being opened up on every flank. It was 1988. The Golden Age of Hip-Hop was upon us. Every week, our store's rap fiend ordered dozens of new 12-inch singles that he'd heard on pirate radio from the US on export: records by De La Soul, Stetsasonic, EPMD, Twin Hype, Monie Love, A Tribe Called Quest, Big Daddy Kane, 3rd Bass . . . a dozen revolutions arriving wrapped in cellophane by airmail weeks, sometimes months before domestic release. All for sale at a premium, all up for grabs by sticky-fingered staff. For about a month, I thought *Straight out the Jungle* by the Jungle Brothers was the greatest album ever made. I'd never heard hip-hop sound so intimate, nor rapping so playful, so wryly political. Then I listened a little more closely and above the music I could hear tapping from beyond the window: De La Soul and A Tribe Called Quest were on the other side of the glass holding *3 Feet High and Rising* and *People's Instinctive Travels and the Paths of Rhythm* . . . this new sound was in fact part of a movement.

On Mondays – sometimes Tuesdays – the shop's resident rave couple would arrive late to work, still high on the weekend's explorations, babbling about a stack of records they'd heard being blasted out from speaker stacks as they hugged and danced soggy-footed in a field near Addlestone or Datchet. We'd order them all in, too, whacking them on full blast late in the day as the weekend approached in order to sell them out.

This enterprising ordering of rap and rave 12-inchers consequently rewarded us with increased licence to call in more of our own stock. Nothing worked quite as well in this respect in Richmond, however, as acid jazz. Richmond and its adjacent suburbs were mad for funky beats, a Hammond organ, wah-wah guitars and some bongos. There were people regularly coming in wearing bead necklaces, sometimes berets. Whenever I spotted anyone of this persuasion in the shop I'd pull out the James Taylor Quartet's recent 'Theme from Starsky and Hutch' 12-inch and put the volume up. For a while in the late autumn of '88, JTQ's version of the seventies cop show theme became our bestselling single, outpacing some genuine national pop hits.

I wanted all these records, and more.

I couldn't afford them.

But I was hearing so much new music that felt fundamental to my being.

I needed the records.

Yet I was earning under £7,000 a year. I really couldn't afford the records.

So I stole them. I'm sorry.

Soon, though, I needed more than just the vinyl I was lifting.

I found it hard to make it to the end of the month with any-thing in my pocket. I was twenty years old and living in a bedsit in one of those grand houses partitioned into tiny boxes with a shared bathroom on each floor in Turnham Green with my girl-friend, who was going to art school in the week and working in the Body Shop at weekends. We ate a lot of lentils and cup-a-soups. Still, though, I had to catch a bus or a Tube to work, smoke dope, drink lager, pay rent, put 50ps in the meter. It all stacked up. We didn't have a TV, so there was plenty of time to fill with music and books in an L-shaped room, but that wasn't always enough. The first weekend of most months I'd go to a club. Sometimes, a football match. Three weeks into each month, I was broke. Then it became two weeks.

I put my hand in the till.

It was not a difficult crime to commit; there was no master plan to execute. I would simply ring in the wrong amount, give the correct change and pocket the difference. Nobody looks at their receipt and if they do, well, in a busy store mistakes will be made: *can someone mark the till roll please!*

Theft unpunished becomes moreish. The limits of what can be achieved are blurred and you start to forget you're even doing it, as if it's an unacknowledged personal tic, or, worse, justified. I even imagined that the till shortfalls were already accounted for by the powers that be, that they had a hippy record store win-some, lose-some mentality, despite being owned by an ag-gressively profit-focused conglomerate who paid their staff in crumbs. That hectic first Christmas I had pockets full of scrunched notes and heavy metal throughout my shifts, but I was not alone.

One evening some heavies from head office came in and gath-ered all the staff in the back room to discuss the huge shortfall after cashing up each day. They read out a list of numbers tied to specific dates and I recognised that some of the dates coincided with my days off. I looked around the room, sizing up my colleagues. Who was it?

'Keep an eye on the temp staff,' whispered the goateed manager to me, with a wink, as we filed out, and I nodded, knowing it was just as likely to be him dipping in. From here, I scaled back operations to the bare minimum required to stay alive between payslips. I liked the job and I did not want to be arrested.

Saturday night in the Bull pub, opposite the station. A whirl of flirtatious, drunk micro-aggressions, teetering upon the lips of chaos, that first weekend after a payday when all the surrounding suburbs piled in to genteel, picture-postcard Richmond looking for love in all the right places, police in riot gear lined up along the high street's length at tipping-out time to prevent the Montagues and Capulets tearing up once again. That's where we drank away a week's wages in four hours as soon as it hit our accounts.

That Saturday in the middle of 1989's high and heavy second summer of acid house, Bea, the blue-eyed star-child from Eltham who had been frying all our minds that year with her boyfriend's LSD, broke out another round of blotters as the clock struck ten. Soon enough, the pub's secrets started to appear from beneath our table. The main bar's brown edges were no longer blurred and smoothed by Stella, but popping out into something more terrifyingly fantastic. The room oozed.

'The park's open all night,' someone whispered, spotting an exit route from the sensory disturbance, so a small group of us headed up through the bright lights of the main drag, beyond the warren of twee shops and portentous domesticity towards the comforting darkness of Richmond Deer Park.

In the park, we explored the outer and inner worlds free from interference, other than the occasional stag, reaching momentous conclusions about the universe and our place in it that are now, unfortunately, lost. We rolled in the dust, laughing so hard our bodies ached. We spoke in tongues. We made pacts. As dawn appeared in the Isabella Plantation, an immaculate garden set surprisingly in the rangy heart of the park, so too did a small rabbit. We were lying in a line facing him on the spongy grass, resurfacing after the night's battle with our vision and reasoning, though barely yet in control of either. The rabbit stepped forward so we could all focus more clearly upon him in hushed reverence. He held our gaze for a few minutes, staring each of us down, twitching from time to time. Then he winked, before hopping away again. He knew. We knew. Life is brief, a flash of light between two chasms of nothingness.

'We should go to Morocco,' I decided, suddenly but audibly, and all present said aye.

On Monday, I told my girlfriend I was going travelling, as she had also done not long before, and the self-centred inconvenience of my plan sounded needlessly like revenge. On Tuesday, I gave the record shop my notice.

'You should stay,' said the manager, 'there's probably a promotion down the line.'

'I'm going,' I replied. 'I've already bought my Interrail pass. I leave for Amsterdam in four weeks.'

He was confused. 'Why don't you just go on holiday?'

For reasons hard to understand, this sound advice enraged me. 'I'm going,' I told him.

It may have been that summer's fine weather and our constant psychedelic drug use, or simply that I was still really just a kid full of whim, but that year you could sense change. We didn't know the Berlin Wall would be down by the end of the autumn, nor that apartheid would collapse soon after, but the world reverberated with renewal in 1989. We could hear mini revolutions in the songs we were living by, in 'I Am the Resurrection', 'Voodoo Ray' and 'Keep On Moving', and I wanted to feel it all even more intensely than those fleeting moments on a dance floor or at dawn in a park. Happy Mondays had changed my opinions about a work–life balance. The road lay ahead. The past's yours, the future is mine.

'You'll be back,' he replied with a shrug.

The Sunday morning shift always sharpened my perspective. Here's how it began. Set the alarm for 5 a.m. A quick splash, get dressed, then run downstairs and board the night bus heading towards Hounslow from Gunnersbury by 5.30. At Hounslow, change on to the Piccadilly Line just after it starts at 6 a.m., alighting at Heathrow Terminal 3. Ride the escalator to the first floor and unlock the shop's shutters by twenty-to, ready for opening at 7 a.m. How can I help?

My pilgrimage through Europe and Morocco had lasted six weeks. Plotted dismally – by me – to take in the best places to score hash, it ended in Rabat, the day after we'd been mugged at knifepoint on the banks of the river Bou Regreg by two guys selling dope. I didn't begrudge them taking our money, it's a calculated risk when buying drugs on the street in an unfamiliar country, but it also included a long lecture about the evils of Western imperialism generally, and Jews more specifically, as well as a prediction of how Islam would eventually triumph over us, that all felt gratuitous under the circumstances.

'See that river,' one asked rhetorically, gesturing with my cash towards the brownish flow behind him, 'you never see anything like that in the West.'

We looked.

'Have you ever seen a photo of the River Thames?' replied my last remaining companion, Barney.

The next day, Barney, who still had money left for more travelling, generously lent me enough to get to Tangier to board a ferry to Algeciras, where I was understandably strip- and cavity-searched upon arrival at customs. From there, I bunked trains up to Paris – a less daring feat than that implies, as nobody checked tickets – and did the same across the city, jumping a train to

Calais, then, using the last of the money, caught a ferry back to England where I called my girlfriend from Waterloo and asked for her help. Jo took me home to her parents.

Within two months, we were living together again in a flat with a friend on Chiswick High Road and I was back working in the same record shop (albeit a different branch, in Hounslow), just as the manager had predicted.

I felt a failure, but at least I was making a success of that. By the spring of 1990, I had been promoted to assistant manager and was transferred to the world's worst music shop: an airport record shop.

It was shift work, on a rota. Some days you started at 7 a.m. and ended at 3 p.m.; others you started at 3 p.m. and ended at 10 p.m. Every other week you worked the early Sunday shift. There was compensation in the form of three consecutive days off, but it was a fairly miserable experience all round. It was summer in an airport. Dreams were coming true in their thousands every day just beyond the doors of the shop, but within it was strip lights, air conditioning, Gloria Estefan and Daniel O'Donnell. There was no piña colada for me.

I rested my hands upon the counter and dropped my head. It was Sunday morning in Heathrow Airport and I had a passport to nowhere. I raised my eyes to serve a short-haired, middle-aged woman in a tight brown raincoat holding a small pile of CD singles. I filled the sleeves and she paid with a twenty-pound note. Hobbled by hay fever I rang in the wrong amount, but gave her the correct change. She thanked me. I pocketed the note. I'd use it to buy some antihistamine at lunch.

About an hour later, the phone rang. It was the manager, Johnny, a small man but a big farter, who asked me to go on a competitive shopping trip to a rival store in another terminal. This was a first for me, but I welcomed the change of scenery so off I strode, leaving the place in the hands of the other staff. I wandered leisurely over to Terminal 2, where I wrote down the prices of various chart albums and back catalogue in my pad, then turned on my heel and strolled back to my own shop.

As I pulled up the counter hatch I was surprised to note that Johnny was there now, alongside the woman in the tight brown raincoat I'd served earlier, as well as two uniformed police officers. The jig was up.

The woman introduced herself as a shop detective and asked me to empty out my pockets. As I did so, a colleague of hers stepped behind the counter. She'd followed me to ensure I hadn't splashed that loot on anything during my trip between terminals. We all took a good look at the £20 note and, what do you know, its serial number matched a number written down in our raincoat friend's notebook. I was handcuffed and placed under arrest for theft.

'I don't suppose you want those competitive price checks now, Johnny?' I asked my manager as they cuffed me. He didn't. I was led from the shop by the police, past my aghast staff, through the terminal and downstairs into a police car.

We set off towards Heathrow police station. As we drove, the officer in the passenger seat turned around and took a good look at me for a few seconds.

'Assistant manager?' he asked.

'Yes,' I agreed.

'Fucking idiot,' he decided, and turned back to face the road again. 'You've ruined your life, mate.'

I thought about this assessment in the cell over the next few hours. My career in retail definitely looked to have run its course. I had just one O-Level, in French. I had also now been arrested in my place of work for theft. I knew, too, that anyone dismissed for misconduct by their employer had to wait six months to claim dole. My short-to-medium-term prospects appeared challenging, it was true. I didn't even have that £20 note any more.

In a fortnight, I'd be summoned to the shop's head office to be officially dismissed. A week after that, I was due before the magistrate in Isleworth Magistrates Court where upon pleading guilty I would be given a reasonable £80 fine and an insight into the industrial, quick-fire nature of petty crime and punishment in West London. Justice was served, swiftly.

That afternoon, though, after I was fingerprinted and released from the police station, I made my way home alone on the Piccadilly Line, let myself into our empty flat and turned on our new television. Brazil against Sweden was just about to start, the second game of the 1990 World Cup in Italy. The grip upon my neck momentarily released. I wasn't going to miss a second of this tournament after all.

7.

Sonic Boom

Oliver Lim called me one day in the summer of 1990 and asked if I was up to much. I had to tell him that I was not.

'Well, all right,' he said. 'I've been asked by this magazine called *Lime Lizard* to take photos of Sonic Boom of Spacemen 3 and they're looking for a writer.'

'I don't know any writers,' I told him.

'No,' replied Oliver. 'You could do it. It's not hard and I know you love music.'

He was right. I did love music. Music held sway over everything I did. It was my religion, my star sign, my fashion designer, my political adviser, my spiritual guru. It had the final say in any decision. When my heart ached, I turned to Edwyn Collins. When I wanted to feel joy, I danced. After I'd left home and was alone in London for several friendless months in 1985, music had taken care of me. In my basement room, Sly Stone and Lou Reed spoke with me. When I ventured out, I went to see the Prisoners who took me under their wing as they played in pubs and clubs across the capital, in Kennington, Deptford, Whitechapel and other postcodes I may not have visited so soon otherwise. They sorted out my wardrobe, transitioning it from scruffy rockabilly to scruffy mod, introducing me to a new crowd of easy-come, easy-go pals. The Prisoners sent me on a deep listening trip back through the psychedelic sixties of their influences, too: the Nuggets compilations, Jimi Hendrix, the Small Faces and the Pretty Things. They eased me through the loneliness. I owe them my life, truly.

I've had friends who don't like football, for whom clothes are not massively important, who don't want to debate the news, who are lazy readers. I have never had a friend who doesn't love music. It's the red line I cannot cross for companionship.

I didn't know Oliver Lim well, but we had a mutual friend called John Brooker who'd brought us together as he knew we both loved contemporary music. I met John at Richmond College because I had bags of weed and he was very keen on drugs. We shared this. Once, we synchronised dropping acid in our separate lessons an hour before lunch, lasting half the class before escaping together, heading towards the river where we lay on its banks imagining the trees were serenading us with Pink Floyd's *The Great Gig in the Sky* until dusk.

John was six foot five, overwhelmingly ginger, stick-thin but wiry, the loud, central figure in any room. He was eccentric and anarchic, surreally funny. We quickly became close. I now realise he was probably manic-depressive and an unsuitable candidate for the rigorous drugs exploration he'd been on since the day I'd met him. Later, he was sectioned, briefly imprisoned and died before his thirtieth birthday after an overdose, alone on the floor of his room, undiscovered for days.

John introduced me to Oliver the day that *The Queen Is Dead* by the Smiths was released. We shared the price of it from Beggars Banquet on Putney High Street and went back to John's home, where John and I dropped a Valium and listened to its towering poetry on our backs in his bedroom, staring in awe at his ceiling rose for an entire afternoon as we repeatedly flipped the record over to cast its spell again.

Soon we became obsessed with the Beatles' *Revolver*, in particular 'She Said She Said', which John was convinced was about masonic influence in the police. He felt he had particular insight into this as his father was a high-ranking freemason. This became such a quest in his mind that one evening while tripping on acid he smashed a shop window in Putney High Street, then sat on the pavement outside and awaited the police so he could ask them about John Lennon. They arrested him.

Every now and then, I'd bump into Oliver at a party or on the street and exchange worried intelligence about John's latest escapade. I think we both hoped that the other was going to be a calming influence on him in the end.

'So,' asked Oliver, down the phone. 'What do you think? Do you want to try it?'

Well, as he said, doing the interview would not be hard. I'd read a lot of music magazines in my life. My subscription to *NME* had been the most important link to the auld country when I lived in France. It continued to exert a spell upon me as a young adult, as I sat with a new issue hidden on my knees beneath my desk in the clerical office in Fulham every Wednesday, and pawed through reviews or gulped down a Mark E. Smith interview, hoping to avoid detection but unable to wait for lunch break. Even now, on the dole, I scraped enough together every week for it. I could transfer some of what I'd learned reading *NME* into this *Lime Lizard* thing, surely.

I liked Spacemen 3, too. I'd seen them at Subterania: oil wheel projections, heavy drones, two handsome men in denim jackets sitting on stools blasting out repetitive, feedback-drenched songs about drugs and revolution.

'OK,' I said. 'I'll do it. Thanks for thinking of me.'

We met at Euston. On the train to Rugby, Oliver gave me a pep talk. You only need to interview him for forty-five minutes at most and then write around 1,000 words. There's no rush to get it in, either, because the magazine is being run out of a flat in Highbury by an American woman with a load of pet lizards, a labour of love, and it's ready when it's ready. Just write it in the next few weeks. There's no money, but just think of the glory.

It was a very thoughtful gesture from someone I barely knew. A photographer for the *Standard*, Oliver was no doubt regularly around other more capable writers. Yet he'd remembered I liked music so much that he'd thought of me. I toasted him again for the gig.

I'd been doing some stints covering my flatmate Jake's holidays and hangovers as a runner for an editing suite in Soho. I loved the running work because it wasn't really work. It was strolling from Dean Street to Argyll Street, flirting, and then walking back to Covent Garden, sometimes with boxes of pizzas. I did it for two weeks, signed on for two weeks, then signed off again in time to avoid being called in for assessment. I just needed something to do in those two weeks on the dole that wasn't sitting at the window puffing on red seal, watching Chiswick High Road go by. Could this be it?

Pete 'Sonic Boom' Kember met us at Rugby station in his fancy fast car, a live Happy Mondays recording blasting out of the tape deck as he zoomed into the pick-up zone. He yanked open the door and told us to get in. I settled next to him as the electronic bass of 'Hallelujah' rattled the dashboard and he shouted at me, 'Do you like the Mondays?'

I'd taped this same concert from Radio One a couple of weeks earlier, but that story seemed too long. I nodded. I loved them.

'Good, good,' he shouted, turned the volume up and off we sped towards his parents' house, Kember singing along to the choruses and laughing knowingly at Shaun Ryder's ad-libs. 'I've seen them loads,' he said. 'Best band in the country.'

The car crunched over gravel as we rolled inside the gates of his parents' home. It was a mansion. He climbed from his motor and made a dash through the afternoon into the house, bounding upstairs beyond the double-fronted entrance hall four steps at a go. We'd be talking in his bedroom. Tea?

Pete Kember had the physique of Jeremy Irons and the philosophical self-confidence of every public school bad boy you meet at full-moon parties or drug dependency units the world over. A lovely bowl-cut, centrally parted. Button-down shirt under a blue crew neck, light denim jacket, black jeans. Desert boots. An MC5 badge. He gestured towards a beanbag and pulled up a small chair, slipping Link Wray on the turntable first. His room was painted a powerful red and upon the walls were framed prints of Warhol's *Marilyn*, Lichtenstein's *Whaam!*, posters of Bo Diddley, Panther Burns, the Cramps. I noted the Cramps poster and described seeing them in 1984, when there was a riot in the audience at L'Eldorado in Paris. Seats were ripped out of the upstairs balcony and used as missiles on those below, as a local dispute between skinheads and rockabillies was settled. The next night singer Lux Interior came on dressed in just a pair of black leather underpants, holding a lime green umbrella over which he proceeded to pour a bottle of red wine. 'Ladies and gentlemen, last night we fought,' he told us. 'Tonight, we make love.' Then he unzipped his pants and let it all hang out.

This tale broke the ice. For the next half hour or so, Kember and I chatted about records we liked as Oliver took photos of him. After a while, I relaxed in his presence to the point where I felt emboldened enough to ask if he minded if I rolled a joint. OK, he said. Go ahead.

I took a small lump of hash from the inside pocket of my jeans, unwrapped it and put my lighter to its edge.

'Woah,' said Kember. 'Let me have a look at that.'

I handed it over and he took a bite of it. He chewed it for a moment, then spat it on the carpet with disgust.

'That's shit, mate,' he said, decisively. 'You can't smoke that rubbish in here.' He put it on his bedside table and removed a box from his drawer. He produced an eighth-of-an-ounce-sized square of golden-brown hash from it. 'Here,' he said. 'Moroccan, freshly arrived. Good stuff. Use this.'

I took his slab and rolled a joint as he inspected my handiwork in progress. I did not falter. This was the day's one task that I had rehearsed sufficiently. I lit it and passed it to him, but he raised his hand.

'OK,' he said, 'let's do this interview now.'

'Oh, I thought this was the interview?'

'What?! No. No. This is just fucking nothing small talk.'

I stared at him blankly. Not only was I in uncharted territory, I was also now a little stoned.

He started to talk to himself, loudly, but looking at the floor in exasperation. 'I told them about just sending me amateurs, I've got too much to do.'

Oliver leapt in. 'Why don't you tell us about your new album, Pete, where it came from, and Ted will start recording.'

'Oh,' I said, gesturing to the mini-Dictaphone I'd borrowed for the day, 'I've been recording the whole time, it's cool.' (*It's cool?*)

Pete Kember shot me a look, but facing back to Oliver started to describe with great eloquence his first solo album, *Spectrum*, which had been released to middling appreciation a little earlier in the year.

The world was waiting for the final album by Spacemen 3 – his real band – that was due sometime soon. But he and his songwriting partner in Spacemen 3, Jason Pierce, were no longer on speaking terms. A few weeks earlier Kember had announced he was actually no longer in Spacemen 3, as he was affronted that all of the members other than him had released a single together under the name Spiritualized, with a sticker on the sleeve that read Spacemen 3. The tail of the dispute was long. It had its roots in money, ego, comedowns in confined spaces, women. Or, specifically, Jason Pierce's girlfriend Kate Radley, who Kember felt was intruding on their own creative bromance. There had been dramatic disputes in splitter vans over the last couple of years, punches thrown in management offices. It was a bad scene.

Lots of great material there to get stuck into. Instead, I asked how the Spacemen 3 album was coming along.

'It'll come out,' said Kember tersely (and accurately: it arrived in early 1991). 'I'm doing one side and he's doing the other.'

Suddenly and dramatically the front door slammed.

'PETER?' called a clear, crisp, upper-class voice. 'ARE YOU HERE? WILL YOU BE EATING SUPPER?'

Fuck. Kember stood up, opened his bedroom door and called down from the landing. 'I'm just doing an interview, Mum.'

He returned and sat back down. Shall we wrap it up soon? No problem, no problem at all. I put my stuff away and stood to leave. Pete Kember picked up my lump of hash.

'I can't see you leave with this shit,' he said. He handed me his lump. 'Take this instead. I'll give you a lift to the station, there's a train just after six.'

I thanked him for his generosity, given the circumstances. Down the stairs, into his car, speeding through Rugby towards the train, Happy Mondays' 'Wrote For Luck' alerting all of Warwickshire to our approach.

I wrote for luck, they sent me you
I sent for juice, you give me poison . . .

I sat at the enormous computer that I had liberated from a friend's rubbish bin for a very long time. Slowly, I composed my report.

The piece of advice I'd have been most grateful to receive would've been to just write what happened. This always works. I did not know that in 1990, though. I tried to spin my own tale, one designed to obscure how ill-prepared I was for this interview with Sonic Boom. Then I printed that off and went to hand my work to Britt, the woman with the lizards in Highbury. She thanked me, showed me Oliver's beautiful sepia portraits and told me they'd be in touch when the thing was printing. It wouldn't be long.

I waited for weeks. Eventually, I called. Not quite yet. Hang in there. I waited more weeks. I called again. Soon. It'll be printing soon.

One day, I was in Virgin Records on Oxford Street, by Tottenham Court Road. They had a large magazine section. As I wandered over, I saw there was a new *Lime Lizard* on the bottom level of the stand. I stood still and imagined for a moment. If only. I took the magazine in my hands. I opened it. I raced through the pages until, there. There was Sonic Boom, an interview with my byline on it. *Written by Ted Kessler.* I levitated.

Oh, there were a lot of mistakes, errors galore. Not all of them mine. In fact, most of the mistakes appeared to have been inserted after I'd handed it in. Misspellings, rogue bits of copy had landed on the spread, a sentence or two was left suspended, unfinished. But the layout was lovely. Look at those photos, too. And whose name is that, in print?

I felt the blood rush through me in the purest elation I'd ever felt. Minutes earlier I'd been twenty-two years old and on the scrapheap, useless, a criminal. Now, I was a twenty-two-year-old writer, published, in print, for all the world to see, though it would be nearly three years before I'd be able to sign off the dole for good.

I took the magazine to the counter, making sure I caught the teller's eye as I paid for two copies. If only he knew.

8.

David

I placed the photocopies inside the envelope and sealed it. Then I addressed it:

David Cavanagh

Select Magazine

245 Blackfriars Road

London, SE1

I put the envelope on the kitchen table. Maybe I should've put down his job title, too. Deputy editor. It could make all the difference. Might do. Oh, they'll know who he is.

I got a new envelope out and started again.

My dad had sent me a book in the post from New York titled *How to Become A Successful Freelance Journalist*. It was full of jazzy tips for idiots such as me, hopeful, unskilled writers without connections to anyone able to commission magazine or newspaper articles. Those tips included terrible advice about how one should word a letter to a commissioning editor in the style of a nineteenth-century suitor wishing for permission to ask for a hand in marriage from a stern patriarch. It also suggested that instead of sending clippings to the editor, you send them to the deputy editor. They'll have more time to inspect your labours.

I couldn't bear the prospect of being rejected by my true love, *NME*, so instead I sent some pieces I'd written for *Lime Lizard* to the deputy editor at *Melody Maker*, Steve Sutherland. I didn't hear back. I was downhearted, but also relieved. I couldn't read

Melody Maker. All the writers wrote in the first person, the music they often championed was wilfully challenging, while the prose seemed flowery, the tone a bit pompous. I didn't enjoy it and if I didn't enjoy it, why would I want to write for it? Everyone who wrote for *Lime Lizard* seemed to be auditioning for *Melody Maker* too and that reinforced my sense that it wasn't the place for me. I couldn't read *Lime Lizard* either, but that was partly because my own writing was so terrible in it.

I needed something to click, though. I'd been signing on for over six months since the personal apocalypse of my arrest at work, blending that with regular stints as a runner in Soho. Occasionally, I'd cobble enough together to buy a couple of ounces of hash, divide that up and sell it at a small profit to a settle a few debts. It was nevertheless a hand-to-barman existence. Life was drab, occasionally desperate. I spent a lot of time calculating how to game the DHSS so that my dole was not suspended. I was permanently on hold to Housing Benefit at Hounslow Council. Home felt like a waiting room.

My girlfriend was studying to become a jeweller. She was either at art school, working in the Body Shop, or at the lathe she'd constructed in our bedroom, bending metal into beautiful new shapes. She was finding herself, alone, and I could only admire her journey. She had a gift. Did I? All I knew was that we were quietly drifting away to sea in separate dinghies, the tide tugging us in different directions.

I would wait for our flatmate, my friend Jake, to return from Soho every day so we could head over the road to the World Famous John Bull (the pub's real name, though that self-proclaimed fame did not save it: the World Famous John Bull is now an office block) and drink strong lager quickly together, before returning to smoke and play each other records. Nothing really made me happier than that.

There were many days he didn't come home, though, and sometimes there would be a lengthy run of those days. He was on an intense rerouting from the sudden death of his true love a couple of years earlier, electrified by grief and fed into an anything-goes whirl of socialising when and wherever possible, a feat made more feasible since acid house had democratised clubbing and after-clubbing. He could live off a bag of peanuts for twenty-four hours.

I was full of admiration, but I missed him when he wasn't there. I was envious, too, of his ability to swerve my cloying, suburban dole reality for a spot drinking after work outside the Blue Posts, Berwick Street, the procession of possibility all around. I needed some purpose.

Looking for another deputy editor to send my stuff to, I had flicked through *Select* in WHSmith. It was a big, chunky new music magazine with a thick spine. The design was not madly inviting but some of the writing was eyecatching. In particular, the interviews and reviews by David Cavanagh were on another level to anything I'd read anywhere else in music magazines. He was cliché-free and often hilarious, but he wasn't playing it for gags. He had a lightness of touch no matter how heavy the story became, bringing his encounters alive with tiny observed detail and a turn of phrase that took you by the collar and tugged you in closer. I wanted to write like him immediately, no matter how unlikely that appeared. He seemed to know his business. I checked the masthead and oh yes, he was the deputy editor. Maybe he'd like to take a look at my gear. I copied the address from the masthead and left the mag in WHSmith.

I didn't send him the Sonic Boom interview, that would remain my secret. Instead, I sent him my next two encounters for *Lime Lizard*, with Billy Childish and Lawrence of Felt. Childish had met me, an ardent, trembling fan of his many rudimentary garage bands, as well as his art and books, particularly his poetry, in the upstairs bar of the Cambridge on Charing Cross Road, bestowing Medway-inflected philosophical witticisms practically unbidden upon my Dictaphone, while sipping neat whisky and chewing a cigarillo. There, he distilled his belief that amateurism was the highest calling in art or music, that the punk doctrine of only needing to know three chords to make a record had been his ethos until he realised he could do it with two, and that producing any kind of art, music or literature as part of a career path or to get paid immediately invalidated it. He treated his own prodigious output as if it was all a childhood game, like playing soldiers in the woods behind his home in Kent. 'Of course, if Kylie Minogue offered me a million quid to make a disco record,' he chuckled through a puff of cigar smoke, 'I'd have to think very carefully about all my principles.' Nowadays, you'd need a fair amount of spare cash to pick up any of his paintings.

He was the most charismatic, singular man I'd ever encountered in the flesh. Handsome, too. For a while, after seeing his band Thee Milkshakes at the Clarendon in Hammersmith as a seventeen-year-old, I had dressed in his 1961 beatnik-mechanic style and assumed a pattern of speech that I imagined mimicked his, based simply upon his beefy between-song banter. Then, after witnessing his blues duo, Billy Childish and the Natural Born Lovers, in a deserted Dublin Castle in Camden, I'd even started wearing a vintage trilby in tribute for a few weeks, until I tossed it high in the air coming home from the pub one night and it landed upon the roof of an Iceland. I took that as a sign to move on from hats. I never really returned.

He took pity upon my worship, recognised I couldn't really vocalise a coherent question, and gave me the goods. The piece wasn't great, but the quotes were delicious and my friend David Tonge took a lovely sepia photo of Childish thumbing his nose, which made him appear as a roguish Stan Laurel. A beautiful spread. It went in the envelope.

Lawrence was another crush, but an enigma to me. I'd come to his band Felt late, when Jake had placed the song 'Primitive Painters' on to the cassette deck and requested I stop talking, just listen, early one Saturday morning after we'd been raving at

Enter the Dragon. The music rose before me as if I was seeing a new form of architecture for the first time, a hit as fundamental as discovering the Velvet Underground or the Fall, something significant to my being revealed. Great columns of guitar and organ blossomed around Liz Fraser's ecstatic affirmation and Lawrence's repeated declaration:

I just wish my life could be strange as a conspiracy
I hold out hope but there's no way of being what I want to be . . .
Me too; me neither.

But by the time I'd heard them, Felt were nearly over. Their first five years between 1980 and '85 had been defined by Lawrence's close work with classically trained guitar prodigy Maurice Deebank, then the next five, after Deebank had left, by him working alongside teenage keyboard prodigy Martin Duffy. I'd missed nearly all of it, but as soon as I'd heard 'Primitive Painters' I ploughed back through their work in its entirety. No two records were alike, but whether melodic art-rock or spectral instrumental, the introspective atmosphere prevailed as reliably as Lawrence's poetic, gently provocative lyrics. I fell hard for his band, but they were already on their last album, *Me and A Monkey on the Moon*. I never got to see them play live.

I arranged to meet Lawrence upon the steps of the Royal Court in Sloane Square one warm midday after that final album. I'd only seen old photos of him, or newer, moody black and whites in which he wore a wide-brimmed hat over his face. How would I recognise him? Oh, you'll know him, replied his PR, Mick Houghton. He stands out in Belgravia.

A small, pale man in denim flares and a sky-blue, pear-collared John Smedley shirt stood alone on the steps of the Royal Court, glaring with a granite expression, his black hair in vivid retreat from the front of his oval head towards its rear. Lawrence greeted me with a nod and a quick, 'Oh, all right.' He looked like a middle-ranking Soviet chess competitor. He held a well-travelled plastic bag filled with glossy magazines, including a copy of *Newsweek* which he'd bought for its piece about the 'new swinging London', an elusive place he was determined to find. 'So many beautiful girls round here,' he observed as we stood on the theatre steps for a moment, soaking in the view, his vowels lightly browned in deadpan Brummie. 'Not that they ever take a second glance at me.'

We went to his nearby bedsit, where we climbed to the roof, sat in the shade and smoked the joint he had had rolled by his friend for the occasion, on the understanding that before I left I'd roll him a replacement. He never rolled his own, he explained. It soon emerged that we had quite a bit in common. We were both at war with the distributors of housing benefit – 'They have to pay. They have to!' – and we both believed Felt should've been much, much more widely recognised as the underground band of the 1980s. Lawrence consoled me.

'Don't worry,' he said. 'Our time will come in ten, twenty years. We'll be like the Velvets, Television, an underground band that become really important after they've split. I might have to die first to make it happen. But it'll happen.'

In the meantime, he planned to give being an internationally adored and lavishly paid pop star a bash. He'd just returned from a short spell living in New York. 'A disaster,' he reported, glumly. 'I thought I'd be hanging out with Lloyd Cole because I read that *NME* cover where he was shooting pool in his local bar, in the East Village, writing songs, part of a Lou Reed scene . . . nothing. There was nothing going down. I mean, *nothing*. I sat in my room for three months then came home.'

He'd had an idea there for a new band, though. 'Denim. We're going to be 1970s meets 1990s, totally against the 1980s.' He explained that he was going to do everything in opposition to his work in Felt. Denim would be signed to a major label, hire expensive studios and producers, use the best session musicians. And they'd have big chart hits, that was guaranteed. 'Nobody can say they were more committed to being an independent artist than me in the eighties,' he explained. 'Ten albums, ten singles in ten years on the indie labels of the decade, Cherry Red, El and Creation. I've done that. I'm going completely against it. This is going to be my childhood meets the future. Middle-of-the-road future-pop. It's gonna be massive.'

In the actual future, Denim made one truly visionary album in 1992, *Back in Denim*, and one very good album in 1996, *Denim on Ice*. They were signed to a major label and they spent a lot of money on musicians and producers and studios. But they were not pop stars. They were actually less commercially successful than Felt. They had a single A-listed by radio stations in 1997 that looked like it was becoming a novelty hit, but the day before release it was withdrawn from the shops and pulped. Princess Diana had died in a car crash that evening and the single was called 'Summer Smash'. Lawrence disbanded Denim soon after.

That late summer day in 1990 on the roof of his bedsit, though, the future was full of possibility for Lawrence, hope glistening upon the horizon. That was the tale I told in *Lime Lizard*.

I stuck the Felt story in the envelope for David Cavanagh too, included a stiff note asking to be considered for commission and hoped for deliverance.

A few weeks later it landed upon the doorstep in a mailer marked *Select*. I could see it from the first-floor landing and I threw myself down the stairs to open it in the hallway.

Dear Ted,
Thanks for your clippings. I read your Felt piece and it was pretty good stuff. I'd like to try you on some reviews if that suits you? Do call.
Best wishes,
David

Would that suit me?! You bet, buddy. I did a little dance in the hallway and tore back up to the top floor and our flat.

London Calling

YES!

Fuck. How do you write a review?

It was amateur hour in the Cock on Great Portland Street, office lads bantering up the path to the bar, gaggles of tourists huddled around a half of Guinness and five packets of crisps in that window of nonsense just after work. I found a seat at a table by the door, tugged a stool underneath with my foot and waited for Alan Cavanagh.

I hadn't seen his brother David for many years, though we had exchanged dozens of emails in the last year or so. I couldn't recall the last time we'd met in fact, but I remembered the first.

He'd emerged into the reception area between *Sounds* and *Select* on the first floor of the Express building and beckoned me towards him. A paisley shirt, untucked beneath a cord jean jacket, fair complexion, wispy hair, glasses, the whiff of an Irish accent worn away over time. He was shyly taciturn and I was terrified. We didn't say much. Instead, he invited me to crouch by his desk, shaded from the scrutiny of the rest of the *Select* team by his tower of promotional cassettes, and suggested I might take an album from his drawer to review. I picked out Carter the Unstoppable Sex Machine because it was the first name I recognised. He hesitated, calculating no doubt the risk of giving a page lead to a review virgin, but he was too kind to take it back. Two hundred and fifty words for Monday, please. Fax it in.

A few days after the deadline I returned to the *Select* office to see David Cavanagh again, as he had some insights he wanted to share about my work. He gave me a copy of the review as it would appear in *Select*, alongside several pages ripped from a pad of notes he'd written, reviewing my review. The deconstruction also contained a list of pointers for the next time I attempted the enterprise. Reading how far off-beam my work had been I was amazed there would be a next time.

It was the kindest, most generous act. My first paid commission would appear in my name, even though it bore little resemblance to my work. If he hadn't saved the copy, if he'd recommissioned it, that probably would've been the end of the line. My confidence would not have recovered. Instead, he opened up his drawer and suggested I try my hand at some reissues for next month. It was a turning point.

Over the years I remained his keenest fan, collecting every issue of *Select* and then *Q* that he wrote in. His feature writing, especially the descriptive detours in his profiles, left indelible marks in my brain: a description of Mark E. Smith, pissed, reaching for his jacket from behind his chair in a Chinese restaurant; a running gag about Paul Weller sacking his bass player on tour in Japan. He found nooks to write about in the access he was afforded, in hanging around waiting for the scheduled interview moment that others missed. His observational style was completely his own. I'm not ashamed to say that when I first found myself commissioned to write features for *NME* I drew on his distinctive style to try and uncover my own. He was a heroic figure to me.

Occasionally we'd cross paths, before a gig, in a pub, and have an awkward pint of no-chat. He was better at writing than talking. Even friends would describe hours spent in silence having been invited to the pub by him. Once, though, in 1996, he went out of his way to speak with me.

I'd written an *NME* interview with Ride that opened with the revelation that an unnamed employee of their label, Creation, had said that they were splitting shortly after the release of this new album. This did not seem a controversial insight to me, as the band had insisted they be interviewed in separate locations on different days because they weren't really speaking any more, but the fact I'd used an unnamed source tripped an alarm at Creation. Their bullish in-house PR Andy Saunders called in fury and threatened to break my legs if I didn't reveal who'd spoken, unaware that as I was awaiting a phone interview on the line,

I had my phone-tap attached recording the call. This insurance policy escalated tensions between magazine and label. It was a tight squeeze.

The next night I was at a gig at Shepherd's Bush Empire. When the house lights came up I saw David Cavanagh marching through the sea of discarded plastic pint pots towards me. He looked serious. Was he about to nab me for biting his style for so long? He leant into me.

'Your Ride piece was on the money,' he said. 'Don't let them scare you, we've heard all about it. Keep at it.'

Then he strode off again. The clouds parted, but I'm not sure we spoke again for decades.

Over the years, I kept in touch with him chiefly through his writing, most notably his glorious biography of Creation Records, *My Magpie Eyes Are Hungry for the Prize*, the set text for all music books, the absolute don of the genre. You'd hear rumours about him. How he fell out with the editors at *Q* and *Mojo* magazines and refused to work for them again. About how active he was on the Fall fan group message board. About his taste for this, his taste for that. At Reading Festival in 1993, a batch of strong ecstasy arrived in the backstage tent. While people carefully split pills in half, I watched him swig two back then march off to the Ramada hotel, where he sat on the floor in the bar with his back against the wall, watching the evening roll away, poker-faced, lost in his thoughts.

Then, in 2017, John Mulvey became editor of *Mojo*. Mulvey had commissioned David at *Uncut* when David had refused to work with the previous editorial regimes at *Mojo/Q* and wanted to bring David back over with him. Cavanagh was keen, but needed to write for *Q*, too, to help make ends meet. Would I be amenable to giving David work? asked John of me.

David Cavanagh dropped me a line and asked how I felt about it as well. He'd be happy, he said, to start on some reviews if needs be.

'David,' I said. 'You're the best music writer of your generation. Perhaps you'd like to write this interview with Luke Haines instead?'

'Of course,' he replied, turning in an exquisite pub-profile with Haines, winkling out a funny, charming story from a couple of hours spent with a famous curmudgeon who'd only recently taken the time to hospitalise me on Twitter for the crime of editing a music magazine. He hated music journalists, but he loved David Cavanagh. Afterwards, the pair made plans to go to the Test series the following year at Lord's together. Once the piece was out, Haines messaged me to thank me for sending Cavanagh to interview him and said he hoped there was no hatchet to be buried between us. It was a fine piece of ambassadorial work by David.

Over the coming months we spoke regularly about getting him on other features. David had an idea to turn in a big story marking a year since Mark E. Smith's death in January 2019. He'd go to Manchester, speak to Smith's partner, his pals, his sister, his bandmates. I excitedly commissioned that, telling him I'd need his copy by early January to get it in the issue out at the end of that month. I bought him a train ticket to the city for early December. In the meantime, I asked if he'd like to interview the melancholic Northern singer-songwriter Bill Ryder-Jones for a six-pager? David spent a few hours listening to Ryder-Jones's melodically mournful music and returned enthused. I took the moment to thank him, once more, for giving me that first break all those years ago and fixing my review, for giving me those notes. The pages he'd written for me, I told him, were my bible for a long time. I returned to them often when reviewing.

He replied that he remembered it too but that I was exaggerating the size of the task. 'It wasn't charity,' he said. 'We all need a little guidance at the start.'

His interview with Bill Ryder-Jones was intense, moving, masterful. He'd travelled to Merseyside to meet Bill at his mother's home in West Kirby, near Bill's own flat. They talked about love, self-harming, his old band the Coral, his bouts of depression, and his elder brother, Daniel, who'd died in an accident when he was nine and Bill was seven. Daniel had fallen from a cliff in Wales during a family holiday. 'He's kind of *the thing* in my life,' Ryder-Jones told David. He had a photo of him on the sleeve of his new album *Yawn* and the word 'Danny' scratched into his hand.

Towards the end of the piece, David wrote this:

> Ryder-Jones, in the end, presents his life with no closed doors or private rooms, leaving it up to you when you've seen enough. The moment arrives when he pulls down the neck of his T-shirt to reveal the words BILL WAS HERE carved into his chest with a razor blade. Like all his tattoos, it was self-administered. 'I don't like needles,' he explains. Then, seeing the look of horror on my face, he laughs. 'It's supposed to be funny, not scary,' he admonishes. 'Picture it, though. Picture me on a slab and you're the mortician. And it says 'Bill Was Here' on the body. You'd think, 'Hey, that's nice, he's put a joke in just for me.'

This piece was published in the issue of *Q* out at the start of December 2018. On 29 December, I checked my emails and saw there was a short, polite message from a woman called Penelope whom I did not know, explaining that David Cavanagh had died suddenly a couple of days earlier. She couldn't say more, but she knew we were close colleagues. She was so sorry to tell me and I was so sorry to hear.

Unsure what to do with the news of David Cavanagh's death, I organised a commemorative drink for his colleagues and friends at a favourite bar in Central London, the Social, in early February 2019. A few days before, an email from Alan Cavanagh arrived. He introduced himself as David's older brother and wondered if I would be able to meet with him for a coffee or pint. I was surprised about this, given my slim connection to David, but we arranged to have a drink before David's commemoration, which Alan declined to attend.

Alan pulled out the stool from beneath the table in the Cock and got down to business. He's strikingly a get-down-to-business kind of man.

'It's all a bit of a mess,' Alan explained. David had died with considerable debts and very little income – he was living in his friend's spare room in Hove – but he did have a large record and CD collection, much of which was now in Alan's home. He wondered if I knew anybody who might want to buy it to help satisfy some of David's creditors? 'There's something else, too,' he added. He asked if I knew what had happened to David. I told him that I did not.

There was a note, Alan said, that David left before he climbed from the platform at Leagrave Station in front of the East Midlands service travelling at 100mph between Derby and London on 27 December.

The note explained that David had gone to see his mother in Bedford for Christmas, deciding to end his life on 23 December. But in order to minimise the disruption to others going home for the festive break, he waited until the 27th to catch the Bedford to Brighton train, cross to platform three at Leagrave and await the high-speed through service.

I am hoping some karma may come my way, David wrote.

'He also mentioned you in the note,' said Alan.

Me?

'He wanted me to apologise on his behalf for not filing the story he was working on for you. He knew you were expecting it.'

I shrugged apologetically, raising my hands. Alan shrugged too. It was more of a mention than their mother had received, he added. I replied that suicidal despair is hard to rationalise after the fact. I wished to tell David not to worry more than anything.

London Calling

We finished our drinks, shook hands and left through separate doors. I crossed Great Portland Street and walked down its sister, Little Portland Street, towards the Social, the bar where tonight everyone knew his name. The room was full, we raised a toast. We all had David Was Here carved into our chests.

Part Three
Pink Press Threat

9.
There's No Limit

All writers – but not just writers, everyone, in fact, involved in creating magic from a vacuum – need to prepare for the profound early disappointment that awaits. They may not achieve alchemy the first fifty times they attempt it. Perhaps it'll elude them a hundred times. They should not give up.

Everyone lacks finesse and style when they start writing. The story will not translate to the page. If it does, it may not be read as the writer hears it, bruising the ego to the bone. This does not indicate a lack of valuable insight or a tale unworthy of sharing. It doesn't mean they're not smart or tasteful enough. The imagination is in working order. All that is missing is skill and experience. The only way to correct that is through practice. Through trial, repeated error. Reading, too, copying admired writers whose work seems most closely within reach. The writing process may not become easier or quicker with time, but it will improve. If trusted advice can be sought, that's useful. Above all, though, write through the confusion. Write on a page, not in the mind where we are all fluent, elegant, successful, untested. Finish what has been started, cut what must be cut, then begin something new. You never know when everything might click.

I was about to quit music journalism after four years of desperate fumbling in search of a voice when *NME* called. It was March 1993. Steve Lamacq had recently left the magazine, along with a load of other high-profile staffers. These staff members had been sulking that the deputy editor of *Melody Maker*, Steve Sutherland, had been appointed *NME* editor, making the quick trip down from the twenty-sixth floor of King's Reach Tower to the large editor's office just within the entrance to the twenty-fifth, a pipe-cleaner clutching boxes of CDs and sporting memorabilia, his bald bonce bobbing through the swing doors, a white T-shirt and pale blue 501s pulled up uncomfortably high in the crotch.

They most audibly complained that, as well as apparently crossing an NUJ picket line of the building, shortly before his appointment Sutherland had written that the difference between *NME* and *Melody Maker* was like that between 'dogshit and diamonds'. If he thought that, they said, why was he coming to edit their dogshit? Fuck him. They left.

Lamacq turned up at *Select*, where I was still toiling away on a small handful of monthly reviews, and asked me out for a pint. I met him – face of a Victorian pickpocket, voice like a Galaxy bar – ready to say that I'd applied to the London College of Printing to study for a journalism certificate, so I could work for a local paper or something similar that would allow me to finally sign off the dole. I was twenty-four. I'd been in the workforce for seven years, but unemployed for at least half of that time. I felt madly dysfunctional and hopeless.

Before I could tell Lamacq that the end was nigh for me in music journalism, he suggested that I speak with Simon Williams at *NME*.

'You're exactly what Simon needs on the *NME* lives desk,' said Lamacq, ridiculously. 'Drop him a line, he'll be expecting you.'

This all seemed very far-fetched to me. Still, I wrote a letter and Simon Williams called me back, commissioning a hundred-word live review: Judda at the Bull & Gate in Kentish Town, on stage at 10 p.m.

Judda weren't the worst band I'd ever heard, but they were the worst band I'd ever heard play live. It was some kind of industrial nonsense, conducted by strobing lights and dry ice, played to a dozen people in a North London boozer, all serious goths in platform boots and cheek piercings. Beforehand, a band associate had spotted the journalist in a duffle coat and Chipie jeans, and offered me two pills to write a positive review. I declined. It was too soon into my *NME* trajectory to accept payola. It was also Sunday night.

Nevertheless, soon after the review ran I received my first piece of hate mail, presumably from the band: a death threat from someone indignant that I didn't like Judda. They wrote that I had a 'baked bean brain'.

I was getting somewhere, finally.

Soon, I was accepting all kinds of commissions from Simon. I was going to review jazz-rap at the Forum, punk-funk at the Jazz Café, Bruce Springsteen at Milton Keynes. I was sitting in pubs and cafés with new acts more nervous than me, interviewing them for 400-word front-section pieces. Suddenly, after four blank years, I felt unburdened, busy, free to write as I imagined. I was too regularly commissioned to overthink my writing. Bosh. Just get it done and in on time. The penny had dropped.

Equally heartening was the fact that I was often invited by Simon and his assistant John Harris into the *NME* office to pick up music, go to the pub at lunchtime and follow them out to gigs at night. The curtains parted and I glimpsed the future: I belonged as a jobbing journalist on *NME* all along. I knew it!

We spent hours talking conspiratorial music biz and office politics twaddle in the Brunswick over two-hour lunch breaks, waddled back pissed to *NME*, listened to the cheery, pleading, furious answerphone messages, ate sandwiches, smoked, wiped the answerphone, went to the Stamford Arms to top up, then headed out to a night of gigs, travelling everywhere by black cab on Simon's expense account. My life had passed through the mirror into a bizarro world in direct opposition to the previous four years: I had too much new paid writing work to get through; I was working collaboratively as part of a large team of like minds;

Pink Press Threat

I was pressed against leather in the back seat, watching London roll by the window.

After gigs, I'd sometimes end up smoking dope back at Simon and John's shared maisonette off Pitfield Street in Old Street, laughing helplessly at Simon's codeword-heavy gobbledegook reviews delivered in real time as we tore through his pile of hush-hush demos, testing them under heavy-resin conditions to see if the bands lived up to their pub backroom promise, before I fell asleep on the sofa and he wombled up to his room . . .

I'd awake with a start. Check the time. Shit. 8 a.m. Appointment is at 9.15. Shoes on, splash face. Quick note on the back of a bill in the kitchen, stuck to the fridge door. *Dear Simon and John, thank you for your hospital. Gotta run. I have to sign on. Ted.*

When I arrived back at *NME* from the Putney DHSS, the note was hanging from the wall divider next to Simon's desk. They thought it was hilariously quaint that one of their regular reviewers was also on the dole. I could see the joke. Here we were, on the twenty-fifth floor overlooking Blackfriars Bridge, an uninterrupted billionaire's view of Central London and beyond, all the way to Hertfordshire, Essex and the wide, wide world, watching the weather roll across the horizon, with our desks and direct phones, our photo bylines in a magazine selling more than 100,000 copies every week, holding sway over the dreams and nightmares of desperate young bands like jumped-up beaks, ferried between freebies in a stream of black cabs. But the truth was that if I didn't sign on and off unemployment benefit between commissions then I would lose my housing benefit, without which I had no hope of paying rent.

There was talk that John Mulvey, the features editor, was mulling over trying me on a bigger story for features. I reckoned, hopefully, that if that was true and it went OK, well, then there might be other features, and if that was also true, then maybe one day I'd have so many features that I'd be able to sign off permanently . . .

Then, I discovered my niche. It turned out that I could write convincingly about techno and dance music, about club culture, about my contemporaries who'd come of age during acid house and were now, five years later, part of a wave of acts making dynamic electronic music of their own. Orbital, Leftfield, the Dust (later Chemical) Brothers, Underworld, Aphex Twin and the Prodigy were all generating enthusiasm well beyond the specialist dance counters in Soho. It had to be covered more widely in the paper, it couldn't be partitioned solely into Vibes, the dance section of *NME* edited by Graham Sherman.

Sherman – as he was universally known – operated Vibes as if he was Asterix and Vibes was that small indomitable village in Gaul holding fast against the Roman Empire. Mirroring the mindset of many in the dance universe then, he believed that techno was a new year zero for music and that guitar music would perish beneath the glacial weight of techno's irresistible 120 BPM. It was just a matter of time. If he could've erected barbed wire around his desk he would've, but instead he commissioned his section from home, calling you at lunchtime and bellowing instructions for mini-interviews he needed over crashing dub reggae in the background, depositing his edited copy on the office server overnight when everyone was asleep. He was a mod and the rest of *NME* were despicable rockers in his mind. I really liked him.

He couldn't be trusted to write about this wave of electronic artists outside of Vibes though, lest it read as campaigning propaganda. Much of the dance writing that transferred to the rest of the paper beyond Vibes was mixed at best. For many of the indie kids and guitar-based men and women of *NME*, writing about techno or DJs presented some notable obstacles: there were no guitars or frontmen; there were no lyrics; the gigs often happened very late in unusual places. I didn't mind any of that. Yeah, I'll go to that all-nighter at the Rocket on Holloway Road. I'd probably go anyway if I could. Sure, I can turn around 600 words on the Drum Club and the Grid. I am more than happy to check out

Pink Press Threat

Andy Weatherall's night at Sabresonic. Yep, I can meet Spooky down at the Brain and Bandulu in London Fields. You need someone to review the Prodigy on Monday night, venue stacked with whistle-blowing teenagers in tracksuits? Brilliant. Yes, I'll go alone. No problem.

I'd interviewed lots of electronic and dance acts for *Lime Lizard*: Aphex Twin, Meat Beat Manifesto, Bomb the Bass, Mark Moore, the Shamen, Baby Ford. They were all complex, often vociferous characters who stood for a way of artistic life beyond the mainstream, and that couldn't be said for every mopey, craven young guitar band I came up against. I'd learned to treat any act as a story to be told in its own right, regardless of the instruments used.

At that moment in 1993, there was a freedom of expression, an idealism, a liberating hedonism present in this new wave of electronic acts that was perhaps not there in your regulation guitar groups, who had a much more tried-and-tested career path. It felt like the start of something genuinely forward-facing and original. They were setting out on a different trajectory, a more democratic creative path.

They didn't need to play an instrument. They didn't need to dress a certain way. They could do what they liked with their hair – baldness wasn't an impediment. All they needed were good ears and an open mind towards contemporary computer, drum machine and sequencing technology. They could create new music based around rhythm that had an audience hungry for it, a constituency born five years earlier from acid house who weren't interested in standing in pubs cross-armed, watching bands retread old ideas; listeners who wanted to be part of a communal experience, dancing to live music in a club environment. It was the evolution from DJ to creator, in its infancy, but nobody went to a techno show to watch the performers. We came to dance beneath the bright lights, enveloped by new sounds.

It was undeniably more exciting than the new rock and indie music of that moment, as evidenced by the fact that even the most committed indie fans on *NME* were coming to Orbital all-nighters to unwind at the end of a busy week soaking in Carling Premier at the Bull & Gate. It was a good time. But could they describe it in 1,000 words? Not so easy.

I didn't exactly have the electronic field to myself at *NME*, but there weren't many other dogs patrolling that plot and the sheep were running wild. They needed herding. I could herd.

My first *NME* feature was an interview with Ultramarine, two softly spoken lads from Essex who had patented a beautiful pastoral-techno sound on their 1991 album, *Every Man and Woman Is a Star*, and were now, in 1993, adding more folky jazz to the mix. I told the tale of their new collaboration with the veteran English singer-songwriter Robert Wyatt called *Kingdom* and was rewarded with the opportunity to write about the forthcoming Megadog Midi Circus tour.

Club Dog was a psychedelic dance night in London during the late eighties and early nineties run by a hippy-looking fellow who called himself Bob Dog. It eventually became so popular that it grew into the huge monthly Megadog parties held at the Rocket. There was no dress code and attendees didn't look much like clubbers, they looked like students, squatters, longhairs, the kind of people you found dancing to a bongo by a bin fire in the stone circle at 4 a.m. at Glastonbury. But a large, eclectic mix of DJs and acts had coalesced around the Megadog brand and, proving that being a hippy need not be an impediment to also being an enterprising entrepreneur, Bob Dog was taking a revolving cast of them on tour around Britain under the banner of the Midi Circus. For a large preview piece, I interviewed Bob Dog and all of the touring acts: the New-Agers influenced as much by *Apocalypse Now* and Cirque du Soleil as Detroit techno, like Eat Static, Drum Club, Banco de Gaia, alongside the two stars of the package, Kent's ex-punk prog-ravers Orbital and the gifted electronic composer Aphex Twin, aka Richard James. After it ran, I was commissioned to write a separate page profile of Paul and Phil Hartnoll, the brothers who operated under the name of Orbital.

I caught a train to Nottingham on 6 July to interview them ahead of that night's Megadog-sponsored Midi Circus show, in the hope that for colour I'd be able to capture some of their live dynamism, alongside backstage japes. The concept of the tour, as told by the Megadog people, was that this was a psychedelic techno circus coming to your town, engineered to expand minds while making you dance all night. That wasn't exactly what I discovered.

It was a Tuesday in the east Midlands, at a venue called Rock City, ironically. Out front, Drum Club – an unlikely duo made up of the son of a High Court judge and a wideboy rave promoter who lived together high on the hog in a vast Brixton squat – were battering a few dozen students clutching subsidised pints at the back of the cavernous auditorium further towards the bar with a grey-faced, repetitive drum-machine minimalism that belonged in a tiny sweatbox club at 2 a.m. It was 8:30 pm. Backstage, the vibes were equally flat and prickly. The 24-hour techno-colour dream was mugged by the humdrum, monotonous reality of soundchecks, load-ins, local promo and general hurrying-up to wait experienced by all touring bands throughout the ages.

Richard James was unhappy that Aphex Twin was billed last on stage that night. There had been a heavy celebration after the London all-nighter at Brixton on Saturday.

'I wish I wasn't doing this fucking tour,' he decided, throwing his big-booted feet on to the catering table in the strip-lit canteen, sending the salad dressing rolling across the top.

'Don't worry, mate,' his companion said, conspiratorially leaning into me, 'we've not really slept much since Friday. He's just grumpy.' He shouted across the table at his companion. 'Aren't you, Richard?'

'I want to go laser gun shooting down the road. Is there time?'

'It's closed.'

'Fuck.'

'Yeah.'

Aphex Twin was gaining a reputation as being a once-in-a-generation talent, a composer capable of timeless, mood-altering melody, who improvised new sounds and rhythmic patterns from his re-engineered keyboards and drum machines. He was way ahead of the pack, digging out his own space. The press – and here I suppose I include myself – were building him into a Brian Eno-meets-Mozart figure. A genius enigma, even if the enigma element was mainly down to Richard James wanting nothing to do with it.

I'd interviewed James twice before and knew him to be contrary, secretive, cheeky, a grubby monkey and mischievous disrupter keen to disappoint all expectations in him whenever possible. He told fabulous stories about his music: that he'd made it ten years earlier as a child living in Cornwall; that the tapes for his masterpiece debut *Selected Ambient Works 85–92* had been released without his permission by his friends. Whenever he was praised too highly or roundly for his work he delighted in releasing something unlistenable in its slipstream or throwing out a really good limited-edition white label under an alias, then denying its existence. Build your own mythology, if you must.

He clothed his basic biography in heavy camouflage, making winkling out confirmation impossible. Once, he arranged to meet me for an interview in the Whispering Gallery of St Paul's, insisting on conducting our conversation from opposite sides of the circular gallery, speaking sotto voce to each other facing into the wall, attempting to catch the echo. When I suggested we go to the pub instead, he refused. 'No way am I letting you get me drunk and accidentally telling you the truth.'

He liked the idea of making money though, because it would provide the means of disappearing further into his own myth. That's why he was doing this tour. He wasn't doing it to make friends.

'Look at these fucking hippy cunts,' he said loudly, as a procession of road crew passed from the stage down the backstage corridors around us. 'Just look at them! Fucking state.'

Another of his friends, a tall skinhead, sat down at the table. 'This is your life now, Rich,' he said, raising his eyebrows behind James's back. 'Year 2000 you'll be on a "Rave's Not Dead" tour for a month in America.'

'Fuck off!'

'It'll be you, Rozalla, 2 Unlimited, the Prodigy, Utah Saints . . . it'll be big, all you old fat raveheads, coining it in Texas.'

Out front, the strobes and expansive, synthesised melodies of Orbital had finally brought the dancers in, arms raised. Rock City wasn't full, but it was no longer empty. People swayed in the green lasers, eyes closed, tugging on joints to 'Halcyon + on + on', the Hartnoll brothers' wordless hymn to their mother's addiction to tranquilisers and Orbital's banger of that moment. I danced for a bit, then wandered backstage to meet them as they came offstage, torch glasses still clicked on, eyes on stalks.

We chatted for a while in the cold white whirl of their post-show dressing room, laughing about Richard James's world-class sulking, the brothers buzzing from their performance. People came and went, gulping down their modest rider. I asked the Hartnolls where they were staying.

'No, we're driving back tonight,' said Phil. 'Crew are all staying.'

Overhearing this exchange, one of the Megadog road crew muttered into my ear. 'If you're staying,' he said, 'have one of these. There's fuck all else to do.'

He handed me a pill which I swallowed almost without realising. It was just so brilliant being paid to go out, to write about it. I was in the moment. I had my toothbrush in my top pocket.

Returning to the auditorium to watch Aphex Twin, I bumped into a couple of members of Seefeel, an ambient guitar band I'd recently interviewed. They'd driven up to watch Aphex from London with their A&R man and publisher because Aphex had remixed them. The crowd thronged towards the stage as we chatted, then the lights dimmed. A roar rolled through the room . . .

The lights immediately went back up full, every bulb lit. The whole room was flooded with white light, no crevice untouched. The mellow, touchy-feely Megadog mood was suddenly extinguished. Bob Dog must have been going mad. The oil wheel projection was switched off.

A drum machine started to misfire at top volume. Then the skinhead, Richard James's friend, appeared topless, dancing across the stage, punching the air and gurning as James stood hunched over his keyboard behind him, pressing buttons seemingly at random, making a punishing racket.

At first, applause. Laughter. Soon, disquiet. What is this dreadful noise? A track ended. Another started. It was indistinct from the previous one, other than it was louder. And again, louder, worse. The audience started flowing out of the venue, which Richard James appeared to celebrate by throwing his arms in the air as if he'd scored a goal.

Seefeel's bassist Darren Seymour turned to me.

'He said he was going to do this. How are you getting back to London?'

Their publisher was driving and there was room for one more in the back. It's got to be better than the Holiday Inn Express, I replied. We hopped in the motor and left before Aphex Twin had wrung the final agonising note from his keyboard.

The night sky was exquisite, inky, backlit by a blanket of stars. Quite a view I had there, leaning against the window, the motorway echoing beside my ears. The driver stuck a tape in the deck, organs and beats enveloping the ride, as we sucked in the sights, a Scalextric racing around the bend towards the capital, orange lights across my eyes, then black, then orange, then black . . . the night, great speed, deep sounds, an eruption of emotion experienced in solitude, travelling through the wee-small-seventy-miles-per-hours.

'Does anyone mind if I open the window to smoke?'

We pulled into a floodlit forecourt and climbed out, lolloping across the car park towards the twinkling café. As we sat at an orange table, the room rushed to greet us, wrapping its arms around me, squeezing. I cleared my throat.

'I'm really sorry,' I said precisely, possibly loudly. 'I took a pill before we left.' Big gulp. 'It's coming on very strongly.'

The table cackled, rippled, shook. The café was a cartoon, every edge rubbed smooth.

'Obviously,' smiled the publisher, kindly, his face exploding into a thousand fractured pieces. 'Would you like a sweet drink?'

Dropping the band off at various stops around south-east London, we circled back up towards the west as dawn broke. We drove down the Mall at first light, swooping by Buckingham Palace to the sound of sparse psychedelic house music, just me and the driver, otherwise silent. The city was yet to wake fully. We had the streets to ourselves.

We nosed through Hyde Park, over the Westway and down towards Hammersmith, along the Fulham Palace Road until we pulled up at Bishop's Park. I thanked him for the ride and walked over Putney Bridge, the warm glare of sunrise baking my face as I held on to a lamp post and took in daybreak's full implication.

I placed my 1,500 words about Orbital on John Mulvey's desk the following Tuesday. The rest of the NME staff and top-line freelancers were crammed into Steve Sutherland's office for the weekly editorial meeting when I arrived. I was not invited, so instead I pulled up a seat in the empty hub at the Live desk, flicking through that week's newly arrived issue.

The door to Steve's office cracked open.

'Ted,' called John Mulvey. 'Can you come in please?'

I stepped into the office. Every head – bored, passive-aggressive, curious, kind, tough-guy – turned to face me. What now?

'Ted,' repeated John. 'How much did you get from Orbital the other night?'

'Well, it's on your desk, so—'

'What we're thinking,' said Steve Sutherland, impatiently, one finger in his ear, his usual tell when delivering a big statement, 'is that we'd like to put them on the cover next week. Photos are great, they're selling tickets, records. It seems like it's their moment. Could you expand what you've got?'

'To around 3,000 words?' rejoined John.

I'd never written 3,000 words. 'Probably not,' I replied, sadly.

'Get on the phone to [PR] Jones, then, and see if you can get hold of them today or tomorrow. We'll need copy first thing Thursday.'

I left the room, dazed. I heard Sutherland clap his hands together and say, 'Any more for any more', and then the staff shuffled out behind me, John Harris clasping my shoulders and whispering *Nice one man!* in my ear.

Two hours later, I was sharing champagne with the Hartnoll brothers in the Strongroom studio in Shoreditch. They were celebrating what felt to them a mighty victory. There had only been one other British techno act on *NME*'s cover when, eighteen months earlier, LFO had appeared smashing up guitars in front of Marshall amps for an 'all you need to know about techno' special. A cringy cover image that appealed to neither guitar nor dance fans and was received commercially as such. Orbital were appearing under their own steam, their only gimmick for the photos being the torch glasses they wore on stage to see what buttons they were pressing in the dark. Otherwise, it was just them: two balding (bald) twenty-something blokes in baggy T-shirts and tracksuit bottoms who looked like they knew their way around a scaffold. They were very happy.

I was nervous though. I had thirty-six hours to transcribe this new interview, write the longest feature I'd ever attempted and hand it in. And for it to be cover-worthy. There was no room for error. I explained my predicament.

'We'll tell you whatever you need, Ted,' replied Paul, the youngest of the two, just a few months older than me. His brother Phil was four years older, a little spikier, but just as accommodating.

They explained their upbringing in Kent, as childhood overspill refugees from south-east London. About their mother's addiction to Halcion, how they'd weaned her off with dope. They talked about Phil growing up an original punk, Paul being into Dead Kennedys and Crass a few years later. About having to miss a shift working in Pizza Express to appear on *Top of the Pops* for 'Chime', about how their career was the very model of doing-it-for-yourself-and-your-mates-and-if-anybody-likes-it-it's-a-bonus. Now, lots of people liked it. That week they were going on the *NME* cover. Next year, they'd steal Glastonbury. They were on a noble road to mega-success while making zero compromises along the way, until sibling rivalry put a spanner in their spokes a few years later . . .

I went back to *NME* and wrote that story in an empty office, putting the final full stop in around midnight. I printed it out, read it back, rewrote it, reprinted it, then stuck it on John Mulvey's desk and the server.

I stepped into the lift and headed down the twenty-five flights to the ground floor.

On the corner of Stamford Street, I scanned both ways for a rare early morning orange light. One approached from Waterloo and I flagged it down, turned it around. The times they were a-changing. My first expensed cab drove me carefully, cautiously towards Putney, as I cursed every meticulous wheel rotation under my breath, one eye on the meter, hoping I had enough in my pocket to cover it as I certainly didn't in my bank account yet.

The following Tuesday, the *NME* with Orbital on the cover arrived at the kiosk by Fulham Broadway station. I stood on the pavement holding it for a few moments, sucking the centre spread in as the commuters bumped by me tutting. I was ecstatic. The cover line was immaculate.

Orbital.
Tripping: the light fantastic.

I stuck an issue under my arm and walked back over the bridge, along the Lower Richmond Road and up the stairs, into the DHSS where I handed over my UB40 card and signed off, this time for good.

10.
Jew or Nazi?

The phone in my flat above Gunnersbury's Tube tracks sounded its alarm. I lifted the receiver suspiciously. It was March 1991, the era of disappointing news.

'Would you like to interview Mark E. Smith of the Fall for us?' *Lime Lizard*'s softly spoken deputy editor Patrick whispered in my ear.

Oh! But this was an unbeatable offer.

My mind's eye flashed forward towards the great event.

A banked seat in a Prestwich pub, floral patterns dancing across the wall, pint and chaser on the Formica tabletop, smoke curling from the ashtray, MES detonating sacred pop-cultural monuments from the corner of his mouth, pinkie raised as he holds his glass just outside of his lips . . .

'You'll have to come into the office next Tuesday. They're putting the call through at three.'

'It's not in person?'

A sarcastic snort. 'It's a fifteen-minute phoner.'

Before the Fall were my favourite group, Mark E. Smith was my favourite interviewee to read. His print personality – adversarial, witchy, contrary, learned, courteous, malevolent, witheringly funny – made any inky product irresistible. I even bought *Melody Maker* to read him when featured.

Over time, the Fall became the avant-garde rock band whose music I would listen to most regularly. I liked the repetitive, disciplined nature of the songs: rhythmic, bombastic, granite-hard, with shards of melody there only to shade, not to distract from the Fall's central focus, namely Mark E. Smith's chipped delivery of his lyrical prose. The words were what really did it. Songs about gremlins. Songs about the Football Association. Songs about Oprah Winfrey, Walt Disney and Cary Grant. About pharmaceutical giants, men of the cloth, minute details of class, corruption and small-time stupidity. About British people in hot weather. About Australians in Europe. About Mancunians in Iceland. About the very business of analysing a song's meaning. I'd read him once reveal his band's formula of 'intelligent lyrics set to primitive music' and yet I could do nothing to resist it.

I knew people so under his spell that they started to speak with the rhythm of his voice, adopted some of his physical mannerisms. I withstood that, but there were times in a pre-rave world where I listened to only the Fall for weeks on end.

More than anything, though, I wanted to sink into a pub with him during a long afternoon session, exploring the outer realms of bar-room philosophy together, capturing those jewels for print.

Instead, I sat in the airless mezzanine of the *Lime Lizard* office in Highbury New Park, sweating. I was extremely nervous. This was my first phone interview, with my Excalibur interviewee. I had no parameters for the experience. It would just be me, on the phone to Mark E. Smith, asking him questions about the Fall.

I stared at the telephone.

We were not friends. Most telephone conversations I had were brief: what time can you get there; why have you stopped my housing benefit, etc. If I could put off a phone call, I always did. I hated speaking into the darkness, listening for the pause to return. Pals only ever called me once for a catch-up.

I stuck the phone mic I'd borrowed into my ear and waited for the telephone to blow.

I had so many lines of enquiry in mind that I had no idea what to say. The vastness of the conversation's possibility terrified me.

Where to begin? I had twenty minutes. Would I be able to crack the code of the Fall in that time?

My pad contained no questions, just prompts for conversational lines we could follow: UFOs, Link Wray, the Labour Party . . . The word 'lyrics' was circled and underlined, with impossible vagueness.

For a time, I'd write long lists of questions for interviewees. Why would you do that? You can't look at a pad of questions as you speak with someone, one-to-one. I learned quickly that I can't interrogate people. But I can go for a walk with them. I can drink with them. Any pub interview became like being drawn at home in the cup. I knew the environment, the crowd were on my side. During one of the earliest interviews I ever conducted in a pub, Francophile singer-songwriter Bill Pritchard rescued a dreadful powwow by trying to drunkenly extinguish a cigarette in my face. My questions had been terrible, but now I had a story.

I realised then that the information extracted from an interviewee was usually secondary to describing what time spent with them was like, no matter how brief. Think about what you'd like to find out about the subject, recognise the limits of what can be learned in an hour's company, go with the flow. Just write what happens. I wasn't sure how this emerging philosophy would work with a telephone conversation.

The *Lime Lizard* phone line started flashing.

'Hello, Ted? I've got Mark here for you, I'll just put him through.'

I gulped an acknowledgement of this reality.

'Is that Ted?'

'Yes, hello, Mark,' I replied to the tight-mouthed Mancunian tone I recognised like family.

'Ted . . . Kessler?'

'Yep.'

'Kessler?'

'Yes?'

117

'Jew or Nazi?'

'Sorry, what?'

'Kessler. It's got to be of Jewish or Nazi origin, hasn't it?'

This was a question I had never faced before in my life, yet its logic was unassailable. Either my ancestors had escaped the Holocaust, or they had contributed to it.

'My dad's a Jew,' I replied.

'Where from?'

'He left Vienna with his family just after the *Anschluss*.'

'Seen Nazis, then?'

'My dad?'

'Yeah.'

'He did, he saw them march into his block of flats.'

'That's a good story, isn't it? Not many can say that. Did you ever see that BBC drama series about a Nazi called Kessler?'

'No.'

'Very good. Kessler's a Gestapo, on the run. Worth tracking it down, you'd enjoy it.'

For many years afterwards, my father would incredulously tell the anecdote of the time his son was asked by a singer in an English group if he was 'a Jew or a Nazi' to cackling dinner guests in New York. The first time I found myself speaking with Justine Frischmann of Elastica, in a bar at an afterparty, I told her the Jew/Nazi story. A massive Fall fan, as well as the daughter of a Holocaust survivor, she too saw the funny side. It became a reliable anecdotal ice-breaker.

In the *Lime Lizard* office, I inspected my conversational prompts again. Could we talk about *Shift-Work*, the Fall's new album, I wondered?

'Yeah,' replied Mark E. Smith, sounding a bit disappointed in me. 'What do you want to know?'

We were racing down the motorway somewhere in the frozen north just south of Rochdale, extremely hungover. Through the cigarette smoke, I asked Andy Willsher to pull over into the approaching services. 'I'll try John Best again,' I explained.

It was January 1994. We'd been on the road for four nights, Paul Moody, Andy Willsher and me, searching for the spirit of rock 'n' roll in Andy's Mini Metro, even though we had not been able to fully define what that meant yet. We now had an idea what it entailed, however.

We'd had the idea, Paul and I, in the Brunswick pub opposite King's Reach Tower one Tuesday afternoon following an *NME* editorial meeting in the run-up to Christmas. We both wanted more work from the paper. We were doing OK, but that wasn't enough. We'd learned in the office that January would present rich opportunity to pitch feature ideas as it was the quietest time of the year – there were even blank covers to be filled. In the pub afterwards, Paul and I discussed options.

Enthused by creamy-topped Carling Premier's 'nitro-poured' 4.7 per cent lager and a mood of festive jollity, we agreed we'd like to work on something together. In an office of big personalities, Paul Moody was among its most likeably charismatic. A psychedelic beatnik from Barnet who'd joined the freelance writing team around the same time as I had, he'd introduced to *NME* the word 'man' as final punctuation to any sentence with such winning charm that by now the office was split into those who also used it and those who did not. Those who did not were invariably thought of as cops by everyone else, man.

Paul was a lightning rod for pub ideas. In another boozer, the Blue Posts, on the corner of Hanway Street and Tottenham Court Road, he'd recently helped dream up the New Wave of New Wave as a catch-all description for two or three punky bands who were playing in London and Brighton pubs around then, including S*M*A*S*H and These Animal Men. He'd come up with the genre alongside two other dominant *NME* characters, John Harris and Simon Williams, whose energetic editing of the live reviews and new band pages acted as a magnet for like minds, as well as a mentoring service in the art of puns and daytime drinking. So taken with their idea for the NWoNW were the trio that they collated some of the acts for a one-off EP called *Shagging in the Streets* that they released on a label Simon named Fierce Panda. Twenty-eight years and hundreds of records later, Simon still runs Fierce Panda, one of Britain's great independent labels.

In the Brunswick, Paul and I considered what kind of *NME* feature we'd like to work on together. We both fondly recalled an *NME* story we'd enjoyed as readers a few years earlier, in 1989, in which Stuart Maconie and Andrew Collins had spent a late-summer week driving the length and breadth of the UK guided only by random choices from *NME*'s Gig Guide pages. They'd spent some nights sleeping in their car, they'd gallivanted through the nights. The lead image had featured the Gig Guide strewn across the heather in the Scottish countryside.

That looked like fun, we agreed.

We can't just nick the idea though, we also admitted. We need a new angle. What is ours?

We took a couple of deep gulps. Lit cigarettes. Ordered two bottles of lemony alcopop Hooch, which we poured into our half-full pint glasses to create Paul's favourite cocktail, the 'turbo shandy'.

Bingo! Paul had it. His eyes widened in revelation.

'Why don't we hit the road in search of the spirit of rock 'n' roll, man?!'

I repeated the idea back as a headline, perhaps even a cover line. It was brilliant. Evocative, mysterious, vague enough for it to mean whatever we needed it to.

The Search for the Spirit of Rock 'n' Roll.

Beautiful. My round.

A month later, on the bleakest New Year Wednesday, we met photographer Andy Willsher outside Bedford's Thameslink station, near where he lived. Andy was an even-tempered and mostly silent man, which were two of several good reasons we asked him to document the quest. He was also a chain-smoker, so he always had cigarettes, and he was an industrious, talented photographer. Perhaps most importantly, he had a clean driving licence and his own car.

Before leaving, we'd looked at the Gig Guide and made a few arrangements with notable local acts. We'd meet Shed Seven in York, One Dove in Glasgow, the Boo Radleys in Liverpool, the Charlatans in Manchester, Moonflowers in Bristol, 60 Ft. Dolls in Newport, Kaliphz (who?) in Rochdale (where?). They could all take us in search of whatever we were looking for: clubs, pubs, after-pubs, after-clubs. We had some very late nights. We had some very bad headaches. We had many amusing diversions and silly adventures even before the car broke down in a blizzard on the Pennines (don't attempt a cross-country Northern road trip in January: go in August). But we hadn't yet discovered anyone who knew where the spirit of rock 'n' roll could be located.

I had one hope left.

Flicking through that week's *NME* on the morning we set out, I'd noticed the Fall were playing in Oxford on Sunday, so I'd put in a request to press agent John Best from the phone box in Bedford station. I explained our mission and wondered if we could ask Mark E. Smith about the spirit of rock 'n' roll in person. Surely he'd know. We could pop in on the way to Bristol, I suggested.

Four days later, we were still awaiting confirmation. We were by now in a rental car as Andy's had died. At the services Andy and Paul headed inside for a comfort break and I picked up the phone to John Best again. We could be in Oxford in three hours if needs be.

'Good news,' I told the other two as they returned to the car park. 'John says Mark E. Smith will meet us at 5 p.m. in his hotel room before the Fall's gig tonight.'

'Excellent, man,' replied Paul. 'He won't know what's hit him!'

'What do you mean?' I wondered.

'I hate that guy! He's so horrible. He's just a bitter grouch. *NME*'s always up his arse, he's the music journalist guru. We'll show him, man!'

I looked at Paul. 'I mean, he really is my guru,' I explained.

'What?!'

'I love the Fall. I love them.'

Paul looked sick. 'Man!'

'What?'

'Not you as well!!' Paul was laughing, but I wasn't. It had been a long four days. I lost my temper.

'I've been waiting years to interview Mark E. Smith in person, so I'm not going in to have a fight with him!' I shouted.

Paul blew out his cheeks, still laughing – but now at me. 'We have to have a bit of fun with him though, man! We can't just fall down at his feet like everyone else.'

Andy blended the car into the onrushing motorway traffic.

Paul was right, of course. This wasn't a Fall feature. It was The Search for the Spirit of Rock 'n' Roll. Turning to the window, I took a deep breath. There was no need to fall out over this. Instead, I sulked all the way to Oxford.

The Fall had booked the biggest suite in a substantial chain hotel in a leafy suburb of the city. Paul, Andy and I pushed on through its doors to discover Mark E. Smith lying on the four-poster bed in the room's centre, the band gathered in a semi-circle on straight-backed chairs around the television.

'All right, lads,' called MES to us as we walked in. 'Don't mind the band, they still think television is a form of witchcraft. They're transfixed whenever they see one.' He patted the divan. 'Take a can and come over.'

Paul and I joined him on the bed.

'So, what's this all about?' he asked.

'Well, what it is,' began Paul 'is that we're going across the country searching for the spirit of rock 'n' roll . . .'

Mark E. Smith stretched back against the pillows and pulled out his cigarettes from the long black leather jacket he was wearing, a smirk dancing across his face.

'Are you really doing this?' he replied, incredulously. 'Searching for the whatever? I thought it was a joke when they told me on the phone.' He leant over and took his pint glass from the bedside table. 'Look, I don't know what the spirit is and I don't really care. I just make records because it isn't perfect yet. I haven't said what I want to say.'

Paul was undeterred. 'But is the spirit Elvis in '56, the Beatles in '63, the Pistols in '77, the Mondays in '89 . . .?'

'The Happy Mondays?' replied Smith, aghast.

Paul started laughing, as we all did. 'Well . . . I mean . . . good band!'

Smith looked at me. 'Are you a Happy Mondays fan too?'

I loved them.

'Fuck me. Well, look, I don't know if we're exactly on the same page then, but I can tell you what the spirit is not.'

Oh yes?

'It's not fucking comedy. Did you read that shit in the papers by Tony Parsons or whoever saying comedy was the new rock 'n' roll? Keep that sort of rubbish away from me.'

'What about Primal Scream?' continued Paul, determinedly. 'Have you heard their new single 'Rocks'? That's got a bit of the spirit hasn't it?'

Mark E. Smith started to laugh again.

'You two are very good,' he replied. 'Maybe comedy is the new rock 'n' roll.' He took a sip of his drink, holding our gaze just a little too uncomfortably long. 'Dead sad, isn't it? All those current groups, Suede and that, dressed like something from 1973, all these fucking idiots playing pub rock . . .'

For a few minutes, he reviewed the contemporary music scene, paying particular attention to grunge. Nirvana had tried to get on the Fall's bus, he explained, but he'd kicked them off. 'I have a rule about not mixing with people from Seattle.' He hated that city. 'It's like Moss Side on a bad night.'

He blamed the English for Nirvana's success.

'The British record industry closes down on 10 December and comes back at the end of January. If there's something wrong with the spirit of rock, it's that.'

He eyed his own group, chomping on sandwiches and cracking open cans around the local news broadcast.

'Can I go now?' he asked us. 'Or should I get the band to beat you up?'

It was too brief, but it was close enough. I'd shared a drink with Mark E. Smith while he slagged loads of people off, me included. It was a dream come true.

In the hallway, Paul put his hand on my shoulder. 'Man,' he declared, wide-eyed. 'What a dude! Lying on the bed like he's the king and the band are his court, throwing out quotes for us to gather up like gold coins. He IS the spirit.'

I knew he'd come round. Nevertheless, we continued our mission a little further westwards all the same.

In the early spring of 2015, I finally went to the pub in Manchester with Mark E. Smith. I'd commissioned myself to write a six-page profile of him for *Q*.

'I used to know the streets of Manchester by the pubs,' he said mistily, as we met outside Gullivers in the Northern Quarter at noon. The city had changed, however. He wasn't even sure if Gullivers was still going to be there when we made the arrangement via his then wife, Elena Poulou. All of his old haunts were being swallowed up by new developments. One of his favourite nearby boozers had been turned into a Byron Burger bar. He took that personally.

Happily, Gullivers had withstood gentrification. As we approached its doorway, a young woman came walking by, pointing aggressively at Mark.

'You're a fucking legend, you are,' she shouted, as she stomped past. 'I fucking love you, I do.'

Mark smiled his appreciation. 'Very gratifying,' he replied under his breath.

We stepped inside the pub, the day's first customers.

Five hours later, as the pub filled up with students and office workers knocking off for the week, we were still there, shut off from the main bar in an annexe that was guarded by the landlord's enormous Great Dane. 'I hate dogs,' had said Smith, as he gingerly stepped over the sleeping hound, 'but nobody's getting past that bastard other than us.'

I wasn't counting, but we had four pints of lager, one bottle of beer and six whiskies each in that time – so maybe I was. Remarkably, Mark didn't leave his seat once throughout our session. I asked him what his secret was.

'I took this orange speed . . .' he began, unbelievably, attributing his bladder control to amphetamine sorcery.

When he died three years later at sixty, I learned that he'd been suffering from kidney cancer when we met. The disease later spread to his lungs but didn't prevent him from performing, even in his final months, from a wheelchair that sometimes didn't get much further than the dressing room, from where he'd deliver his lines while the band played on stage.

Outside the pub, as we stood swaying in time to the landscape around us and prepared to go our separate ways, he'd unwrapped a packet of Marlboro for us both. I asked how he was.

'I'm all right,' he replied softly. 'Compared to what I have been, I'm good.'

What had we spoken about inside the pub all that time? Richard Madeley. Internet trolls. The evil of antidepressants. His Irish mates who were very good with computers. How, as usual, his current band was better than any previous incarnation, and how his most recent fans were more his kind of folk than their ancestors.

'There's always some cunt who wants to ask me about a masterpiece I made in 1982,' he said to me in reply to my enquiry about his 1982 masterpiece, *Hex Enduction Hour*, 'but I'm making better records now.'

Even before we were drunk, his speech was slurred, occasionally incomprehensible. He looked a decade older than his fifty-seven years, walking with a stooped limp on account of a twice-broken hip. You sensed the meter was running out.

Yet his company was magical, hilarious. The dream. He told me shockingly libellous tales about other Mancunian musicians of his generation, as well as going into detail about his own not-inconsiderable legal woes, about which Elena forwarded me a message from Mark few days later.

Dear Ted,

Re: last Friday

Constant repeating of stories due, probably, to my legal issues. Sorry to bore you. Talking of legal issues, can't mention.

See ya soon for MES Age 1–12.

Yr pal,

Mark E.

Outside Gullivers, I lit his cigarette and asked what his plans for the evening were.

'I'll probably go to the pub for a sandwich,' he replied. We shook hands. 'Kessler?' he asked. 'There's a very good BBC drama about a Nazi called Kessler. Ever seen that?'

I told him I had not. He smiled and nodded, then I watched him wander off into the sun, his faint bald patch bobbing through the commuters towards his minicab back to Prestwich.

11.
What It's Like

Ian McCann was a heavyweight presence in the *NME* office, someone whose writing about reggae, soul and rap I'd devoured before joining. Sometimes I'd find myself in the subbing room, where Ian freelanced, looking at printouts of the next issue. As I leafed through pages searching for my name, Ian would sidle up to me.

'What's it like?' he'd whisper theatrically in my ear, his drawled Cockney tang spread thickly over the query.

The conversation never went any further, but we both knew what he was talking about. Often the other subs would snigger along.

Everyone understood.

He wanted to know what it was like to move in with a conflict of interest.

A flight across the Atlantic, all the way to Atlanta, photographer David Tonge, PR Jacqui and me. We're going to meet Jeff Buckley at the Point. His first full album *Grace* is out in a few weeks.

Did I like Jeff Buckley's forthcoming debut long-player? Yes, very much. Had I seen him perform already? I had, at the Garage in Highbury, upstairs, cross-legged on the floor, as he blew minds with the range of his voice, his handsome presence, his intensity. Was I prepared for the task at hand? Not at all. My mind was elsewhere.

Pink Press Threat

Tomorrow, 7 August, I'm due on a flight to San Francisco to meet up with Lush, the quartet of melodic English shoegazers and *bon vivants* whose guitarist Emma Anderson has also been my girlfriend for the last year or so. Lush are playing the famous Fillmore Theatre. The next day they're due in Los Angeles for a show at Grand Slam, a club apparently owned by Prince. Then they're continuing their ten-week US tour in Dallas, at Deep Ellum. I'm going to all these shows with them. That's where my mind is.

My priorities are completely up the spout.

In the earliest days at *NME* we'd laugh at the other, older saps on staff who'd put their personal affairs on a par with or even on a shelf above *the life*. Why would you do that? The life was amazing. Nights without end. Last-minute flights to interview rock stars in exotic climes. A toothbrush, notepad, Dictaphone, passport, bank card and a wallet full of receipts. Occasionally, clean pants. What else did you need? Work was all the social life and adventure required, more so. Why would you complicate it with phone calls seeking whereabouts, with extra-curricular arrangements? Deadlines were piled upon deadlines upon hangovers. When did these idiots find time to romance?

Ah, well.

We were living together in Emma's Notting Hill flat within weeks of meeting, first at a festival, then at the ICA after an anniversary party for her label, 4AD, every encounter rushing us ever more quickly into that second-floor apartment in a white stucco building just off Portobello Road, behind the Rough Trade shop. Emma's flatmate Polly was there too, until she wasn't much because she also had a new boyfriend, and then Emma wasn't there much either because she was recording an album, in Wales, for six weeks. So a train or a lift to Monmouthshire every Friday to visit, meaning that oh no, so sorry, I can't do that piece, I'm at Rockfield this weekend . . .

I became one of those saps at lightning speed. I let it envelop me. It was so easy.

I thought Lush going on tour in the US for nearly three months in the summer of '94 would mean I could focus more clearly on the really important stuff, like the piercing arc of my *NME* career. Instead, I spent a lot of time studying Lush's tour handbook. What dates are days off, which are the best times to call the hotel – *sorry, did I wake you?* – for grumpy chat about the soap opera of tour life, when am I going to be able to come visit and, if so, how can I fund it?

Would you like to interview Jeff Buckley?

I would – where? Atlanta, you say? Let me check the Lush tour diary.

I can definitely make this work.

Beyond Atlanta's identikit American central business district in the back of a cab from our hotel, up through the verdant outer reaches of the city to the east, out into Little Five Points' warren of alternative therapy centres, head shops, vintage stalls, international eateries and bars. Push the doors of the sprawling Point music venue and climb down a staircase to the basement kitchen on to a stool opposite sweet-faced, softly spoken, earnest-as-a-preteen Jeff Buckley.

'So good to meet you. Thank you for coming all the way over to talk to me.'

Before leaving for the trip, there had been strict stipulations from Jeff Buckley's US management that no mention could be made in person nor in print of Jeff's father Tim Buckley, the similarly gifted singer-songwriter who had died at twenty-eight of a heroin overdose in 1975, when Jeff was eight. Tim had long been estranged from Jeff's mother Mary Guibert at the time of his death, but his DNA was nevertheless stamped indelibly through his son for all to admire. They looked nearly identical, for one. They sounded staggeringly alike too, in a manner that seemed impossible for Jeff to avoid but that could not be replicated by any other artist, no matter how many have subsequently attempted it. They both wrote poetically romantic songs informed by their era's cutting edge, played guitar in a fashion that embraced improvisation, and possessed voices of similarly unusual range and power.

How was I going to write this without at least mentioning his dad?

I said I wouldn't, but then I did. I lied. I asked Jeff Buckley what he thought he'd taken from his father.

His eyes tightened. 'I knew him for nine days.'

The sentence hung in the air for a moment, wrapping itself around my throat. Then Jeff Buckley picked up the thread, pulling tighter.

'I met him for the first time when I was eight years old over Easter and he died two months later. He left my mother when I was six months old. So I never really knew him at all.' A sad, light shake of the head. 'We were born with the same parts, but when I sing it's me. This is my own time and if people expect me to work the same things for them as he did, they're going to be disappointed.'

I was neither smart nor sharp enough to reply that no, in fact, he was working exactly the same way that his father had done for listeners, and that that was OK. In no way did it diminish his work. It was just part of the story. He was his father's son, but he was writing his own songs, living in his own time. I might have even mentioned that despite my best efforts and my father's long absence from my life, I was a journalist and that my father was also a journalist. It was a coincidence, but also not at all. We are what we are, Popeye.

Instead, I awkwardly changed the subject. We spoke about the music that he *did* want to be associated with. We spoke about what influenced him.

'The words come from here,' he said, touching his top pocket. 'From memories, from dreams, from people I've known. I'm always writing and reflecting on life. I want to suck it all in.'

'The music,' he continued, 'comes from within and outside. Within is the big mystery of life, we've all got it. The outside bits are easier: the Beatles, Led Zeppelin, the Smiths – man, I'd fight for their honour, for the words of Morrissey and the music of Johnny – Edith Piaf, My Bloody Valentine, James Brown, Lush . . .'

'Oh, I go out with Emma from Lush,' I blurted. I couldn't stop myself. It was idiotic. He gave me a slightly embarrassed, you-don't-say look, head cocked to one side.

'Miki was at my gig in London.'

Please, I thought, we can't talk about Lush in this interview.

'John McEnroe was also there,' I replied instead.

'He came with Chrissie.'

'Hynde? Yes, I saw you all talking afterwards. What do Jeff Buckley, Chrissie Hynde and John McEnroe chat about?'

'That's kind of private,' he replied, wincing. He considered just how much could be discreetly revealed. 'I told him he was the Johnny Rotten of tennis, the punk genius. He was why I watched tennis, there was art in what he did.'

A head popped around the door, puncturing the awkwardness. It was time for Jeff to warm up for the show. He shrugged apologetically and, as we stood in farewell, he opened his arms to hug me. We entered a clinch. Then Jeff Buckley stepped out through the kitchen and I left via the stairs.

I forlornly watched Weezer pack up their van for the drive to Houston for that night's show supporting Lush from an armchair in the lobby of a large business travel hotel in Dallas. I had an hour or so to kill before my ride to the airport, so I took out my notepad and began to write a note of contrition.

We have all enjoyed the comedy motion picture *This Is Spinal Tap*, laughing at the clichéd indignities and ego realignments that bands on the road in the USA must endure over the peaks and troughs of a career. For many, singer David St. Hubbins' girlfriend Jeanine Pettibone is a touchstone character, an enduring butt of all jokes. In the language of misogyny that rock speaks so fluently she is a 'Yoko', the femme fatale who is breaking up the fraternal bond of the band with her astrological charts, styling suggestions and mispronunciation of 'Dolby'.

Walk a mile in Jeanine's shoes.

Over the previous year I had entered many rooms cast as Jeanine Pettibone, a role I was just as awkwardly inept in. Like Jeanine, I trod upon the landmine of band politics on what felt like a daily, sometimes hourly basis. On occasion, I was asked my opinion as a partner and a journalist and, like Jeanine, I had foolishly voiced it.

I had been in control booths in Wales, in Sussex, in France, in London as producers and technicians grappled with levels that never quite worked and the room buzzed with silent resentment between band members, as I glanced anxiously at my wrist trying to work out if I should mention we might miss last orders (don't mention that we might miss last orders).

I had regularly faced the long trial by bass drum of soundcheck while attempting to form an opinion that could be useful later. I had left places I wanted to stay in and stayed in places I wished to leave because the swirl of band history dictated it. I had rolled along the motorway in the curtained tomb of my tour bus bunk, drunk/hungover, wishing I'd chosen one less date to visit. I had been a sap, trying to control a romantic narrative that was not mine to steer. Worse, I had become an unreliable narrator. My written work was not good.

Our time together on the US leg of Lush's 1994 tour, meanwhile, was not a roaring success, either.

The Fillmore in San Francisco had been reassuringly full of spectators, but that number was swollen by fans of support act Weezer who were enjoying a hit with their debut single 'Undone (The Sweater Song)', the Spike Jonze-directed video which was on *MTV* all day and all night. The phenomenon of the headliner being upstaged by the upstart support act is only briefly covered in *This Is Spinal Tap*, but it's a seam to be further tapped in any sequel. I also massively misjudged the post-gig mood by piling into a toilet with a member of management and hoofing up a load of coke. OK everyone, let's get on the bus to LA, we'll be there in the morning . . .

I really wanted Lush to do well, and not just for domestic harmony. Before I met Lush, I'd never really listened to them. They weren't on my radar. I'd heard the single 'For Love', which had a lovely yearning melody and harmonies, but at that time I was in a dance fog; I was into beats, bass. Melody was something you sprinkled sparingly on top; structure was the intro and the outro. I was mad about old reggae and contemporary rap. I was a snob about indie music. At *NME* I'd dug into that niche.

Emma was a songwriting disciple; the song was all. She judged a record on the quality of its songs, which seems like an obvious marker, but wasn't really my primary concern before we met. She opened my eyes to that. She played me the 5th Dimension, Tim Hardin. She turned me on to Laura Nyro, whose soulful, curtains-drawn melancholia I became obsessed with. I heard Burt Bacharach's precise songwriting perfection in a whole new light via her. She was my song Sherpa.

I could hear great craft in the songs that Lush wrote. A song like 'De-Luxe' relayed a story about rushing on a powerful drug through abstract guitar sounds, but at its core was a delicate, delicious vocal melody. That writing was rarely remarked upon in print as the press preferred to focus on the group's humour, personal chaos and availability, and that was because the band often went to the same shows, the same aftershows that the press went to in London. It diminished Lush in the eyes of writers and editors, but the more I saw them, the more I heard them, the more I recognised how good they were. They were a female-fronted band steeped in sixties songwriting nous, post-punk emancipation and contemporary sonic architecture. They were atypical.

Lush weren't quite getting their just desserts in 1994, however. Their new album *Split* had had a long, trying gestation, as I'd borne witness to, and was receiving mixed critical appraisal. Some of their shows were a bit bumpy to begin with too.

One day, when they come to write the illustrated history of Los Angeles' best nightclubs, there may well be a long section on the Glam Slam. But in the harsh light of soundcheck in August 1994 it didn't appear to be an ideal choice for a performance by Lush, an indie-rock band fronted by two forthright feminists.

'What the fuck is that?!' said singer Miki Berenyi as we followed her inside the venue and stood in the middle of the floor, mouths ajar. There before us were two massive pillars that bookended the stage, made up of statues of naked, writhing women.

Once it had been ascertained that neither the statues nor the venue could be moved, matters nosedived. It was a Lush-only club date, but sold out nonetheless. Unlike many of their British indie contemporaries, Lush had toured extensively in the States since their first shows there in 1990. They'd popped their cherry on a long first tour alongside kindred spirits Ride, following up with epic, multi-month journeys, with US underground veterans Flaming Lips and then as the odd one out on the coast-to-coast Lollapalooza stadium trek with mega-names like Red Hot Chili Peppers, Pearl Jam, Ice Cube, Soundgarden and Ministry. They'd paid their dues. They had a following. *Split* had recently debuted in the US college top ten.

So the crowd of LA indie kids and hipsters were excited to catch a first glimpse of album number three being played live in their town. There was whooping as the lights lowered. However, four songs in the onstage power cut out. Silence. Nothing. A void filled with silhouettes shrugging, pointing. The whoops turned to boos as the band trooped apologetically from the stage . . .

No sound, but the lights were working just fine backstage as the band and immediate entourage (i.e. me) sat in sullen, furious silence awaiting electricity for half an hour or so. Fat men in beige clothes made urgent calls to electricians and spoke on walkie-talkies while English voices periodically called them cunts behind their backs. Has anyone tried the Dobly button?

Eventually, defeat was admitted and we emerged from the dressing rooms with the remaining rider to distribute to the crowd, promising to return the next night, a nominal day off, by which time the electricity was flowing like victory through Glam Slam. We drove the streets of downtown LA afterwards, sucking in the petrol and night lights through open windows, before a celebratory drive-in In-N-Out burger and a sad little cocktail in the Mondrian bar. Then, star-shaped sleep.

I wrote a news story about the event for *NME*, imagining that I was earning my bunk on the bus in some small capacity. In fact, it just provoked a stern note from Prince's UK lawyer warning us about directly blaming the singer for the venue's shortcomings. At which point, sensibly, I should've caught a cab to LAX, changed my flight and returned home to write my Jeff Buckley piece for the deadline, which was just days away. Instead, I remained on the Lush US tour for the great tequila Olympics of 1994 after a thinly attended show in the city of Dallas. By now, even the American road crew were blasting *Definitely Maybe* whenever you walked in a room, pressing play on 'Rock 'n' Roll Star' for load-in and 'Slide Away' at the end of the night. You could feel Oasis rising from across the ocean, sweeping all aside. For a band like Lush who'd put so many hard yards in across the US to look out at a half-empty venue at that moment was dispiriting – even if that venue was in Dallas (not a big college town, apparently).

That night we drank the night away in a hipster tequila bar and fought like deranged cellmates back at the hotel until dawn. I waved off the tour bus before breakfast, then sat to compose my apology in order to catch the mail.

What was I apologising for? My presence. What was I doing here, tagging along on tour, caught between the two worlds of reporter and performer in a Jeanine Pettibone purgatory? If only I'd known then that to scratch a scab reopens a wound. Distance is valuable. Don't waste it.

I necked two G&Ts on the plane and then, finally, took out my Dictaphone to transcribe the Jeff Buckley interview. Back home, jet-lagged in W11, I quickly wrote the piece and handed it in the following day, bang on time.

Three weeks later, on 24 August, I stood with Emma in the late early hours outside the lift on one of the Reading Ramada's floors. We were going up but we were also coming down. It had been a long night in various rooms after Lush's festival performance. The lift doors parted and there before us in perhaps even more advanced disarray stood Jeff Buckley. He blanched. We stepped in.

'Jeff,' I said, 'this is Emma.'

This was a high-stakes introduction on my behalf, as well as a low blow. My piece about Jeff Buckley had drawn fire from the Buckley gatekeepers, including his management and label, Columbia. This was understandable as I had arrogantly described what I'd been banned from writing about in the piece, and by whom, before then offering a description of asking him anyway. I still flinch at the memory, mainly because the writing is bad, but also because it dumped his blameless PR Jacqui in the fire at work.

In the lift, I used Buckley's fondness for Lush as a diplomatic bridge.

'Pleased to meet you, Emma,' replied Jeff, with a wan smile.

The doors opened again. As we made to leave, I turned back and offered my hand out to shake.

He looked at me for a moment and, with the faintest shrug, shook my palm before the doors closed upon him. It was the last time I saw Jeff Buckley. He drowned in the Mississippi River three years later, aged thirty.

*

Back in the *NME* office, I heard the familiar jingle-jangle of Steve Sutherland's keys and coins in his jeans rolling down the corridor to the art room where I was looking at a printout of that week's cover.

'Ted!' he called. 'Long time no see! Have you been away with Jeff Buckley all this time?!'

'No,' I told him. 'I've been with Lush in California and Texas.'

'Ah,' he replied, wincing and retreating swiftly, as he did whenever personal lives came into play, jangling his coins as he wandered away. 'Right, well, good to have you back anyway.'

A familiar voice suddenly appeared in my ear.

'Cor! On tour *in Texas*,' Ian McCann whispered, stagily. 'What's it like?'

We both laughed, but no matter how many times he asked, I never told him. I never told anyone.

12.
Down and Out in Paris and London

Emma and I caught a flight to Paris in November 1994, subconsciously aware that our relationship was probably ending but prepared to nevertheless enact the final manoeuvres. Oasis and Elastica were playing and we both wanted to see them. Why let a bad time get in the way of a good one?

There would be work involved for me, watching a load of British bands play at La Cigale as part of the four-city touring festival Les Inrockuptibles, so that I could turn around a 2,000-word report. Some of the bands I liked, some I didn't, but it wasn't taxing work, standing in a concert hall for two consecutive nights and then drinking the night away, picking up titbits to flesh it out.

I'd been sent because I'd met guitarist Noel Gallagher several times in the line of duty during Oasis's earliest days. *NME* was now milking that Oasis cash cow for all it was worth. An appearance by them on the cover already spiked sales in a manner disproportionate to all other acts before their first album had even arrived.

The most recent alternative British bands to demonstrate any grand commercial ambitions, the Stone Roses and Happy Mondays in the late 1980s, had come unstuck in the glare of the really big stages. Unable to convert local mania into global appeal, they had retreated to lick their wounds (among other substances). Subsequently, British alternative music reverted to its cottage-industry status: success was playing theatres and the corn exchange; a hit record meant breaking the top ten for a week and then disappearing. Oasis viewed number seven in the album charts as defeat, not victory, and they let the world know that. It was a shock to hear.

For some, it was welcome grandstanding. Damon Albarn took the boasts as encouragement, a challenge that he figured his songwriting could take on, so he adapted Blur for the fight; in this new light, Manic Street Preachers saw that their own grandiose ambitions were perhaps not just art statements to be paraded in front of journalists, but something to really aspire to. Most other established alternative acts shrunk away intimidated.

The first time I saw Oasis, at London's 100 Club in April '94, the week their debut single 'Supersonic' came out, it was clear to all that they were about more than just talking a good fight in the press. It was magisterial. You could hear the lineage immediately, back through to all the other bad-boy British rock bands who'd stood on that stage, but despite those echoes they appeared entirely contemporary. They hadn't studied the music press, they didn't look like they'd ever hung about in a guitar shop. Their performance was wordless, practically motionless, yet every sense was overwhelmed by the noise with which these poker-faced Mancunians faced you down. They had an animal magnetism the like of which we hadn't witnessed from a band that decade. Singer Liam Gallagher was a malevolent doll. The songs were really good, too – you've probably heard a few of them.

One or two songs in, I turned around to see the faces of everyone else gawping at the stage and caught John Harris's eye just off to my left. He raised his fingers in an A-OK toke gesture and nodded furiously, lips pursed. Everyone knew.

In my review I wrote Oasis were destined for *Top of the Pops* before the end of the year ('if the singer stands up straight'), which at the time seemed a big call for a band who hadn't yet released a single. Now it reads as ludicrously safe. A few months later I lay on the floor of the packed bar in the Hilton in Glasgow after Oasis had detonated the tent at T in the Park and listened to Noel as he calmly explained why Oasis were going to be the biggest group in the world.

'We're not worried about some student twat in London singing about pantomime horses,' he said, describing Suede – the dominant indie band in the press at that time. 'We've got a song called "Cigarettes and Alcohol". Wait until the American truck drivers get hold of that. Driving along singing that out the window. Kids buzzing on E to "Live Forever". We're gonna be massive, man, biggest band anywhere.'

I'd never heard talk like it. Yet having just watched 10,000 people rapturously sing every word of their unreleased album, it seemed plausible, likely even.

Soon, the shutters would come securely down upon Oasis as all those promises came true, but presently the access was freely available if the elder Gallagher recognised you and didn't object to your presence. He didn't mind me too much, so off I went.

Emma was there because she knew several of the bands better than I did, especially Elastica, having gone out with their sweet-natured drummer Justin Welch before me. There was a lot of last-minute mingling possible before Lush's own touring restarted and I could sense Emma gritting her teeth ahead of that work.

I also made sure that we travelled with the most important tool for any reporting trip, a happy-go-lucky photographer. This is a vital ambassadorial role on any overseas job where access to talent is reliant on goodwill, as most music journalists have substantial personality defects that need covering. Often, the photographer can rescue the mission from a writer too socially inept to instigate contact (hello) and a PR too timid to spell time requirements out to talent.

As soon as we arrived at the hotel alongside *NME* photographer and friend to the indie stars Roger Sargent, he was greeted with hugs by Rick Witter of Shed Seven, that night's headliner. Witter announced he was furious with Noel Gallagher. They'd crossed paths the previous day as Shed Seven checked in and Oasis headed off to their first show in another city.

'I don't know what their fucking problem is,' said Witter, an otherwise amiable fellow. The niggle seemed to be that yesterday when Witter had asked Gallagher if he was enjoying the tour Gallagher had replied, 'Yes, but there's a lot of shit bands on it.' An inferiority complex had (correctly) convinced Rick Witter that Noel Gallagher meant Shed Seven.

When told of this twenty-four hours later, after Oasis had had the venue's roof launched into space by several coachloads of drunk Brit daytrippers, Noel Gallagher raised a thick eyebrow. 'First of all, Shed Seven are shit,' he reiterated. 'Secondly, we're playing the same venues the day after they play and each place we arrive at the local journalists all say, "Oh, you should hear what Shed Seven said about you." So excuse me if I don't want to stand around making small talk in a three-star hotel lobby in Paris with some dickhead from York who's been slagging us off to French people.'

He suggested we should go to a bar. There was an Oasis knees-up organised by the promoter above a nearby strip club, but Noel wanted to avoid that for now. This was a moment of great change for Oasis, a power-dynamic shifting definitively towards Noel and away from the other members. Two months earlier, in Los Angeles, he'd walked out of a disastrous show at the Whiskey a Go Go in fury and disappeared for two weeks, sending all into meltdown. When he reappeared, any nominal idea of democracy was quashed for good. He was responsible for the songs that had recently seen *Definitely Maybe* arrive in the album charts at number one and, without him, there would be no more where that came from. I asked him what had happened.

'One day I will tell you,' he said, 'and you will have the greatest story ever.'

We ordered a round of shots.

'I will tell you completely off the record that the band all did fucking angel dust when they thought it was coke, which is why the gig was so shit. That'll never happen again.'

If I wrote that, however, he would not speak to me again. And he'd have my legs rearranged. I promised not to mention it. (Decades later, the truth came out anyway in the documentary *Supersonic*: in fury, Noel shacked up with a woman in San Francisco while he let his colleagues stew.)

One knock-on effect of Noel's LA disappearance and a few other skirmishes, including a punch-up with fans on stage in Newcastle, was that Oasis now had a security guard, a staunchly posh ex-army parachutist called Iain Robertson, who was tasked with maintaining discipline and safety around Oasis on the road. Practically, it meant that he spent a lot of time trying to track down Liam and Noel Gallagher, who toyed with him like small boys with a magnifying glass terrorising ants. As we spoke, we saw Robertson jogging down the road looking frantically in the windows of neighbouring bars and bistros.

'Oh, watch out,' said Noel. 'Here comes that twat from Sandhurst in the cowboy hat.'

Robertson stormed in and begged Noel to come to the official drink. All the band were there and it was secure. He had been given just one task by manager Marcus Russell and that was to make sure everyone was safely in the same place. Noel took pity on him and we went to the bar.

I stopped to get some cash out and as I caught up, I saw Roger Sargent arguing with the drummer from Echobelly, Andy, just outside the entrance to Lili la Tigresse's topless bar where the Oasis party was. Roger was telling Andy how good Oasis were tonight and Andy was disagreeing.

'Yeah, they're a laugh, I couldn't stop laughing. Are they a joke band?' he shouted from the bottom of the stairs, as Roger patted him on the chest in an attempt to quieten him down. This didn't work.

'You see Bonehead? I could have him. He thinks he's hard? No problem. That bloke from Sandhurst? I could have him.'

The bouncers may have proven a tougher prospect for him, though, and as Echobelly were not invited to the Oasis party – the subtitle to their career, unfortunately – I climbed beyond the velvet rope into the snug upstairs bar, where Liam Gallagher fixed me with a glare upon entry.

'Who are you?' asked the singer for neither the first nor the last time in our lives. I interviewed Liam Gallagher at least seven times over the following years, usually for cover stories. It wasn't until the sixth time that he didn't greet me with 'have we met before?' This time when I told him that I was with *NME* he made the sign of the cross and hissed. Luckily, Noel gestured towards the tables.

It was a small, tired gathering of drunk people in a very dark room. The band were there, their tour manager Maggie, PR Johnny Hopkins, Emma and Roger. For Johnny I presented a problem. He had a *Melody Maker* Christmas cover in the can and my presence, uninvited by him, threatened that.

I set his mind at rest by assuring him that this Paris trip would not become an *NME* cover, that I was just there reviewing the whole caboodle for the paper over a spread. He relaxed. Noel ordered rounds of champagne, toasting each arrival ('To my brother Elvis!' 'To the Welsh!' etc.), eventually becoming so bored with that that he and guitarist Bonehead started chucking the ice buckets across the room at each other, soaking everyone. Later, as Bonehead slept on his chair, Noel placed a bucket victoriously upon Bonehead's head. He didn't wake.

At 6 a.m. I decided to call it a day and left the bar with Emma. On the way back to the hotel she loudly described in detail all of the things she'd come to understandably dislike about me from twenty feet behind as dawn broke weakly upon Pigalle. I put her to bed and lay down beside her, muttering pathetically . . .

I was awoken at 10 a.m. by the room's phone.

'Morning, Ted, sorry to wake you, old chap,' boomed Iain Robertson down the line. 'Noel's not with you is he?'

I checked the room. No, Noel Gallagher is not in my hotel room. I could hear the air being deflated from Robertson down the line.

'Fuck. Where is he?'

I repeated Robertson's question back to him.

'Not in his room and not in any of the band or crew rooms, either. He's missed lobby call and we have to leave for Marseille now. Balls. Gotta go, if you see him get him to call me or Maggie please.'

I left Paris without seeing Noel Gallagher again, but with his final words to me pressing a small buzzer in the back of my mind without halt: 'I'm staying at the Hilton in Kensington next week. Give us a ring if you fancy doing it again . . .'

My work was published in *NME* every week but it was hard, even then, to make ends meet. I had three days in the office assisting on the live reviews desk thanks to the largesse of that section editor, Iestyn George, who went out of his way to help me, just as Simon Williams had before him. But I still needed a big feature at least every fortnight to keep up with my outgoings. A cover story would last longer.

I'd been given the 'singles of the year' panel feature to organise for the Christmas issue. I knew I had a few weeks to nail a panel of stars for it, but Noel's parting words lingered. I called the Kensington Hilton and asked for Noel Gallagher's room. Surprisingly, they put me straight through. Even more surprisingly, he answered.

'All right, Noel,' I said. 'Ted Kessler here.'

'All right, Ted, how are you?'

I told him that I was well. That I was organising the *NME* singles of the year feature. That Justine Frischmann of Elastica and

Jarvis Cocker of Pulp were on board. Andy Cairns from the band Therapy? too. Did he fancy it?

He did. He did fancy it. Tell him the time, tell him the place. He'd see me there.

I scrambled all jets. Three days later I was sitting in the bar of the Kensington Hilton at noon with photographer Peter Walsh as Noel Gallagher wandered down the hall alongside Paul 'Guigsy' McGuigan, Oasis bassist. Generally, Guigsy didn't do any press but the pair were staying together and he didn't have much else on. Guigsy rolled a joint and I asked Noel what had happened in Paris.

He gave his only sheepish reply of the day. 'I woke up in the right room, but on the wrong floor,' he explained, unbelievably. He said he'd been able to catch a flight in time for soundcheck all the same. 'And I totally shat up Iain Robertson, so bonus.'

In the ground-floor hotel meeting room of the Kensington Hilton everyone drank quickly, heavily, perhaps a little nervously, as one does when in a room full of whisky and brandy with strangers listening to you talk. But our awkward blind date went smoothly. Many young rock bands are clannish, but Noel Gallagher has always been happier crossing the room to see if there's someone new to meet, keen to extract novel allies from his elevated circumstances. As nobody present was in direct competition with each other, all quickly became very friendly.

Six hours later, Jarvis Cocker was on his knees covering a small pile of vomit he'd deposited in the corner of the room with some serviettes. 'I need to go home and hose myself off,' he decided, very quietly, dragging his coat through the sick. Noel and Justine had become firm friends and emerged from a private conversation with plans to continue at Elastica's rehearsal room. They were all pulling on coats just as Emma arrived, hoping to have a similar night on the town to the one she had enjoyed in Paris, one final shebang before another slog sleeping in a bunk on the road in a different time zone. She was to be disappointed, however, as everyone promptly split, leaving just me and a bowl of noodles under the bright lights of a Queensway diner for company, our dinner-table conversation long since extinguished.

After she left for Japan a couple of days later, I transcribed the interview. This seemed better than the usual round-table discussion. Here was Justine Frischmann talking about Courtney Love standing outside her London home screaming for her while Damon Albarn hid behind the curtain. There was long judgement passed upon records by Suede and Blur, groups containing both future and present enemies of Noel Gallagher as well as past and current lovers of Justine Frischmann. Jarvis Cocker said Michael Stipe of REM sounded like Larry the Lamb. Noel Gallagher declared Tom Jones should be banned from music. Guigsy broke his media silence to occasionally embarrass Noel, like an elderly relative in front of school friends. He hasn't been heard from, media-wise, since.

I had an idea. I quickly topped and tailed the transcript – reading it back now, I should've spent longer on that, as with so much else – and then I took it into the office.

The *NME* issue with the round table on the cover hit the shelves the Tuesday before the 1994 Christmas issue was due. The shit hit the fan before the afternoon was over.

Steve Sutherland came wandering out of his office and down the corridor to our desks, chuckling and ferociously jangling the change in his pocket, a little after our mid-afternoon return from the Brunswick.

'I have just had Johnny Hopkins on the phone,' he said to me, wincing. 'Not happy with you and not happy with me, it must be said.'

I had not told Johnny nor anyone associated with Oasis or their label Creation that we were putting Noel Gallagher and Justine Frischmann on the cover the week before the bumper Christmas issue. In fact, I hadn't told him about the feature at all. Worse, neither had Noel. The first anybody at Creation or management Ignition knew of its existence was its appearance on the London news-stands.

I pressed the play button on the live desk answerphone. After wading through the usual pleas and threats, there was Johnny Hopkins calmly voicing his surprised disappointment in me. Could I give him a call? Three lunchtime pints said yes, wiser heads said no.

Don't worry about it, Sutherland decided. 'It's a genuine scoop. He's just flapping about the *Maker* cover but that will happen, and you can imagine the calls he's had from (Creation's Alan) McGee and Marcus (Russell, manager).' Another wince and off Steve strode, jangling furiously. He thrived on empty confrontation like this.

The issue sold well and, since I also had a long interview with Andrew Weatherall in it, I personally did OK too. But it was a pyrrhic victory. This was the last time access to Noel Gallagher would be so direct.

Further layers were immediately added to Oasis's protection, on managerial and security levels. Press negotiations in future would be long and painfully laborious. By the time I became features editor it would take months of phone tennis and pleading to get anything Oasis-related, and sometimes that turned out to be nothing. Johnny Hopkins enjoyed his revenge, though I am led to believe he shared it out with all commissioning editors, not just me, before one day he too was dispensed with.

A Sunday soon after, Emma returned from tour with something to tell me. Little did she know that I too was returning, from Brighton, with something to tell her.

She had met someone new, though that was not the reason it was over. It was just time. I paused at this and allowed that to be the reason. I did not mention that I too had met someone else. I was too cowardly. Also, I was tired. I hadn't been to bed.

We agreed we'd remain great friends and went to sleep on it on the mattress upon our old bedroom floor one last time. Sadly, as it turned out, we did not remain great friends. The next mid-morning I set off for work, but only made it as far as Doggett's pub by Blackfriars Bridge, where I called the live desk in the office. John Harris answered and I asked if he wanted a pint. He came down.

As I told John what had happened, I started to cry. This surprised me. I wasn't sad about the end of the relationship with Emma. She was right. It was time. I knew this. I was relieved. I sensed, though, that this was the start of something, too, and perhaps that's why I found myself awkwardly tearing up in front of my embarrassed colleague in a near-deserted pub.

It was the end of the new, of turning everything up, of any suggestion being an opportunity, of all the young acts being funny and artistic and odd. The chart positions had started to gain significance for the established acts in the wake of Oasis, while bigger development deals were now being offered by major labels to new guitar bands – some of whom didn't even exist ahead of the deals being offered. Dance acts were moving beyond clubs into theatres and traditional venues, away from one-off singles, towards the concept album.

The early days were drawing to a close. The era of careful consideration was approaching. I felt it. John too. We were entering the second act of our *NME* lives. The bands we'd arrived with were crossing over or dying out. We were all growing up. Look out of the window, you'll hardly recognise the place.

We finished our drinks and went up to the office to prepare for our new reality.

13.

Our Man in Havana (*part one*)

Happy Mondays rearranged the terms and conditions of my existence.

I had seen them play at Dingwalls in the autumn of 1988, the week that their second album *Bummed* came out, a couple of months after I'd returned from the summer of working the beaches in the South of France, and that was that. No way back.

How old are you, are you old enough?

Should you be in here watching that?

I'd turned twenty a month earlier. The perfect age, as it turned out. Old enough for autonomy, young enough to not have a clue. Blank. Bored. Full of beans. Ready for action. And here it comes, Sly & the Family Rolling Stones; the Sex Floyd; James Brown's Funky Joy Division People. I belonged here.

They only played for thirty minutes, but I signed on the line. Our interests were in sync.

Maybe things were going to change anyway. We've all read the witness statements now. We know our history very well. Maybe acid house was rewiring youth culture and maybe Happy Mondays were just the first physical embodiment of that regime change in band form. The documentaries are there for all to view. The conclusions seem very firmly of that opinion.

I just know that I went to see Happy Mondays in Camden on a rainy night in November and everything changed. It was my personal year zero. I've measured every subsequent band I've seen in the flesh against that night.

Pink Press Threat

It's hard to imagine, isn't it, when you see them now on those TV sofas, on *Gogglebox* or *Good Morning Britain*, cuddly and giggly, joking about aliens and alopecia. Old. Goofing off, messing around, playing up for the cameras. Loveable rogues. Big men, out of shape. Last of the summer fortified wine.

In their twenties, though, on nightclub stages, singing songs about drugs and orgies, freaks and fannies. My lord. Advocating hedonism with such zeal it felt like a revolutionary cause you'd die for (some did).

I was there because I couldn't stop playing their latest single 'Wrote for Luck' in the shop. It just went round and round and round. *I wrote for luck, they sent me you . . .*

And here I am. And there you are, Shaun Ryder, spliff in hand, hunched over the mic wearing a chunky-knit cardigan and brown cords, barking out rhythmic slang poetry, eyes closed, smile wide, love and violence floating in the air. Bez at his side, skin and bones and maracas, like a cartoon alley cat from a yet-to-be-invented Pixar film, limbs on strings, the band cutting the most psychedelic, kinetic groove I'd ever seen performed by white Englishmen holding guitars. It was Chic, reimagined by inner-city Lancastrian pub pirates.

Happy Mondays didn't look like a band. Jesus Jones, who were supporting them, they looked like a band: rock hair, nice guitars, branding, matching shirts. Clean. Happy Mondays looked like the kind of men you saw through the steel fence at away matches making cut-throat signs at you. This isn't a recommendation, of course, but it made a change. It seemed more relatable than the *Melody Maker* small-ads guitar-shop boys who normally trod the boards for your pleasure. All the band's mates were on stage too, dancing, gurning behind them, demanding the audience throw coins on stage for an encore that never arrived. That could be you up there, you know. You aren't that different. It's not a million miles away. You wear high-street knock-offs as well, just smart enough to bypass the door policy, whizz stuffed down your sock.

Afterwards, minds blown, Jake and I walked the eight miles back to Chiswick in the drizzle. We'd missed the train and there wasn't a night bus, but that was OK. We were already on board.

I became heavily involved in Happy Mondays' limited recorded materials: the chewy Mancunian garage-funk of their first album, 1987's *Squirrel and G-Man*, as well as *Bummed*, the sound of cold British towns having very hot times. Their music was glued to my ears. I stole the old 12-inchers from the record shop shelves, I cheered the new releases on to television like a victory in the cup away at a fancied Big Six club. Happy Mondays were very influential. Inspired by their freedom of expression, I quit my job and travelled on a six-week drug pilgrimage through Europe to Morocco. They were a revelation for hedonistic herberts everywhere, grotty outsiders who'd nevertheless snuck inside. They changed a generation's wardrobe.

As I started writing about music, I wondered if I'd catch up in time to have some nights on the road with Happy Mondays. They were very funny on the page. I liked that, turn it up. I wanted to share a quiet moment with Shaun Ryder.

But they queered their pitch before I got within sniffing distance. Just four years after my first sighting, Happy Mondays were done, cooked in their own bad habits – mostly Shaun Ryder's – with the final nail in the coffin hammered by *NME*'s Steven Wells when he coaxed wretched homophobia from them during a cover interview to publicise their tired fourth album in 1992, after the hits from LP number three *Pills 'n' Thrills and Bellyaches* had pushed them over the good-times edge. They were kaput. They hated each other. They needed to get away. So they called it a day, sent in the lawyers and went for a Kit-Kat.

Farewell rainbows, hello grey skies.

1 December 1995

As we were booked on a morning flight to Havana, it was decided that it would be prudent if Bez stayed in the Hilton attached to Stansted Airport. He could oversleep, jump out of bed at 8.45 and still meet us at check-in by 9 a.m. that way. Safety first.

At 9.20, Anton Brookes, the PR nominally managing the trip, was persuaded by photographer Kevin Cummins that he'd better check Bez was on his way. Anton called the hotel.

'Er, there's no reply from his room,' Anton reported upon his return from the payphone. He looked around the airport, sweeping his long hair into a ponytail as he did so. 'But he's not checked out either.' Sheepish grin. 'So . . . what do you want to do?'

Anton was the archetypal gentle giant. As huge and as physically intimidating as a rugby league player, but as softly waggy and easily distracted as a golden retriever. He'd been Nirvana's press officer from their earliest days and was swept along in their slipstream, as temperamentally unsuited to mainstream success as Kurt Cobain had been. Nowadays he did the press for most of Nirvana manager John Silva's other acts too, including Foo Fighters and Beastie Boys. Big-time groups who needed a lot of external press management. Not Anton's forte. He was better at chatting with a band about Barnsley's chances of promotion from Division 1. A kind, empathetic Yorkshireman who drove all journalists mad when they needed him to produce the goods. I once missed an interview slot because, as he was escorting me backstage at a US festival, he became distracted by a Native American merch stall and stopped to discuss at length what he believed to be his own Native American heritage, lifting his sleeves to slowly annotate his corresponding tattoos. Despite that, I loved seeing his big grin come bouncing around the corner – that baked-in charm was no doubt the secret of his success.

He also did press for Black Grape, Shaun Ryder's new group which included rapper Paul 'Kermit' Leveridge and Ryder's long-term foil, the dancer Mark 'Bez' Berry, as members.

Improbably, Ryder had pulled himself free from the wreckage of debt and heavy drugs which surrounded Happy Mondays upon their demise. With the help of American producer Danny Saber and a new group of session players he delivered Black Grape's upbeat party manifesto *It's Great When You're Straight . . . Yeah*. I was handed it to review for *NME* at the end of July 1995 and gave it a gushing, ten-out-of-ten full-page lead review. It was exactly what I'd been waiting for ever since *Bummed*. I thought it was brilliant. I wasn't alone. The album's druggy funk entered the charts at number one.

Soon after, Anton suggested an *NME* cover story with Black Grape could take place in Cuba. As Ryder was prevented from entering the US on a work visa at that time due to historic drugs convictions, Black Grape thought it would be amusing to invite *MTV* and assorted interested American publications to Cuba for the band's round of US publicity. Communist-ruled Cuba, of course, was on the banned list for American citizens. The American journalists would have to travel via other Caribbean islands and not disclose their full itineraries to US immigration. I'd been recently made staff writer, so I was commissioned to tell the story for *NME*.

The fly in the ointment of this practical joke was that the band themselves had to make it to Cuba. Black Grape were all travelling from different locations. Shaun Ryder was coming from Mexico, where he was on holiday with his fiancée, Oriole Leitch, daughter of sixties folk superstar Donovan. Kermit was flying from Manchester. And Bez was coming from Stansted with us, to make sure he arrived. Except he wasn't here.

Kevin Cummins, the only real adult involved in the whole enterprise, told Anton he should call Black Grape's management to find out what was going on with Bez. Anton agreed with him. Presently, he returned with more bad news.

'So,' he began, grinning ridiculously. 'Nobody's heard from Bez.'

Right. Massive, gaping pause.

'And Kermit's in hospital.'

'What?! What's wrong?'

'Dunno. But Shaun's definitely on his way! He's leaving this afternoon. He was meant to arrive yesterday but he's had food poisoning in Mexico.'

'So we're still going?'

'Everyone's looking for Bez. At worst you'll still have Shaun in Cuba.' Big grin. 'Hopefully!'

Kevin rolled his eyes at me. He'd shot Happy Mondays many times, most famously taking the photo of Ryder hanging from a giant letter E on the roof of a hotel in Spain for an iconic *NME* cover at the height of the Mondays' powers. He was used to their shenanigans.

'That's reassuring, Anton,' replied Kevin, dripping with soft Mancunian sarcasm.

Ninety minutes later, our Cuban Air DC10 was bouncing its way through the clouds as the pilot clicked off the seat belt signs and the cabin crew made their way down the aisle with complimentary rum.

While Kevin and I said cheers, Anton unclipped and bumped off the seats along to the facilities. Kevin immediately leant across the aisle and rooted through Anton's hand luggage, gleefully removing a lingerie magazine. Shaking his head sadly as he leafed through, Cummins opened it upon the centre spread and lay the magazine across Anton's seat table for all to see.

I turned to face the window, bringing the rum to my lips as we fought to hit altitude. The flight was choppy, but worse turbulence surely lay ahead on land.

At 10.30 that evening, Kevin, Anton and I found ourselves at a long table on a raised platform at El Floridita restaurant in the old town of Havana enjoying one of their famous daiquiris.

There was a large bronze bust of Ernest Hemingway behind us that sported an inscription of one of his famous quotes: '*My mojito in the Bodeguita del Medio and my daiquiri in the Floridita*'.

'Do you get the hint?' asked Kevin, ordering another round for us alongside a water for Anton.

Cuba had only recently opened for some very low-key tourist business and there were a small number of designated night-time locations for foreigners, one of which was El Floridita. The only other people in the restaurant were smartly dressed politicians, men in fancy army uniforms, some women who appeared to have been paid to attend, as well as the dozen American journalists and envoys from their US label Radioactive who were sharing our table. Just beyond the doors of El Floridita lay acute deprivation, the ongoing US embargo of Cuba that began in 1962 having had the desired effect of freezing the country in the year of its commencement. In December 1995, *El bloqueo* meant that Cuba was starving. But within El Floridita the fish, vegetables, ice cream and cocktails were plentiful.

Neither Shaun Ryder nor Bez were here to enjoy them, however. We'd been in the country for a few hours and had only contradictory rumours about their whereabouts to go on. Nerves were jangling audibly amongst our friends from Radioactive. Without the main event, this could be an expensive weekend of pointless sanction-busting for them.

The doors swung open.

Shaun and Bez entered the arena, accompanied by their A&R man Brendan and Oriole. Bez had a little rucksuck on his back and a big loopy grin sloshing across his chops.

'Fucking hell!' he shouted loudly across the table, dropping his bag on the floor. 'Cuba, man! Good to see ya. I've had a proper nightmare journey.'

Behind him, Ryder shuffled in holding Oriole Leitch in one hand and his guts with the other. He appeared green, sweaty, deeply unwell.

'Kevin fucking Cummins!' he growled at us, as Oriole swept by and into a seat on an adjacent table. 'What are you doing here?!'

'What do you think, Shaun?' Kevin answered.

'Nobody told me you were coming, man. I'm the last to know anything.' He grimaced. 'I've been shitting and puking for four days on end, I nearly didn't make it. I'm wazzed up on antibiotics and all sorts.'

'Shaun!' whispered Oriole. 'Come and sit down, try to eat.'

Ryder looked at the table and belched, popping his shoulders and rolling his neck. He didn't look ready to eat. Still. Best try. 'Kevin, we'll catch up later, have a drink, man.' He shuffled over to his table and gingerly lowered himself down between Brendan and Oriole.

Bez, meanwhile, explained that he'd been in his hotel room in Stansted all along. He hadn't heard the phone ringing next to him. 'I went to bed quite late.' He'd subsequently been flown to Havana on a new ticket via Dusseldorf at great expense to Radioactive, only just making each connection by minutes. 'It's a miracle I'm here.'

Once Bez sat down alongside Ryder, Oriole and Brendan, their table was immediately furnished with food. It was getting late and El Floridita wanted to close. Ryder raised his cutlery, dug in and attempted a mouthful of meat. He lowered his knife and fork over his plate and held them above it as he slowly masticated. Every chew appeared to cause him immense pain. He looked in turmoil.

'Has anybody got weed?' he asked of our table, huskily. 'I haven't eaten or slept for three days.'

Obviously, nobody had. How could they?

'Come on, man,' Bez said urgently to Anton, standing up, keen to help his friend. 'Let's go score. They'll think you're a Rasta, we'll tell them you need a smoke for religious reasons.'

Anton Brookes was teetotal. He had never smoked a joint nor popped a pill in his life. However, he pulled on his jacket and stepped out into the Havana night with Bez, armed with just his ponytailed hair as a clue to his newly discovered Rastafarianism. Neither of them was carrying a phone or a map of this unfamiliar city, nor could they speak a word of Spanish. It was a bold adventure. Bez, after all, had failed to catch a flight from the same airport he was sleeping in just that morning.

As soon as they left, so too did the American press corps. They'd seen enough for one evening. Shaun Ryder picked his plate up and moved to our table to say hello more peacefully. Kevin ordered a round of daiquiris, but Shaun raised a finger and looked warily over at Oriole. 'Best not,' he said. 'Antibiotics.'

We asked him what had happened to Kermit.

'Well,' he began, 'the silly cunt's been using a dirty needle and has given himself septicaemia. He's in an isolation ward with bits of his heart flaking off, bits of liver flaking off. He's touch and go.'

He caught my eye.

'You,' he said, very seriously, raising a thick index finger and pointing at me. 'Don't write that he used a dirty needle otherwise I will track you down and kill you. Say he got it from dirty water or something.'

There are many sides to Shaun Ryder, no doubt. The two that I have borne witness to most often are A) the loquacious, hilarious Mancunian raconteur and rascal most familiar from his public image – smart, surreal, edgy but loveable; B) the screw-face Ryder who'd bite your nose off when crossed. For a brief moment, I looked into the eyes of the latter. I assured him I wouldn't. (Years later, Kermit would publicly recount how he caught septicaemia from injecting drugs, lifting this fatwa.)

Every other customer in the restaurant had long left by now, but through the power of the regularly unpeeled dollar we remained. They wished to shut, though, and began flicking the lights off.

As if by magic, the shoppers reappeared. 'I've got the weed,' Bez told Ryder. 'Let's go.'

We waited outside El Floridita for our cabs. Bez took two wooden blocks from the one-legged beggar using them to crouch on and tapped out a little rhythm which he danced to, Bez-style. Chuckling along, Anton turned to me. 'That was actually quite scary,' he confessed, quietly. 'We found a guy who said he had dope, so we went with him through all these flats and then he dropped us off somewhere else.' These other men were armed with knives, said Anton. They'd wanted to take the money first and return with the drugs later. 'Bez told them to fuck off, he'd go with them. And somehow he got the drugs in the end.'

As our cabs pulled up, Bez took a £10 note from his wallet and pressed it into the beggar's hand as he returned the wooden blocks.

'You're a good man, Bez,' Anton told him, twisting around in his seat as we lurched off down the road.

'Aye, you've got to help beggars,' replied Bez, serenely, 'because what goes around comes around.'

Havana rolled by the window. We made our way from the warren of the old town down to the moonlit harbour road and on towards the looming Hotel Nacional.

Jet-lagged the next morning, Kevin, Anton and I took a stroll through Havana scouting locations for photos. Cuba had entered a period of severe economic austerity in 1992 following the collapse of the Soviet Union. A new ministry for tourism was devised in 1994 to help navigate this austerity, but until 1997 all contact between visitors and Cubans at large was outlawed by the government. We were only really meant to leave the hotel with government-appointed guides.

All these factors combined to mean that everywhere we went we were besieged by desperate, fascinated locals. Our scouting trip involved a lot of scuttling quickly from doorway to doorway for Kevin and me.

'Where's Anton?' Kevin suddenly asked as we wandered down a road in the old town towards the port.

We scanned the horizon. Anton appeared around the corner. He had ten, maybe twenty small children hanging from each arm shouting at him as he peeled off notes from a wodge of dollar bills and handed them out. He passed by laughing and saying 'no' repeatedly to them, but handing out the cash anyway. Kevin raised his camera to his eye. Click.

We got back to the Nacional for the noon meeting to begin our coach tour of the city alongside *MTV*. Neither Shaun nor Bez were present, however.

After we'd returned to the Nacional the night before, Shaun and Bez had sat in the large leather armchairs in the bar area chatting amiably with us for an hour or so, Shaun describing the precise mechanical details of his Mexican food poisoning, day by day, movement by movement, while Bez had given an update on Kermit's condition.

'I went to see him in hospital before I left,' he recalled. 'Bought him some amino acids, some ultra-fuel. He's in a really, really bad way. You wouldn't recognise him, he's that thin. But he didn't want anybody to know. He was saying, "Promise you won't tell anybody I'm in hospital Bez." It doesn't matter now. Cat's out of the bag!' He paused, thoughtfully. 'I'm glad he's not one of those things . . .' He searched for the description. 'A dead legend.'

Shaun Ryder had uncharacteristically remained on mineral water throughout, until Oriole announced she was returning to their hotel room. Ryder then instructed Bez to 'break out the brandies'.

Kevin and I retired in the early hours, but Shaun and Bez had apparently pushed on through.

At 2.30 p.m., Bez appeared in the lobby saying that Shaun was asleep in his room. Details were sketchy, but Bez had now popped down to fetch him a cocktail pick-me-up, aware that there were a coachload of twitchy Americans suffering massive schedule failure over them. Eventually, about three hours late, they appeared holding Campari and oranges in round glasses. Ryder may have been asleep previously, but he had not rested. Evidently weed hadn't been Bez's only purchase the night before.

'I feel about ninety years old,' groaned Ryder, climbing slowly aboard the coach. 'Brendan, can we sack off the interviews and get some smack instead?'

Brendan turned to the scandalised American journalists and camera crew behind them on the bus. 'It's a joke,' he said, raising the palms of his hands. 'A joke.'

Arriving at El Morro, the imposing fortress that sits on a hill over Havana Bay, the pair shuffled next to each other on a wall for their *MTV* interview. Before and during the conversation there would be a lot of impressive gobbing from Shaun Ryder, as he attempted to breathe through his hangover.

MTV had only sent a camera crew, so the Radioactive PR read the supplied questions in a monotone voice. It was windy up there. Every time Shaun spat, his phlegm sailed for miles down to the harbour – progress he cheered occasionally, forcing the deathly question to be repeated.

MTV: 'Black Grape were due to tour the States now, can you tell us what happened, how you feel and if you have any message for your fans there?'

Bez: 'We was totally made up. If you've got tickets, you'd better get your money back, we're not coming.'

Shaun: 'It's getting sorted. It was pretty obvious we weren't getting in because all the other times we've come over with the old black passports they've got no barcode and you don't say, "Yes, I've done this, yes, I've done that." You lie. But with the new ones your record comes up on the screen from Interpol and ours goes drugs, drugs, drugs, drugs, drugs.'

MTV: 'Honesty isn't always the best policy, then?'

Shaun: 'Well, that's what happens when you tell the truth, so . . .'

[He stops to cough a massive ball of gob up and spit it over the wall before shouting 'FUCK THAT, KIDS, LIE!']

The *MTV* cameraperson turned over his shoulder and looked at Brendan. 'We can't use any of this,' he whispered.

Brendan shrugged. What do you want from me?

We all trooped back on to the bus afterwards and drove through the streets of Havana on a poverty safari, periodically stopping whenever Kevin Cummins' haranguing about photo opportunities cut through. All the Americans aboard the coach were extremely polite and sunny, but officiously square. All the Brits other than Anton were rude, sarcastic and hungover. It made for a tense ride.

As we watched Shaun and Bez pose for Kevin next to one of the vintage 1950s cars that lined the streets of Havana, unserviced with new parts since the start of the blockade, a young guy in a Bob Marley T-shirt approached Anton to chat. He'd picked the right candidate. Ten minutes into their conversation about the restrictions and difficulties of daily Cuban life, Anton had dropped at least twenty dollars on him. I wandered away back down the tight street towards the photo session.

Kevin finished his shots and we all climbed back aboard the bus. After a quick head count, we realised one person was missing: Anton, of course. The bus driver suggested that he'd seen Anton follow his new friend into one of the blocks of nearby flats, so Brendan and the *MTV* crew also entered the building to track him down. 'We're desperate for B-roll material,' an *MTV* person said to Brendan, thanking him.

The rest of us sat on the bus.

By now, Shaun and Bez were growing restless waiting for their PR who had vanished. It was an unusual role reversal for them. Last night's buzz was also wearing thin.

'Fuck this,' announced Shaun Ryder loudly. He'd noticed that we'd parked next to a barber shop. 'I'm going to get my head shaved.'

He climbed back off the bus, strode across the road and straight into the barber's chair, with Kevin Cummins in pursuit. As the surprised, bequiffed young barber wrapped a sheet around Ryder's neck, the Mancunian explained through signage what was required. The barber put his cigarette into the corner of his mouth and shaved. Kevin started clicking.

A few minutes later, as the cut was being finalised, Anton emerged from the flats accompanied by the *MTV* crew. He was clutching a painting he'd bought as a means of escape. Shaun climbed back aboard the bus, shaved baldly number one all over. 'I just see those clippers and they start whispering, "Shave me Shaun, shave me."'

The MTV crew were distraught.

'But this will ruin our continuity,' the director complained to Brendan.

Shaun answered loudly on his behalf. 'Tough fucking titty.' He leant forward and tapped the driver on the shoulder. 'Let's get back to the hotel, pal. I need a drink.'

6 February 1999

On each of the three occasions I interviewed Shaun Ryder between 1995 and 2003, he took the opportunity to describe how he'd recently quit heroin or methadone. The process as he described it was always painful, stressful, difficult. It involved residential therapy and medical procedures. He'd been taking both drugs since his teens, after all.

It wasn't clear at the time, but now I can see that it was all part of the same cycle of attempting to get clean with varying degrees of determination. I have subsequently read later interviews where he is again newly shorn of his habits, proclaiming himself hooked on mountain bikes or shellfish instead. When we last spoke, in a Ladbroke Grove pub around his first solo album in the early noughties, it seemed he had some more work to undertake before being quite as remade as he proclaimed. He left the interview midway through to go to the toilet, remaining locked inside for over thirty minutes until his friend retrieved him.

'Sorry about that,' he said, sitting back down. 'I had a really large steak for lunch.'

For a time, this was code we subsequently employed at *Q* when discussing a bad hangover.

When I arrived at a photo studio by the river in Hammersmith to interview Shaun Ryder in early 1999, he was again keen to describe his process of detoxification. Dressed head to toe in a baggy grey Admiral tracksuit that he'd been given as part of a new sponsorship deal, Ryder was here to promote the reunion of Happy Mondays in an exclusive *NME* interview. It was the first time I'd seen Shaun since leaving him in the bar at the Nacional in Havana, spinning tales about alien visitations and complaining about his bowels. He looked like he'd spent the intervening four years in a tumble dryer.

'I went into hospital last January, 1998,' he explained of his most recent detox. 'They stuck rods in my guts and pumped me full of stuff to break my habit. It was hard. I've been on methadone since I was sixteen. But it worked . . .'

He was lying on a sofa with his eyes closed and a finger stuffed up each nostril, his other hand rummaging around his pants. As he spoke he started to drift off. And then he was asleep. His tour manager spotted this and dashed over.

'Shaun!' he shouted, shaking his shoulder, and turning to me. 'Sorry about this, he's been up all night with his lawyer.'

Shaun Ryder awoke. 'I have, I have, been up all night . . . with my brief, not doing what you might think. What was I saying? Where was I?'

Hospital.

'Oh yeah, hospital . . .'

Also present was Bez, who I had last seen launching a flying kick at the window of a Bureau de Change in Madrid airport, as we awaited our separate connections home, because they wouldn't change the Cuban currency he'd somehow ended up with.

Bez had signed up to this first Happy Mondays reunion tour two days earlier, along with original drummer, the mild-mannered Gaz Whelan and bassist Paul Ryder, Shaun's younger, more introspective brother. The other founding members, guitarist Mark Day and keyboardist Paul Davis, had not been invited to this reunion: those wounds would take a little longer to heal.

Whelan, Paul Ryder and Bez were nearly as surprised to be here as I was. 'We haven't even rehearsed yet,' explained Whelan. The invitation to re-form had come through a fortnight earlier and then, forty-eight hours ago, they'd signed the agreements, agreeing their promo duties – including this interview, which I'd only learned of when Anton pitched a quick-turnaround cover two days earlier.

'We signed the new Mondays contract on the sixth anniversary of us splitting up,' said Whelan, ruefully.

For Paul Ryder, the reunion had arrived at just the right moment. He couldn't have done it any sooner. 'I've been committed to two mental hospitals, sectioned twice since the Mondays split. I've been in rehab four times. And I got divorced. Kept me pretty busy.' He popped out two pills into his hand. 'The National Health hospital in Prestwich really sorted me out. I'm fine now.' He swallowed his pills. 'Got to keep taking these though.'

Shaun Ryder had long said that he wouldn't re-form Happy Mondays under any circumstances. The band had split citing his unreasonable behaviour and he bore a hard grudge towards the others. The universe had now convinced him otherwise. Black Grape had dissolved after two albums a couple of years earlier, via financial disputes both between band members, and between Ryder and the group's management. It was messy. Shaun now had an issue with his tax that could be costly, and he too was getting divorced from his wife, Oriole Leitch.

'Do you know that snidey bitch?' he asked.

'I do,' I replied. 'We met in Cuba.'

'You know she's Donovan's daughter? Anybody who writes that amount of happy music has got to be evil in my book. I am in and out of court with her. Someone suggested we get the Mondays together again and I said, "No chance." But the tax bill cleaned me out.' He shrugged. 'What can I do? I said, "Go on then, we'll do the Mondays tour, do a single."'

I watched them goof around for the photographer, Derek Ridgers. Shaun was making everybody laugh by performing a spoof acid house dance, but as Paul Ryder and Gaz Whelan exchanged glances at the back of the picture it seemed that the passage might not be entirely smooth. So it proved. This line-up split eighteen months later, with Paul Ryder saying he would never appear on stage with his brother again. Subsequently, there have been at least four incarnations of Happy Mondays, including for a while from 2012 the full original line-up after differences between Shaun Ryder and his brother, the guitarist and keyboardist were finally ironed out. That didn't last either.

'Hey you!' Shaun Ryder shouted at me across the studio, as Ridgers changed his camera roll. 'Got any whizz?'

'Sorry, Shaun, no.'

He sized me up, cocking his head to one side. 'Do I know you?' he asked. 'Have we met before?'

'Of course. I came to Cuba with you and Bez four years ago.'

'Cuba?' Shaun Ryder looked quizzical. 'I've never been to Cuba, man.'

'You have. It was on the cover of *NME*. You both were on the front, leaning on a car in Havana.'

'Bez, this dude says we went to Cuba. I don't think so. Do you remember going to Cuba?'

Bez held his chin. 'I remember going to Jamaica.' He thought about it for a moment. 'I don't think I've been to Cuba.'

Shaun Ryder shook his head. 'I think I'd remember going to Havana, man. It wasn't us.'

He looked me up and down again. 'Sure you're not holding any whizz?'

14.
Karma Police

Bash it out: that was the mantra of any productive *NME* journalist. Just get it done. There are fifty-one issues of the magazine to send a year. Many other people are willing to fill those issues with words if you are unable to supply them, so get on with it. Struggling with an ending? Tough. Need an extension to rework that intro? Sorry. Bash it out.

Later, when I worked on monthlies, I'd marvel at the section editors who'd take a 'writing day' at home to compose a 350-word album review. On staff at *NME*, I'd write a 1,500-word feature in a day and a 3,000-word cover story over the weekend. You soon became adept at writing quickly to tight deadlines.

The caveat to that machismo is that the writing was often rubbish. It could've always been improved by taking more care and space, with more inquisitive editing, but the clock was running. There was no time for any of that navel-gazing. There's another issue to fill in seven days.

Who reads last week's *NME* anyway?

Bands read last week's *NME*, that's who. And, unlike you, they never forget what you've written about them.

If I'd been paying closer attention to Thom Yorke in Madrid, it would have saved me a lot of pain later in Barcelona, Berlin and Birmingham. He'd let me know very clearly where he was going with all this.

It was May 1995. We were sitting in the basement of an Italian restaurant in the Spanish capital sharing bowls of pasta with the other members of Radiohead at the time, which was approaching midnight. I'd spent the afternoon in the lobby of their hotel watching them being ground into the dust by promotional duties. They weren't even playing in the city. They were on an international promo tour, calling in at several hubs over a fortnight to satisfy the growing, constant interest in them. I joined a queue of journalists from Spain, France, Norway, Brazil and Holland to talk to each of them in turn as members of the Barcelona basketball team milled around us awaiting their coach, before interviewing Thom over drinks and dinner that evening.

I was there to write a cover story about Radiohead, which Steve Sutherland had somewhat grudgingly granted at the second time of asking, having already demoted one such commission from the cover at the last minute a few months earlier. Like many observers – me included – he'd had to swallow his initial assessment of them as one-hit wonders after the international smash 'Creep' from their so-so first album *Pablo Honey* was followed a couple of years later in 1995 by *The Bends*, an album which was not just a big step up in terms of writing and delivery, but also contained several hit singles. I was there to make amends for *NME* having pulled out of our initial *Bends*-related cover in February. They were a British guitar band with a platinum second album, an album that had quickly sold a million copies across the globe. They were huge in America. We couldn't ignore them.

Even as we now praised Radiohead, though, we underestimated them. *The Bends* wasn't their true manifestation, their destination. It was their first giant leap forwards. They would make several other preconception-smashing albums over the following decade or so, shapeshifting beyond any pigeonholes journalists such as I could dream up for them. We were blind to their true potential.

It was an easy mistake to make. Generally, music journalists on the weeklies in the eighties and nineties were prejudiced against geeky, awkward-looking public schoolboys from Oxfordshire playing histrionic indie rock. We thought that was what monthly magazine journalists on Q or *Empire* looked like, not rock stars. Radiohead's songs were driven by angst, both existential and physical. What did they have to worry about? Their lives were gilded.

It wasn't just how inky music writers viewed them, either. Many musicians ahead of them in the cultural pecking order then were snobbishly suspicious, too. When I interviewed Bobby Gillespie of Primal Scream in 1997, he asked me what I was listening to. I told him I was addicted to the forthcoming Radiohead album, *OK Computer*. He'd wrinkled his nose.

'No,' he said, shaking his head as if I'd asked him a question rather than made a recommendation.

'It's going to really surprise you,' I told him. 'They're going somewhere totally new with rock music here.'

'No, I won't listen to that shit,' he told me, decisively. And that was that.

In the end, none of our prejudice affected the impact Radiohead made. The music they produced, the concerts they delivered so far surpassed any expectations critics had for them at each stage. They were an arena rock band playing to rooms full of lighters held aloft for a while around the first two records, but they soon became the best at that. Then they remerged as a more progressive rock band, but found a way to translate that windiness to stadiums, becoming the biggest group on the planet for a while for their third album. They turned their back on that, too, and metamorphosed into a partly electronic art-rock act, touring the world in their own huge tents. They grew rhythmic, experimental, political – yet they could still engage directly with a 100,000 fans at Glastonbury. Radiohead were on a distinct path, even if none of us could read their map. They didn't need us. In the end, that critical resistance was irrelevant to them.

Well, nearly. It was all going somewhere, being buried for karmic revenge. The band were logging it.

In Madrid, I was afforded good time with each member. They were very generous, thoughtful. Talking with bassist Colin Greenwood it felt a little as if I was being interviewed by him, he was so interested in *NME* and its writers. He knew everyone's tastes, all the weekly in-jokes from its pages. He wanted to know what Johnny Cigarettes was really called (Johnny Sharp), whether Steve Sutherland hated them (unlikely), if Steven Wells was as terrifying in real life as his furiously funny prose (no, he was a very noisy puppy). Colin was friendly, flamboyant with his adjectives, open.

His brother Jonny, the extravagantly gifted guitarist, gave a more instructive glimpse into Radiohead's future relationship with the press.

'I got really despairing in Canada about three weeks ago,' he said, slumped in his seat opposite me, describing the North American leg of this promo tour. 'I hadn't seen an instrument for weeks but still had been talking about Radiohead every day . . .'

The first signs of the future dislocation were there. Later, Thom Yorke predicted exactly what was coming down the line over the next decade from Radiohead. Though I reported his quotes, I didn't really see the bigger picture. How could I? At that moment they were just a big alternative rock band on their second album about to obtain a coveted first *NME* cover.

'I get really envious when I hear stuff on Warp Records,' he said, invoking the then Sheffield-based avant-garde electronic label which was home to Autechre and LFO. 'I get the sense that they're made in isolation and that there wasn't this need to be a bollocks rock band going, "I want my guitar solo." It's not that there isn't anything new to be done with the guitar, it's just that I'm not hearing it from bands. I hear it with Jonny every day.

There's this sense of adventure working with computers that's so exciting. I'd like to explore that more. Depends on the songs.'

The songs that they'd started sketching for album number three wouldn't really fit with this electronic direction that he was advocating, but it would be fully reflected by the albums they delivered in the noughties. He was five years ahead of his time.

I just thought he was riffing for the interview, though. I didn't realise he was laying out his entire blueprint for the future of his band. In the midst of his long promotional tour to satisfy a growing international audience, he was already thinking of ways to survive the onward journey. Radiohead had actively sought international success with a lust that most British bands (other than Oasis) had not, but having tasted it they alone wished to change the rules of engagement for the sake of their own longevity.

'What we're most conscious of is a need to stop being a tumble dryer spewing stuff out,' outlined Thom over dinner. 'There'll be a point when we say enough, otherwise we could be selling margarine, anything. We've got to engineer enough room not to be kissing ugly arse any more. I think all the work we're doing now will allow us that space to grow.'

They'd spent the late afternoon taking photos with Steve Double throughout Madrid for the *NME* cover shoot, the epitome of kissing ugly arse for five men who hated posing for photos. It was their second *NME* cover shoot in four months. For the aborted first cover, Thom had especially worn a fluffy fake-fur coat and zany shades. Now, when Double asked him to put a large red flower in his mouth for the cover photo, Thom Yorke obliged. He knew what he had to do to get this over the line.

Back in London, I joined the weekly editorial meeting. I was surprised to learn that in my absence there had been a change of heart over the cover. It had been decided that Dodgy, a cheery power-pop trio from Hounslow who'd been knocking about at sixth on the bill at festivals for a few years already, were going on the cover instead.

How come?

'The Radiohead photos are not cover-worthy,' came back the verdict from Steve Sutherland. 'Thom looks a dick with that flower in his mouth.'

'He's wearing shades too,' continued the art editor. 'Pictures are a bit dark . . .'

These were compelling answers. The previous year, I'd had a Beastie Boys story knocked off the front at the last minute for an *Absolutely Fabulous*-meets-Pet Shop Boys interview which I'd felt was a mistake at the time – the Beastie Boys' third album *Ill Communication* was sweeping all before them, those Steve Double Beasties photos were fantastic and I really didn't believe any *NME* reader bought the magazine because comedians Jennifer Saunders and Dawn French were on the front. I'd sulked, briefly. Occasionally, I'd bring it up when moaning about the powers that be in the pub even years later – 'how can you believe in a magazine that thinks *Absolutely Fabulous* matters more to music fans than the Beastie Boys?!' etc.

This time, though, I looked at the photos and knew they had a point. The Dodgy shoot was sunny, triumphant, the three of them throwing salutes on the quay of some Mediterranean port. They were about to reissue their 'Staying Out for the Summer' single. It had reached number 38 last year, but with a bit of production spit and polish and a gust of prevailing, feel-good Britpop wind in its sail, surely they had a seasonal hit on their hands. Thom had a big red flower in his mouth. There was no eye contact. The lighting was very gloomy.

I didn't put up a massive fight, but I did sound a note of cautious protest.

'Radiohead are a much more popular group than Dodgy,' I suggested. 'They're not going away. We've promised them the cover twice and have broken that promise both times; they're going to be really pissed off . . .'

Steve shrugged. 'Dodgy and Radiohead, it's the devil or the deep-blue sea,' he decided. 'It's the start of the summer. This week the story is going to be that Dodgy single, not old misery guts. Radiohead will get their chance.'

Dodgy went on the cover, with a drop-in of Thom with that flower in his mouth sitting in the top right-hand corner.

In the end, 'Staying Out for the Summer' only reached number 19 in the singles. It was very disappointing. Nobody could understand it. *The Bends*, meanwhile, has now sold nearly two million copies in the UK alone, three times that worldwide.

When *NME* did eventually put Radiohead on the cover at the end of 1995, the writer opened the piece describing a moody backstage scene against the band's wishes. Yorke vowed to never speak to the magazine again. Enough was enough.

It was March 1998. The phone on my desk rang. This was not unusual. The phone on the *NME* features desk, which I was now the editor of, rings all day long. It was like a reverse Russian roulette. One call out of six is a lifesaver, the other five make you want to blow your brains out. This call, unusually, was neither.

'Hello, Ted, it's [*insert name of go-getting young production assistant, classically a Chloe or a Will*], we just wondered how you were getting on with that release form?'

How I was getting on with the release form was that I'd filed it under a stack of other bits of paper I didn't want to think about three weeks earlier. I told them I hadn't got to it yet. I was still thinking it over.

'OK, understood, but we will need it back in the next week otherwise we'll have to cut your contribution out.'

'Can I see my bit yet?'

'I'm sorry, no. Grant's not showing anything for approval. It's going to be really good though. What we've seen is amazing.'

One person's amazing is another's humiliating, of course. How good could my contribution be, I wondered.

A year earlier, in March 1997, I'd been the live reviews editor for *NME* when an unmissable commission arose. Radiohead were launching their new album, *OK Computer*, on 22 May in Barcelona with a small club show. Their label Parlophone would take a writer from *NME* over to document it. There would be no access to the band as they were also doing a *Mojo* exclusive cover there, but we'd be welcome to review the show, spending a couple of nights in the city.

I immediately commissioned myself. The album was clearly a work of era-defining genius and Barcelona in late spring is one of the best places to spend a couple of easy-paced days. It seemed like a win-win. And if the *NME* reviews editor can't from time to time commission himself to do a sweet trip abroad, what was the point of any of it?

I went to the gig. I went to the aftershow party, where drink removed the legs from at least two visiting music-biz bigwigs. I walked throughout the city wearing shorts. Afterwards, I bashed out 600 words overnight and forgot all about it.

A few weeks later, I was promoted to features editor when Mark Sutherland left to edit *Melody Maker*. I thought when applying for the role that it was an ideal time to be commissioning the *NME* features and cover stories. Britpop was in bloom. The bands and artists I'd spent the previous four years covering were now all becoming household names. Some were even entering imperial phases, known globally as headliners. Acts like Oasis and Radiohead. My guys.

Quickly I realised that the time to become the *NME* features editor is when the good groups are on their way up, not when they've arrived in first class. More alarmingly, while first class was full, Coach was looking tatty. We had passed the tipping point of Britpop and the explosion of electronic dance acts by about eighteen months. British music was no longer in bloom. It was starting to rot, if you inspected the roots. The funny, interesting, gifted, big-mouth musicians who'd been in reception at *NME* for around three years – Jarvis Cocker, Richard Ashcroft, Justine Frischman, Noel and Liam Gallagher, Damon Albarn, Liam Howlett, Tricky, Polly Harvey, Björk etc – were no longer a call away. Now, you got one interview every two years if you were lucky and they dictated the rules of access. The job was clearly more attritional. And rather than fighting for access with just *Melody Maker*, we were up against all the monthlies who viewed these acts as mainstream enough for covers now, as well as broadsheet magazines who also fancied a bit of Jarvis Cocker winking on the front of their Sunday magazine. *NME* was the bigger fish in the weekly music paper market, but now that this rabble of misfits were all bona fide pop stars, *Smash Hits* wanted a bite of that apple too. Suddenly, *Q*'s 250,000 copies every month alongside a *Sunday Times Magazine* cover became a very attractive counter-proposal for a PR pitching for business to a label meeting.

Filling the year's fifty-one issues was less straightforward than before because the new acts were worse, so we had to engineer some smoke and mirror effects around them. That was easy enough. You could always dig deeper into the experimental margins, or into the US underground. The covers were harder. Ideally you required three core acts on the cover every month and one flyer, an outside bet. That was the cover ratio when I'd joined *NME*. Now that order was reversed. You aimed for at least one core act on the cover every month, the rest were hopeful punts or some kind of fluffed-up live review or news story. Death was dined upon for weeks.

This cover ratio was not helped by the two British guitar acts that *NME* really needed from the summer of 1997 onwards not really talking to the magazine any more.

Oasis had ascended to the stratosphere. I interviewed them for a cover in April that year. A quote by Noel Gallagher stating that he thought Oasis were probably bigger than God for kids at that moment – which was true: the church would struggle to fill Knebworth, even if it charged less than £22 a ticket – was lifted for the front pages of the *Mirror*, *Daily Star* and the *Sun*. BBC One's *Six O'Clock News* ran it as a lead item. It all seemed so hysterical for a throwaway reply to a speculative question about the lyrics in 'D'You Know What I Mean?'. The day the interview came out my colleague Paul Moody bumped into Noel striding down Marylebone High Street. Noel had passed by shouting, 'Sorry, Paul, can't stop. I'm being chased by the God squad!'

The issue sold well, the biggest of the year by a distance, nosing sales back over 100,000 after a slight dip. Joy and relief soon gave way to anxiety, however. That was our bash on the Oasis Teddy Picker. There was a host of international media now in line for them – we'd have to wait our turn, possibly at Christmas but more likely the following year. Noel had long ago taken offence at Steve Sutherland's combative backing of Blur, amongst other things, so now he enjoyed making us dangle.

Meanwhile, Radiohead's *OK Computer* was the year's runaway hit album. Miles ahead of the rest. But they didn't want anything to do with *NME* either, despite James Oldham giving it ten out of ten in our review. I called their idiosyncratic PR Caffy St Luce many times about this deadlock. Caffy, like Anton Brookes and other long-term independent PRs to the best acts, was an enthusiast, someone whose genuine love of the groups she handled was the reason she did them even after they became big business. She wasn't a careerist, she was a diehard fan. That's what Radiohead and Manic Street Preachers liked about her – they could trust and relate to her instincts. She, in common with many weekly music writers, with me, was a happy amateur suddenly playing a professional game. No doubt we all appeared endearingly out of our depth when confronted with genuine pros in management, at labels. It often seemed as though patient allowance was made for our kooky enthusiasm. None of which made securing an urgently necessary Radiohead cover any easier.

I'd call. I'd beg. I'd cajole. I'd use some of her other acts as bargaining chips, which was a no-no but I was desperate. I'd leave message after message. Caffy would apologise and say they couldn't give an *NME* interview right now. Sometimes she'd say they were too busy. Eventually she just said that Thom was still too fucked off with you.

'With me?'

'No! Not just you, not you in particular.' With the whole thing. The covers being pulled, the snidey picture captions, the stuff that had been printed when asked not to.

It all seemed fair to me.

I didn't stop hassling her though.

Eventually, in late October, I suggested an idea that gave them pause for thought. *OK Computer* was going to win *NME*'s album of the year. Radiohead were on the last leg of that year's mammoth world tour. Why don't I come to the Berlin date and the final show, in Birmingham? I'd already been to the first one in May. I could write a piece for an end of year issue, along the lines of Barcelona, Berlin, Birmingham: six months with Britain's best band. Something like that.

It went back and forth for a bit. It was unlikely that Thom or Jonny would talk to me for an interview. Drummer Phil Selway was probably sitting it out too. But Colin Greenwood and the other guitarist, the affable Ed O'Brien, would chat. The band would pose for photos, too, and I could hang out, go to the gigs. Soak it all up. How does that sound as a compromise?

I packed an overnight bag and took a cab at 5.30 a.m. for Stansted. Roger Sargent, Caffy St Luce and I were going to Berlin.

We arrived in the mid-morning of 2 November at Huxleys, a hangar-like Berlin venue where in 1930 Adolf Hitler had addressed an audience that included his future first architect, Albert Speer. For the first six hours or so that we were there that was the most interesting thing that I learned.

As soon as the band heard we'd arrived, they locked themselves in their buses. Jonny Greenwood, emerging from his bus, had accidentally bumped into us as we pulled up in a cab. In his haste to escape, he'd let the door lock on him so he was forced to greet us and show us the way into the venue. He immediately took flight once he'd deposited us with the road crew who were setting up the rig.

It was very cold. Roger Sargent set up some lights in a doorway and waited to take photos. I smoked a lot of cigarettes. We watched the soundman rollerskating around the venue's floor as roadies coughed into microphones. Though no doubt enjoying herself, Caffy left us to get on with it, joining the band on one of their nice, warm buses.

After all our reserves of banter and bitching had run dry, Roger and I fruitlessly sought some warmth in the band's empty dressing room. Eventually, Caffy arrived with Colin Greenwood in tow ahead of their soundcheck. Colin was very tired after a long run of shows, and I too was dopey as I wasn't used to waking at 5 a.m. to stand in the cold for six hours, but he was nevertheless friendly.

We settled into chairs behind a small round table next to their changing room and spoke for forty-five minutes about how the year had been for the band, about the future for them, about his favourite albums of the year. That kind of thing. It was all pretty jovial. A few minutes before wrapping up, as I started to run through any topics in my mind I might have forgotten to raise, I became distracted by a bright white light entering the room behind me. I turned my head to face it and became aware of a camera crew walking slowly around the perimeter of the room with one tall man next to the camera operator rolling his hands at me to keep talking.

'Are they filming us?' I asked Colin. 'It's a bit weird having them walk in on us like this.'

'Not at all,' he replied. 'Life's so short, especially the life of a band. It's nice to have a record of it for when we're old and grey.'

Grant Gee, a documentary maker who'd worked with U2, was on tour with Radiohead filming everything they did for a film that they hoped would show the dual realities of touring and promotion. Later, they'd film Roger taking his photos and me interviewing Ed O'Brien too. They were recording everything.

'Just ignore us and carry on please,' said the tall, posh man at the front of the crew who I assumed was Gee.

The interview was pretty much over by this point, but we battled on for a few more minutes. I dredged up a question about the band's schedule and Colin drifted off into a complaint about interviews and being interviewed, that ended with him apologising and pulling his hat over his eyes. I didn't really know why he was apologising and told him so. He was the bassist. In normal circumstances he wouldn't need to do quite as much heavy lifting in an *NME* cover story. It was all fine. I knew I could make it work. Don't worry.

Grant Gee and his gang kept the cameras rolling. I shook my box of matches. Come on, please. Let's stop filming.

I looked at the release form one more time. Most people said I should just sign it. What's the worst that could happen? You'll be in a Radiohead documentary. Biggest band in the world in 1998. You'll be on telly.

In the back of my mind, I recalled something my dad had told me he regretted when I was growing up, about how he'd been involved in a car crash while covering a Middle East peace conference in Cairo in which his cab driver was killed and he received substantial head wounds. Afterwards, upon awaking in hospital, he recalled being distraught that he'd failed in his reporting.

'Why?' I asked.

'Because a reporter should never become the story.'

A reporter should never become the story.

I signed the release form. Who was I kidding? I was no reporter. I was an egomaniacal *NME* writer.

Less than three minutes into the premier of *Meeting People Is Easy*, Grant Gee's film about Radiohead, I knew what I'd let myself in for.

In Berlin, before the band's encore, Thom Yorke had thanked the audience for coming. 'You've been good,' he told them. 'It's a shame I haven't been able to see any of your city today but our lives don't seem to allow that any more. Our lives consist of just press, soundcheck, gig now . . .'

At the time I'd thought, *Yeah, put a holiday request form in to HR with the rest of the mugs here*. Now I knew it was a precis of the documentary his band were making about a year in their career.

Our lives consist of press, soundcheck, gig now. Look how miserable it is, living like this in black and white. Look at all the idiots we have to deal with.

A little way into *Meeting People Is Easy*, I appear: the last few minutes of the interview with Colin, when the camera crew have suddenly turned up and I'm desperately trying to think of some questions to string the conversation out as they're instructing me to. Colin complaining about interviews, covering his face with his hat. Our apologies. A little bit of my chat with Ed, too. A passive-aggressive shake of my matchbox. Throughout the film, copy from their print interviews run down the screen. At one stage, a section of my cover story in which I poke fun at them avoiding me tumbles across the action. *Even the drummer is giving us the bum's rush, nicely . . .*

Three thousand words for first thing Monday. Just bash it out. Nobody reads last week's paper.

Meeting People Is Easy sold over half a million copies on DVD and VHS. In his *New Yorker* review, Alex Ross wrote that *Meeting People Is Easy* was a 'counterstrike against the music press, recording scores of pointless interviews with dead-tired members of the band'.

We were all tired, man.

In May 1999, Channel 4 screened it in full. In the days after, I was contacted by all kinds of blasts from my past. I went for pints with people I hadn't seen since school. I was called by a couple of old girlfriends, and nearly girlfriends, who wondered how I was doing. Some Radiohead fans wrote mad letters in coloured crayon and blood to me at *NME*.

When Niall Doherty joined *Q* and took a seat opposite me twelve years later, he said that he felt as if he already knew me as he'd watched the Radiohead documentary so many times as a teenager. The passive-aggressive shake of the matchbox always made him laugh. *Meeting People Is Easy*. Radiohead meant the title sarcastically, but it actually became a prophecy for me. That film made contact with many good friends old and new possible.

I never met any of Radiohead again though, sadly.

15.
To Be Someone

May 1995

The phone on the Live desk rings. I answer.

'Hello, *NME*?'

'Ted, it's Pippa.'

'Pippa! How are you?'

'I'm OK, thanks. Look, I have a message from Paul that he's asked me to deliver directly to you, so I apologise in advance.'

'Right . . .'

'Paul says this, I've written it down: "Tell that Ted Kessler that if he wants to give me a kick up the arse, he's more than welcome to get on a train to Woking and try. I'll be waiting for him."'

'Is he very unhappy about the review, then?'

'He is. He thinks it's really unfair.'

'It's a six out of ten. That's 60 per cent. It's a decent pass mark.'

'I don't think that's how Paul sees it. He thinks it's more of a ten out of ten album. He's really cross about it.'

'Ah, look. I'm a massive Paul Weller fan. I was in the Jam fan club, Pippa. I love that guy. He was my hero growing up. It's not personal, it's just this record.'

'I know, Ted. It doesn't make any difference to him. He's taken it very badly.'

'But I don't think *Stanley Road* is a terrible album. Some of it is brilliant. "Broken Stones" is great. "The Changingman", "Stanley

185

Road" itself are both great. It's just those M.O.R. ones, like "You Do Something to Me". They're a bit bland for me.'

'Ted, you wrote it was "an old fart blues record".'

'Did I?'

'I don't think Paul likes being called an old fart or you writing that he needs a kick up the arse.'

'Fair enough.'

'It'll probably blow over, but I'd steer clear of him for now.'

'Understood. Sorry.'

'Bye, Ted.'

June 1997

The phone on the Features desk rings. I answer.

'Hello, *NME*?'

'Ted, it's Pippa.'

'Oh hi, Pippa! How are you?'

'This is a difficult phone call, Ted.'

'Not again.'

'Yes.'

'Does he want me to come and try to kick him up the arse?'

'No. He's still not over that *Stanley Road* review, though.'

'That's a shame.'

'I told him that you were the *NME* writer for the cover but Paul's not up for you interviewing him. He's already offered to fight Stuart Bailie over his review this time.'

'So I hear. Stuart's quite up for it, you know. He's from Belfast.'

'I wouldn't fancy his chances against Paul. Not in his current frame of mind about *NME* journalists. Look, he's asked me to read you another message.'

'OK, all ears.'

'He says: "Tell Ted Kessler that he's not a good enough writer to interview me, so they'll have to find someone better."'

'Message received! I will commission someone else to interview Paul Weller in that case. Any preferences?'

'As long as it's not you or Stuart, we'll be fine.'

April 2000

Paul Weller looks at the grey brew I have placed in front of him.

'Bit fucking anaemic,' he summarises.

It looks terrible. Weak. Like me.

'I'll make us another round, shall I?'

Weller walks over to the sink in the kitchen, pours our teas away and refills the photo studio kettle.

'This new bloke you've got,' he says, dropping two fresh bags into our mugs. 'Young is he?'

He is, I confirm.

Ben Knowles, the new *NME* editor, is twenty-six. *NME*'s youngest ever editor, as he likes to immediately tell everyone he meets. He's the editor, I'm the features editor, an elderly thirty-one, and we are delivering some truly atrocious editions of the paper together. John Mulvey, thirty-two, is the deputy editor and trying to get away without being too tarnished by what is going out of the office on to the shelves every week, but these issues stain everyone. We are all complicit: editors, writers, designers, Stereophonics and Limp Bizkit. No one gets out alive.

Steve Sutherland had been shuffled upstairs after two years of nosediving sales, partly because *NME* looked like a midlife crisis, partly because music was in a devastating post-Britpop slump that was hospitalising all magazines, and partly because those in charge of publishing the likes of *NME*, *Melody Maker* and *Select* had collectively lost their minds. It was the overdue comedown. Nerves were shot. Talent was drained. Sales had plummeted. People were panicking.

When advertising the editor's job, *NME*'s publisher Robert Tame encouraged all senior staff to apply, asking us for detailed documents about what we'd do to arrest decline, what roles would be changed, who was in, who was out. Then he gave the job to Ben Knowles, a *Melody Maker* writer who'd previously been on *Smash Hits*.

'I've read all your documents,' Ben told me with a grin when we first met. 'Some interesting career ideas for each other there.'

His own pitch was simple, he told me. Much shorter than mine. He was going to bring all the best writers on board. And he would put all the biggest names in music exclusively on the cover. The publishers had loved these innovative ideas, he explained.

Reality had now refocused those ambitions somewhat. The week before this Paul Weller interview, the *NME* cover was made up of a screengrab of Sacha Baron Cohen's comic hip-hop character Ali G alongside the legend 'why Ali G is the most rock 'n' roll show on TV'. This week, London mayoral candidate Ken Livingstone was on the front pretending to DJ in a brown suit with a yellow floral tie. The cover line read 'Ken he kick it?'

'He's twenty-six,' I reply to Weller. '*NME*'s youngest ever editor.'

'That's the way it should be,' nods Weller, approvingly. 'It shouldn't be old cunts like me and Steve fucking Sutherland in charge of music.'

He places our brick-red mugs of tea on the Formica table. 'What's this interview about?'

'We've got a new series called [swallow hard] "The Greats", where we talk to living legends about their life's work.'

'Oh, I'm a great, am I? Fucking hell, last year *NME* said I'm a cunt. I think you wrote that.'

'I didn't!'

'Now they say I'm a great. That's how it goes with you lot. I've seen it all before.'

We take a moment to recap.

1979: Climbing through my mother's cupboard trying to feel for my Christmas present hidden behind the shoes and dresses. Cardboard square in a crinkly bag. Bingo. Drag it from the back into my parents' bedroom and carefully pull out the album from the Our Price wrapper. *Setting Sons* by the Jam. By New Year's Day I know every line by heart.

Saturday's kids play one-arm bandits,
they never win but that's not the point is it,
dip in silver paper when their pints go flat,
how about that – far out!

Still do.

1980, March: Cross-legged on the floor in front of the TV on a Thursday at 7 p.m., as ever. On Sunday, 'Going Underground' by the Jam had exploded the chart by landing directly at number one. A 60/40 split of punk and the Beatles blasting all competition to smithereens. I'd taped the top forty run-down as usual and listened to 'Going Underground' a few hundred times over the following four days. It was the best song I'd ever heard. I couldn't understand why it was louder than every other entry. How they made that bass wobble sound at the end. What was eating Paul Weller – kidney machines? Atomic crimes? – but it was so sleek, its fury so precise, a bullet of melody and violence straight to my eleven-year-old heart. Here's Paul Weller wearing an apron inside out on *Top of the Pops*. Should I be wearing one too?

1980, September: Climbing from the bus outside my new French school for the first day. I am wearing tassel loafers, grey Sta-Prest trousers, a black Fred Perry polo with a gold logo and a black Harrington jacket. On my lapel, there's one badge: The Jam. I am hopeful that by wearing my very best budget-Weller outfit I will impress my new classmates. That does not happen. There are no other Jam fan mods in Saint-Germain-en-Laye. But there are lots of greasy metalhead teenagers who spend most breaks looking to hang me from the toilet door by my underpants.

1982: The Dear John letter nobody desires. Paul Weller is split-ting the Jam up at the tender age of twenty-four, but he needs us, his loyal official fan club members, to hear it directly from him. He'll be back, he explains, but in the meantime he urges us to *stay cool, clean and hard. Paul x.* I promise I'll try.

1983: He has kept his word and returned with a new band whose aesthetic is moulded from a romantic vision of Parisian culture. That's weird, I think. I live in Paris. One of the Style Council's first EPs that I buy is called *À Paris*: in Paris. It is ac-companied by a lavish set of photos of Weller and colleague Mick Talbot wistfully drinking espressos on Parisian café terraces or mooning around on Place d'Italie at dusk. Its release coincides with my own relationship to the city vastly improving, of also taking young companions to drink two-franc coffees, of marching through Paris with pals on silly night-time adventures, and I can't help thinking he's trying to tell me something. When the Style Council come to town, I sleep in a doorway huddled up to fellow English teenagers near L'Eldorado because I missed the last train after watching their encore. We shiver through to dawn singing 'You're the Best Thing', off-key.

1995: I write in *NME* that Paul Weller's new album *Stanley Road* is 'old fart blues' music and that he should expand his influences, that he needs a kick up the arse.

Without wishing to scare him off, I now explain to Weller my relationship to his back catalogue, to his sartorial philosophy, to his sound and vision, and apologise for using unkind language in my *Stanley Road* review. I wasn't mad about the record, that's all. I know lots of other people loved it. The review made no tangi-ble difference: it's his most commercially successful solo album. I thank him for allowing me to interview him after all that. He accepts this and explains why he offered to fight me.

'I'm naturally very defensive,' he replies, 'because I've had to defend my existence to people like you since I was eighteen. It's been constant. I'm very defensive but if they could see it from my stick they'd understand. *Why have you done this? Why have you said that?* Always trying to catch you out, trip you up, letting me know how crap they think I am since I was eighteen. It ain't easy having everyone scrutinise you.'

I apologise for my language again, suggesting his life must have been as pressurised at times as David Beckham's, whose existence in 2000 was much discussed.

'Yeah, it has,' he agrees. 'Only with much better hair.'

Before leaving, I hand over a mix CD of new music I've made him and he signs a CD of his current album, wishing me all the best. We have a cordial agreement.

A few weeks later, the Features desk phone rings.

'Hello, *NME*?'

'Hi, Ted, it's Pippa.'

'Pippa.'

'Paul liked the piece, so thanks for that. We wondered if you wanted to do his EPK [electronic press kit] next week?'

We are reconciled.

December 2000

An email arrives from Ben Knowles inviting me to a meeting with him in an hour, at 5 p.m., in his office. It's very formal. Robert Tame is copied. Ben's office is about ten feet from my desk. Why is he emailing?

John Mulvey has also received the same invitation, timed for ten minutes earlier. As John leaves the office and passes by me on my way in, he shakes his head, his eyes wide.

I step in and take a seat. Robert Tame is sitting on the other seat next to me wearing a black polo neck and pinstripe suit trousers. Poker-faced, he looks like an estate agent dressed as the Milk Tray man.

'There are going to be a few changes at *NME*,' Ben explains.

I am not surprised, but it is still hard to hear. John Mulvey will no longer be deputy editor and I will be leaving the features editing job. It's time to change the staff dynamic for the new year, he explains.

'What I'd like to suggest for you,' says Ben, 'is that you become our senior writer.'

'Senior writer? Is that a job?'

'You'll be paid exactly what you are now. It'll be on a year's contract.'

'And then?'

'Then we see where we are.'

'Right. What about John?'

'John's leaving.'

'Will I still have a desk?'

'No, we can't do that for insurance reasons. You'll be based at home, but we'll still expect you to come in for meetings and to fulfil a set number of words every month.'

'Can I write for other publications?'

'Within reason. No EMAP titles, obviously.'

'So I'll be freelance.'

Robert Tame steps in to close this down. 'What we're offering, Ted, is a unique opportunity. Nobody else has this deal in IPC. You'll be paid a year's salary, you are guaranteed high-profile work with *NME*, but you can also top that up with work elsewhere. It's a really good resolution. Ben does need to make the magazine his own.'

'We could have offered you just the settlement money,' adds Ben. 'But I really feel that you have a lot to offer us as a writer. A magazine like *NME* needs a senior writer, someone who leads from the front informing the paper's voice, someone to help guide the younger writers. It's a vital role and you are the ideal person for it. I really need you to do it.' I look at Ben. He's good at this, the chat. I can see finally how he got the job. I'd approached my interview for the editor's role like a conversation under police caution.

'OK,' I reply, 'well, give me the weekend please to think it over, but it sounds like I'll be senior writer.'

'You should think of this as an opportunity,' Ben continues. 'You know when I first thought of you for this role?'

I don't.

'After that Paul Weller interview. I was talking to my mum about it, she loved it, the fact you'd mentioned I was the youngest *NME* editor as she was such a huge Jam fan. And I thought, well, I wonder how we make the most of those writing skills, it's probably not chained to a desk commissioning features, editing copy, it's getting out there . . .'

And here we have it.

'And here we have it.'

I'm out on my arse with the rest of the clowns . . .

As I leave the office, I wonder if I'll ever get another staff position anywhere again.

February 2006

We cannot always comprehend the eras of great personal change when in their midst. Heading over the Brentford flyover Paul Weller is charging towards his new self at eighty miles per hour. Despite the great speed he is travelling at, it will take him some years to arrive at his new destination. The journey has begun, however.

He rolls down the window in the front passenger seat and lights a cigarette, passing the packet back to me over his shoulder.

'Roger,' he shouts to his faithful guitar tech Roger Nowell, who is holding the wheel. 'Rog, stick "Razorblade" on again.'

On Monday we went to a shisha café on Edgware Road, right around the corner from my childhood flat, and spoke into my Dictaphone for the *Q* Interview slot while sucking on fruit-flavoured pipes. His final words to me as we embraced by his bus stop were 'we'll have a drink Thursday'.

Today, Thursday, we have had a drink. First, we had a drink in his Black Barn studio control room while he blasted me music that he's been working on. Afterwards, we went to the pub around the corner in the village of Ripley, a leafy nick upon Surrey's stockbroker belt. We had a few drinks there. Then, hungry, we knocked back a curry at the local Indian restaurant. While we waited for Roger to return with his car so he could drive us back to London, we returned to the pub and enjoyed a couple of quick-fire pints and chasers.

Now, we're heading to the K West Hotel in Shepherd's Bush for a nightcap.

Throughout our afternoon and evening together, our companion has been 'Razorblade' by the Strokes, a song from their recently released *First Impressions of Earth* album. 'Are you having that Strokes album?' Weller asked soon after I'd walked up the gravel path to Black Barn. '"Razorblade"'s a tune, man.'

In four years, the hangovers will defeat Paul Weller, the black moods that accompany the binges will need to be banished. Sodden and exhausted, he will renew as a sober man. Softer, kinder and more aware of those around whom he orbits. Even more productive, too. Hard to imagine right now, but it's coming at him in the distance, ready to swallow him up, demanding change.

Now, though, he leans out of the window as we flash over the motorway into West London at midnight, singing the words to 'Razorblade' by the Strokes at the top of his voice, lost in melody and the moment. *Oh, razor blade, that's what I call love . . .*

He twists around to check that I'm singing too, and I'm singing too. He takes a smoke from the pack on the seat next to me and turns back towards the highway.

'Stick it on again, Rog!' he shouts.

Stoic, gothic man of Yorkshire Roger presses play and the

drums roll, the guitars race through the vehicle at top volume and, heads thrown back, we all sing. We all sing.

Occasionally, when he has a new album due, he'll text. Turns out he wants to know what you think after all.

> Monday 11 Jan 2021: Ted did Polly send u the album yet? And if so any thoughts on it!!

I reply that I have just played *Fat Pop* for the first time – which I have – and that I think it sounds great so far.

> Ah good! Well spk soon and take care man x

A month later, on 15 February, I leave my East London postcode for the first time since November, when the most recent Covid-19 lockdown was pronounced. I climb into a record company cab and make the enjoyably long trip across the city and out into the Surrey countryside to visit Paul Weller at Black Barn Studios. I'm going to interview him for *Mojo*. When I arrive, he's outside having his photo taken for the cover, smoke travelling up the red Harrington sleeve from his fingers behind his back. He gives me a firm, modsexual welcome hug. I'll never get used to Paul Weller embracing me.

His hair is longer and his manner gentler than ever. As usual, he wishes to know how you are, how your family are, what any mutual acquaintances may be up to. Heard any good music? He is warm and welcoming, despite the provocation of the various pieces of Chelsea Football Club memorabilia that vie for attention in amongst the old Motown, Beatles and pop culture artefacts proudly on show throughout his studio and the cottage at the end of the garden. He stays in that whitewashed villa while working down here, with his band living in the adjoining house, like the Monkees.

A decade of sobriety has softened his edges, but you can also more clearly see the melancholia seeping into him as he ages, like water eating at blotting paper. He started work and creating early, he did everything he could to beat the clock. He has produced hundreds of recorded pieces of original music, as well as many beautiful children across a spectrum of ages, from adult to nipper. But here he is, aged sixty-two. He's not getting any younger. None of us are. 'I feel the weight of mortality very strongly,' he agrees.

We ask the photographer Nicole Nodland to take a picture of us together outside in the winter sun. Who knows when I'll see him again?

A few days later, on Sunday, a text arrives from Weller at 22.58, as I'm reaching for the bedside lamp.

As I was ruminating earlier can I add that my gratitude to music is boundless. I'd still be scratching about in my old town if it wasn't for music! I possibly would never have travelled, met so many great people from all over the world, seen beyond the confines of the UK & how much we have in common. When soul heads say 'keep the faith', that's exactly what it is: a faith. Pure & simple. Music's forever giving, it's a living thing, it's not started wars (fights, yeh), it cuts through all cultures, it's information, education, entertainment. And generally it tells the truth! That's all . . . just had to say that! X

For a day or so, I've been contemplating an ending to the piece, but now I climb from bed and walk to the kitchen table. There I transpose the text and tap in the open goal of the pay-off he'd laid on for me. *The heart has many desires,* I write, *but for Paul Weller there is just one constant, uncomplicated, lifelong love. That's just how he is and why he needs you so.*

I feel the unbeatable satisfaction of a final full stop and return to bed, silently praising Paul Weller's exquisite timing in my head as I drift off. He's always been there for me.

Part Four
Post-Millennium Tension

16.

The Bay of Ligs (*Our Man in Havana, part two*)

The streets outside bristled with ferocious morning birdsong. My neighbours were yet to rise: I had NW6 to myself. I sat down at the kitchen table, removed a pinch of Golden Virginia, dropped it into a Rizla paper, rolled, lit and exhaled. Coughing, I started to write.

Saturday, 17 February 2001
The whisper tears out of central Havana, through the police roadblocks around the Karl Marx Theatre, and smashes into the teenage throng outside the venue. It goes: 'Castro is coming, Castro is coming! Fidel Castro is coming to see the Manic Street Preachers!'

It soon sets the backstage car park alight, too. The Manic Street Preachers' management start ushering the group's immediate entourage inside, into the warren of stageside hallways, keen that nobody from the inner circle should miss any possible meeting with the iconic Cuban leader. Back outside in the car park, burly men wearing white suits and earpieces arrive and peer beneath parked cars. It is 8.15 p.m.; fifteen minutes to show time.

Suddenly, a delegation of Cubans sweep into the Manics' dressing room. 'Good evening,' booms the Minister of Culture.

'Would you like to meet someone very, very important?' Nicky Wire raises his eyebrows: 'Of course.'

'OK, just the band and management,' nods the Minister, clapping his hands together with finality. 'Follow me, please.'

And they're off, walking at pace down a corridor that runs parallel to the stage and into a small, brightly lit antechamber. Those not in the band or management are left on the other side of the stage looking desperately across into the room, aware that history is being etched close by.

'Bugger that,' says Rob Stringer, Epic Records' UK chairman. 'I'm not missing this.'

He bolts across the stage. Those remaining – fellow label bigwigs, a Channel 4 film crew and me – take one look at each other and run in his slipstream. The first door is slowly but firmly being closed as Stringer arrives, so we chase around to the side door where a security man stands guard. He looks at us, looks across at the tour manager, who nods urgently, and then beckons us inside.

The Manics sit on the edge of one side of a square couch, grinning hysterically. On the other side, behind his famous long beard and wearing his trademark green military uniform, sits Fidel Castro.

The atmosphere crackles as the revolutionary dictator waves his arms expansively, talking to the band in Spanish. Fidel Castro is the face of Cuba. He is also one of the twentieth century's most remarkable and enigmatic figures. In January 1959, after a brutal guerrilla war against a corrupt, right-wing government, he led his army down through the Cuban mountains into Havana, where he seized power to the delight of the masses – and to the horror of the Cuban ruling classes and their allies, the United States. He has been in power ever since. He has survived many attempts on his life, several reportedly masterminded by the CIA, presiding over a communist state only ninety miles from the US for over forty years.

He is a seventy-four-year-old mass of living history with thick, grey hair. Right at this moment, though, he's apologising to the Manic Street Preachers.

'I wanted to come early to be able to meet you,' he says through an interpreter. 'Because I'm afraid that at 10 p.m. I will have to leave for an unavoidable engagement. But if you start at 8.30 I will be able to listen to your performance.'

'It might be a bit noisy,' says Nicky Wire.

'I will try to adapt my ears to the noise,' Castro replies. 'It cannot be more noisy than war, can it?'

'Maybe,' laughs Wire, blushing.

Like the Manic Street Preachers, I was pleased that Fidel Castro had decided to come to their gig. I needed an intro to the *NME* piece I was writing and they needed a reason to be there. Until Castro rocked up, we were both struggling.

Though we were operating at slightly different levels of commercial success and expectation, both our careers had entered choppy new waters.

I was no longer the lord of all I commissioned, able to fill *NME* with whatever I fancied while landing myself with all the plum jobs, ideally in Los Angeles on a major label dime, staying at a fancy Hollywood hotel with a nice pool. Now I was at the mercy of whatever my more skilled, scrupulous replacement from *The Face* Alex Needham needed to plug the features well with each week. I had to fulfil my word quota, after all. So I became the semi-reliable, jobbing *NME* writer once more, accepting every commission thrown my way and consequently interviewing some artists about whom I was ambivalent at best. I did not want to sleep on a tour bus between Glasgow and Newcastle with earnest hardcore punks Amen, nor listen to Lostprophets' future sex criminal Ian Watkins intensely detail his philosophies over lunch, but I knew the rules of the game. As long as that £2,000 after tax hit my bank account every month, then I would churn out 1,500 serviceable words about Incubus' needy pop-rock if asked to. My reward for this ego readjustment was a juicy cover story from time to time, such as this trip to Havana with Manic Street Preachers.

The Manics, meanwhile, were also enduring their own status turbulence. They had evolved from the situationist punks who'd sprung out of the unfancied Valleys town of Blackwood in South Wales in the early nineties into a chart-topping anthem-rock band by the decade's second half. Now, though, they were searching for a purpose and meaning beyond being a band whose albums went platinum. This was unusual in an arena-sized band. Normally, the purpose of a big group was to continue being successful. The Manics' quest had an existential element too. What was it all for?

In the beginning, it was to deliver lyrical messages and a world view generally unrepresented in rock music with a commercial purpose, etched in the most starkly poetic terms by lyricists Richey Edwards and bassist Nicky Wire. Songs critical of global capitalism, the monarchy, detailing anorexia and mental illness. About child prostitution, the Holocaust, capital punishment, totalitarianism. Not the usual bye bye baby, baby goodbye schtick.

Then, after Edwards had disappeared from his London hotel never to be seen again in February 1995, the mission became to claw their way free from the unresolved grief, to endure. They hit upon a less abrasive sound in Edwards' absence, something more melancholically epic for two huge albums.

By 2001, though, they knew they needed to break the pattern. They were looking for a reason to be. A way to be, too. Now in their thirties, they were entering a period of existence that they hadn't mapped out together when teenagers dreaming up their band's trajectory: middle age. They wanted to stand apart again and what better way to differentiate yourselves from every other big group than by launching your album in Havana with a historic concert, the first Western band to play in communist Cuba? It was mould-breaking.

And yet, once we arrived in Havana, it became clear that the mission had grown far beyond the group's control. This was state business. The country had opened up for tourists in the late nineties and the city of Havana was being rebuilt significantly with that influx of foreign currency. It appeared unrecognisable from my previous trip there with Black Grape in 1995. Chunks of apartment buildings were no longer falling off unannounced into the streets. Beggars had been swept under the paving.

This time, Cuban officials were keen to deliver as much exposure for Havana as possible. Dozens of media organisations from around the world were flown in and put up at the lavishly revamped Hotel Nacional, where arriving guests were greeted with warm towels, cold mojitos, a mariachi band in full garb playing 'Guantanamera' and a printed itinerary detailing the multiple organised visits to cultural centres we'd be expected to join. Mine also included an invitation aboard the band's sightseeing tour of Havana the next morning.

I hopped on the coach alongside seasoned *NME* photographer Tom Sheehan, a dozen record label people, a two-man HTV camera crew and the band. Sheehan, a widely loved anecdote machine with his own bespoke range of Cockney rhyming slang, was charming the Manics with some tale of yore when the band's security Steven Head jumped on board.

'What are you doing on here?' asked Head, an outwardly gentle giant who also took care of Oasis among other vulnerable mega-acts. 'Band are in that convertible.'

We looked out the window. Beside us sat a 1959 red Cadillac with its top down and a cameraman sitting in the passenger seat.

'I'm in the Jeep with the rest of the Channel 4 crew,' continued Head. 'Everyone else is following in this coach.'

The convoy set off, the convertible leading the way. The trio of Manics sat in a row in the back seat, their hair blown erratically in the sea breeze as they were filmed both from the passenger seat and by the Jeep behind. The artifice of the set-up typified the jaunt to Cuba for the Manics. What had started off as wheezy blue-sky thinking from the band had grown into a huge banquet of opportunity for all. So, instead of the band quietly sightseeing a new city, it had become a three-vehicle, thirty-person, two-film-crew caravan.

It was not the fault of the band that everything had grown so overblown. It was the era they were trapped in, the spirit of the age.

Music culture was clogged. The clogging had started towards the end of Britpop, around 1997, when British groups a little way into their careers felt compelled to deliver Big and Important statement albums: *OK Computer, Urban Hymns, Mezzanine, Be Here Now*. These huge sellers set the tone. Everything had to be Big and Important: albums, tour production, string arrangements, videos, coats. Soon, Big and Important morphed into Dark and Heavy, an affliction that affected British rock music in particular. This was very bad news for a magazine like *NME*, whose stock in trade was the British youth culture associated with kids making zippy, chaotic alternative guitar and rhythmic music. That kind of carry-on didn't really exist in the late nineties. Everyone, even new groups like Starsailor or Embrace, were playing acoustic guitars, recording at Abbey Road and hiring string ensembles.

NME was always at its best when the writers, bands and readers were roughly the same age. In 2000, the writers were old, the bands were often older and the readers were retreating. Historically, the paper could shake off any such cultural lethargy by engineering scenes around new acts. All they ever needed was two or three bands in vague geographic, sonic and sartorial proximity to each other. Baggy, Shoegazers, Grebo, the New Wave of New Wave . . . each made-up movement provided weeks of copy and momentum, delivered by the youthful exuberance of new bands overjoyed to be recognised in print, until that thrill wore thin and we moved on to a new made-up scene. The nuclear blanket bomb of Britpop had pretty much killed all that off, though. The earth was scorched.

I was sent to report on one scene cooked up in desperation by the paper in 2001: the New Acoustic Movement. Not everything had to have the impact of punk but NAM was never going to catch alight. Shaggy-looking blokes in woolly hats sitting on stools mumbling about break-ups to an acoustic guitar in a cellar filled with friends and family members. Nobody was changing their hair or wardrobe for that. (Eventually James Blunt and then Ed Sheeran a decade later did manage to jazz the concept up successfully for the mass market.)

Meanwhile, there was a steady flow of dynamically brilliant rap and R&B drifting across the Atlantic, but our interest was always a one-way street. England was just another boring stop on the deathly European promo schedule for the bigger American stars. I set off to interview many rappers while in a state of nervous devotion and left their company disillusioned, fearful of trying to turn our disastrous meeting into a cover story. The Fugees turned up nine hours late and gave me ten minutes each in a hallway backstage in Wolverhampton. Eminem greeted me on his tour bus in Dallas before pulling his hat over his eyes and shrugging disdainfully through our conversation. Puff Daddy invited me into his five-star Park Lane lair and spent our allotted thirty minutes picking out photos of himself with his entourage. I flew to Seattle for a fifteen-minute audience with 50 Cent squeezed between his TV commitments. Two star rappers actually went the whole hog and fell fast asleep in the midst of our hard-hitting summits: Warren G, recently arrived from LA, drifted off in an armchair in the moodily lit bar of his Kensington hotel, while Ja Rule greeted me with the words 'I was at the club last night', then lay down on the sofa of his West End hotel suite, pulled a cover around his shoulders, rolled over and fell soundly asleep. I let myself out.

Maybe it was me. It probably was, though few if any of my contemporaries fared much better. We were just variously skilled at covering our tracks. Only the eloquent, ferociously engaged Chuck D of Public Enemy lived up to expectations.

And yet I kept putting myself in the firing line because I loved hip-hop. I wanted it to be covered on an equal footing in *NME*. Did our core readership want to read it though? The dismal truth that nagged at successive *NME* editors about hip-hop was provided by the sales figures. No matter how many cutting-edge or hit rap stars made the cover, the only news-stand spikes were provided by young men holding guitars. Nothing else pushed the needle. In eras of solid sales, *NME* could withstand a few dips for the greater good of musical breadth and diversity. In a time when the figures were generally on a determined decline, those sudden plunges were disastrous.

Flicking through the first four months of 2001's *NME* covers is chastening. The editorial team were trying to readjust the age ratio, but the poverty of the run clearly demonstrates what the paper and the labels were up against, and why the Manics playing Cuba demanded such a feeding frenzy: the story provided nourishment in a desert. There was nothing going on. They were living on vapours.

OK. If you insist. Let's inspect the damage.

NME *2001 cover run through April:*

6 Jan: 32 New Stars for 2001

13 Jan: 100 Events That Will Happen in 2001

20 Jan: JJ72 (*who?*)

27 Jan: Sex, Drugs & Rock Journalism: The Outrageous True Confessions of *NME*'s Greatest Writers! (*£6.26 on eBay, to inspect the full horror*)

3 Feb: NME Awards Tour: Amen/Starsailor/JJ72 (*who?*)/Alfie (*I wrote this, but have no memory of JJ72*)

10 Feb: Hip-Hop Special (*a drawing of a young man in a baseball cap next to the graffitied legend How Hip-Hop Stole the Show. News-stand apocalypse*)

17 Feb: NME Awards Special: Bono and the Gallaghers

24 Feb: Popstars (*a cover about a TV talent show to unearth the future members of pop band Hear'Say*)

3 March: Manic Street Preachers in Cuba (*hello*)

10 March: Stereophonics

17 March: Gorillaz & Daft Punk, *an illustrated cover*

24 March: (*I will simply relay the cover exactly as it appears, yellow and white text on black background*): BRTN'S YTH: 2FCKD 2CARE

FEATURING: OXIDE & NEUTRINO, SUGABABES, THE GOVERNMENT, IRISH SPEEDFREAKS, GLASGOW MET-ALLERS, LONDON GAYBOYS & DRUGS

31 March: Missy Elliott

7 April: Miami Dance Conference (*the word MIAMI spelled out in cocaine on cleavage in a pink bikini*)

14 April: Starsailor

21 April: We Love NY: Your Guide to the Most Rock 'n' Roll City on Earth

28 April: Destiny's Child

The culture was unmoored. It appeared as if the Manic Street Preachers were holding the first four months of the year on their back.

By coming to communist Cuba to launch their album with an unprecedented gig, the Manics were at least trying to kick against the flatness of the age, to create a new angle for big-band rock music to operate from. But as an A&R man at Universal Music was fond of saying at that time when discussing potential signings: the shit was bigger than the cat. The era couldn't be so easily fixed.

'Next time,' suggested the Manics' MD at Sony Rob Stringer dreamily, as he watched the band's *NME* photoshoot be filmed by both UK TV crews in Plaza de la Revolución, beneath a massive iron mural of Che Guevara, 'why don't we have the album launch in Monaco?'

Singer James Dean Bradfield shrugged. 'It would be no more uncomfortable personally, Rob,' he replied.

'Or how about Barbados?' continued Stringer, enthused. 'We could say that it is ideologically imperative that we stay at Sandy Lane Beach Resort. What do you think?'

After the concert at the Karl Marx Theatre, there was a bash in a grand hall in the gardens of the Nacional. As we gathered awaiting the band, a small-talk rumour quickly swept the party that the hall was the same location as used in *The Godfather Part II* scene when Michael Corleone tells his brother Fredo that he knew he'd betrayed him. 'You broke my heart, Fredo!' Then the army arrive. The revolution had begun. In fact, though the scenes were set in the Nacional, filming had taken place in the Dominican Republic, not here. It became an incidental fact to strike with disappointment from reporters' notebooks upon our homecoming embrace of Google. Looked similar, though.

As in *The Godfather Part II*, Fidel Castro had also crashed our do, entering the balcony of Karl Marx Theatre's auditorium to the dramatic drone-rock strains of Queens of the Stone Age's 'Regular John', which was coincidentally cued by Manics' tour DJ Robin Turner at that precise moment. Castro stood on the balcony and waved along to the music, absorbing his three-minute standing ovation before the Manics walked on. Fidel skipped the aftershow, but the party was star-studded with local legends nonetheless.

Waiting to greet the band as they entered the Nacional ballroom were Olympic champion middle-distance runner Alberto Juantorena and three-time gold medallist heavyweight boxer Félix Savón. For full-time sports nut Nicky Wire, this seemed a bigger thrill than meeting Fidel Castro.

'You're a legend you are!' Wire said with a squeal to Savón, as the granite-jawed fighter repeatedly patted diminutive drummer

Sean Moore on the shoulders, expressionless. 'You're a legend because you always beat the Americans!'

As Savón drifted across the almost-busy dance floor with a salsa shuffle, I stepped out into the gardens to take the air and write a couple of quotes in my pad in case I forgot.

'Night, Ted.'

I turned round to see Nicky Wire striding up the path to the hotel. Why was he leaving his own bash?

'Oh, it's not really my thing, partying,' he replied, with a smile. 'Besides, I wouldn't want to tarnish any of it. It's been such a lovely evening.' He gave me a little wave. 'Good night, then.'

With that Wire headed along the path, back into the lobby towards his room, the reupholstered penthouse with its view of the glistening harbour, to call his wife and tell her all about his evening, the night he played his music for Fidel Castro and threw his arms around Félix Savón.

I finished writing the piece and flicked the kettle on. What now? The crushing silence that stalks a freelance writer between jobs settled upon me once more. I was either rushing to get something finished in time, in panicked mental overload, or I was bereft, blank, staring for hours from the kitchen window at the little pile of cigarette butts my neighbour had forced through the fence, uncertain if I'd ever work again.

I was idly hitting the send and receive button on my email, hoping that it might squeeze out a reply from the *Observer Magazine*, when the door knocker sounded.

Postman. My little mate Keith who was always happy for a few moments of chat on the doorstep about QPR's latest calamity. He'd introduced himself as a fellow supporter when delivering my season ticket and usually had plenty of insight to share about the club's steep slide from London's top team to the foot of the second tier in less than a decade. Neither of us realised that much worse was soon to follow, as relegation and financial apocalypse in the form of administration awaited that summer.

'Have you got anything for me?' I asked eventually.

'Oh sorry, mate,' he said, rustling through his sack. 'Here.'

He handed me a small but heavy brown mailer. It had been sent from New York. I recognised the handwriting. I thanked Keith and walked down the hall, back into the kitchen, where I unpacked the mailer at the table.

It was from my youngest brother, Daniel. Daniel had gone to New York University after high school in DC, then he'd landed jobs at a couple of small indie and electronic record labels in the city. The previous summer he'd come over to London with his girlfriend to visit, a trip to Reading Festival high on their list of attractions. There, we introduced him to Laurence Bell who ran Domino Records. They got on so well that soon after his return Daniel opened the US office of Domino, operating from a desk in his Union Square apartment, with visiting bands often crashing on his floor when touring. I assumed this package was something to do with Domino, a first US signing perhaps. I tipped it out on to the table.

Out fell ten or twenty identical grey CDs in slipcases. In white lettering stamped across each read the word *Interpol*.

There was a card. It wished me well, sent me love and respect, and wondered if I might want to listen to Daniel's newest demo EP from his own band Interpol, with whom he played guitar, wrote music. Maybe I could pass a few copies around my circle of music friends?

Flustered, I put the CDs back into the mailer for later and walked down the corridor to the bedroom, where I changed into my running gear. I needed to clear my head. I didn't have time for this right now, for my brother's band. I was just too busy.

17.

I Happen to Like New York

For music journalists, there was just one beacon of hope that appeared through the heavy new millennium gloom.

I first spied it in that short, excruciating, dead-man-walking era between being told I was coming off the features editor job and my last day in the *NME* office around Christmas 2000, when a PR, Tim Vigon from Coalition, came into *NME* with a demo to play for the editor Ben Knowles and James Oldham, who was to be promoted to deputy editor from reviews in the new year. I knew it had to be good. Nobody came in to play a demo.

Maniacally enthused, James rushed from the editor's office after twenty minutes and put the CD on the main office stereo. 'This,' he said, fiddling with the tray and buttons, 'is absolutely brilliant.' He pressed play on *The Modern Age* by a band from New York City called the Strokes.

Five years earlier, James had sent me his fanzine when I was editing the live reviews. His rag had pizazz, so I invited him for a chat and a pint, minded to get him started on some reviews. He arrived from his parents' home outside Wycombe on a spiky winter's afternoon, pale with inky hair, skinny, dressed entirely in black, an Oxford-educated ex-goth with a dry, flinty sense of humour. He was clever and funny, cheeky and inquisitive. He had an anything-goes attitude. Massively into books and music. People enjoyed spending time with him, as did I. We soon became good friends.

There was now to be a slight readjustment in the balance of our relationship, as I left the office staff and he was elevated up the masthead. Once, I'd have snaffled this exciting new band's demo tape, but now it was James's time to shine in that light. It was the cycle of editorial life. I was getting used to that idea. He already was.

As the music played, we could hear the plug being pulled on all the scummy, stagnant American rock music we'd been forced to editorially bathe in in recent years: Korn, Limp Bizkit, Marilyn Manson, the Bloodhound Gang and other groups whose names I do not wish to repeat lest we meet again. Their time in *NME* was over.

The Modern Age was pumping through the twenty-fifth floor main office like a laxative: guitars a jagged mix of two of the greatest New York rock bands, the Velvet Underground and Television, drums that resembled thumped cardboard boxes, no cymbals, motorik, soulful, urban, the mysterious baritone poetry of the voice:

Up on a hill, here's where we begin
This little story, a long time ago . . .

It was the start of something. Please be as charismatic and handsome as the music. James took a plane to New York to find out alongside photographer Pennie Smith, famous for her work with the Clash amongst others, who was there to ensure that whatever they discovered had the requisite smudgy, classic-looking black and white documentation to illustrate it.

In June 2001, timed for the band's first single, 'Hard to Explain', the Strokes appeared on the cover of *NME*: story by James Oldham; pictures by Pennie Smith. Five beautiful boys in thrift shop denims, canvas and leathers, leaning on a lamp post in New York City. The slate was wiped and the cover flew from newsstands, a cool, refreshing drink for parched indie and college kids across the land. It's not a huge leap to imagine that the arrival of the Strokes saved the life of the magazine (*see the 2001* NME *cover run as detailed in 'The Bay of Ligs'*). It certainly changed the window display in Topshop.

In July, James called me at home.

'We're doing the Strokes on the cover again, for the album in August,' he told me. 'They're taking us to Los Angeles for a show and a couple of days hanging out. Do you want to write it?'

I thanked him and accepted the commission.

From around 1990 onwards, my dad would tell anybody who asked, and many who didn't, that this was the greatest ever time to live in New York City, in Manhattan.

'Enjoy it,' he would say. 'It's never been better. And it may not last.'

The city was no longer bankrupt. The streets were cleaner. You were much less likely to be murdered. The cultural and culinary life of New York was in the absolute pink.

'I've seen the worst of the city,' he'd say. 'Now, right now, today, this is the best.'

He'd grown up in Queens, in Forest Hills, post-war, and in Manhattan in the sixties. 'More spicy,' he'd say simply of both comparative experiences.

He'd returned to the city of his youth after a sixteen-year absence in 1985. First, he lived in a small Midtown apartment where I'd sleep on his sofa when visiting. Then in 1989 he got a short-lived job teaching journalism at New York University. Through this, he managed to snaffle an NYU apartment, a sweet first-floor, two-bedroom corner spot in a university building on Bleecker Street by LaGuardia, right in Greenwich Village. His wife Jair began a job working for the French Institute at NYU and so, with my sister Gaby growing up in the second room, they stayed in that flat for over thirty years, long after my dad left NYU. There was no way they'd give up that place, subsidised, in my old man's dream location and otherwise out of their budget if on the free market. It came to define them, in so far as bricks arranged in a particular location can.

In the mornings, he had a ritual of making a pot of powerful coffee very early, by 6 a.m. He'd bring in the *New York Times* from the mat outside the door, slap it on the dining table and then he'd stand for a few moments watching the sun appear over Lower Manhattan, the light rippling, reflecting across the buildings and settling upon the central attraction from my dad's living room, the Twin Towers of the World Trade Center just a mile down the road. Each tower was 1,350 feet high, 110 storeys, once the tallest buildings in the world. They dominated his landscape. They were right there. Dead ahead.

That morning, 11 September 2001, my middle brother Mark was in his office on Park Avenue, towards Union Square, where he worked at a literary agency. As usual, he was there by 8.30. He was drinking coffee at his desk as he watched American Airlines Flight 11 streak noisily across the city and slam into the North Tower of the World Trade Center soon after, at 8.46. He was still there half an hour later when United 175 flew into the South Tower.

He remained in his office until the afternoon, watching the aftermath of the attack upon those towers a short subway ride away on TV with his colleagues, as well as American Airlines 77 flying into the Pentagon. After he spoke to my mother who was locked down at NBC in Washington and my dad at his apartment, he left work and snuck beyond the security cordon to meet up with our youngest brother Daniel, who lived beneath the line.

Slave to caffeine, Daniel awoke that morning jonesing for his usual first fix. His boss Laurence Bell of Domino was over from London staying in his home office, so Daniel left him to negotiate his jet lag and stepped out on to 3rd Avenue to buy breakfast with his girlfriend, Danielle. As they walked down the avenue a large plane swooped above, making Daniel jump. Danielle chuckled at him. 'What's up with you?' she asked.

'Didn't you think that was flying low?' he replied.

As they ordered their coffees and food, Mark called to say they should make them takeaway. They'd want to get in front of a TV immediately. Back home, they awoke Laurence and watched the second plane hit the tower live together.

After Mark met up with Daniel, they wandered through the streets, punch-drunk, walking by the soldiers erecting barricades, air heavy with smoke and dust, the unusual silence of Downtown regularly punctuated by sirens and wafts of something new and dreadful on the breeze. Eventually, they wound up at Max's Fish, a favourite East Village bar frequented by their friends and many of the band members who'd go on to make their names in the coming decade. Somehow, Clinic, who had been due to play in New York that week and the reason Laurence was over, had made it to Max's too. The Liverpudlian band's resourceful tour manager Morgan Lebus had managed to uncover a way back into the city from Boston when all the routes in were supposedly closed off. Everyone gathered around the pool table, seeking something abstract and familiar to distract from the new reality beyond the door.

After some fraught emails with both of my parents, I managed to speak to them on the phone in DC and NYC in the days after. My mother was on a high-alert war footing. She told me she was considering retirement. I suggested she take a few days off, not to make any irreversible calls right now.

My father was more phlegmatic about the whole thing. 'My God, what a thing to witness,' he said. 'In New York, of all places.'

After years working as a Middle East correspondent, reporting wars and subsequent peace talks, the irony of watching a new conflict unfurl so horrifically from a window in his living room bit deeply. Three thousand deaths, just in front of him. I asked him how he was.

'I'm fine, but the city,' he replied. 'We're in a new era now.'

*

Before the eras changed, just before the old America abruptly passed and the modern US came to be, I went to Los Angeles for a final sip from that cup.

It was 3 August 2001, and the Strokes were living the best version of their young lives, poolside at the Roosevelt Hotel in Hollywood as one day tumbled warmly into the next. At the time, it felt like a silly dream you awake from laughing. Now, I can only remember it as a final, carefree dance in America before the disco lights were unplugged.

Earlier that evening, they had played an extremely sold-out show at the Troubadour, with hundreds left out on the pavement and everyone from Sofia Coppola and Keanu Reeves to Joe Strummer and Courtney Love crammed inside. I'd seen them play half a dozen times in England that year, in London, Oxford, Colchester, and the response had been increasingly lovelorn, but the reaction that night in LA, the week their first album *Is This It* hit racks, was overwhelming. The band appeared taken aback.

'Fucking A!' exclaimed singer Julian Casablancas, a soft-cheeked twenty-two-year-old, shaking his head and taking a puff of his cigarette between songs beneath a prominent no smoking sign. He laughed and pulled the collars of his white suit jacket together. At this, a front row filled with young girls screamed at him, like in a movie from the 1960s. 'Incredible,' he said, before counting in the next number.

Afterwards, there was a record-company party in a long, dimly lit bar attached to the Troubadour. The bar was free but nobody other than the band seemed to be drinking, which made the aim of being invited back to their hotel that much easier for everyone else present.

Soon after Casablancas stuck his tongue in my ear at the bar and asked if he could kiss me, I hopped in the minibus back to the Roosevelt with him and wide-eyed drummer Fabrizio Moretti. As we awaited twenty-year-old guitarist Nick Valensi to gather his bag from the dressing room, I made small talk with Valensi's mother at the stage door. Danielle Valensi held my hand through-out our chat, keen for her message to cut through.

'Only write nice things about my son, sir,' she implored. 'Don't take advantage of their good nature.'

'We have this under control, Mom,' said Nick upon his return. 'Love you!' he called, as we waved her off. 'I bet Bono never introduced you to his mom.'

He climbed into the bus. 'OK. Let's get wasted.'

Back at the hotel, Fab Moretti stripped down to his underwear alongside *NME* photographer Ewen Spencer and climbed into the warm pool. They started to execute slow, happy lengths in the under-lit water.

The rest of the party got business under way in Valensi's room, but he soon narrowed the guest list down to two so people wandered off to different poolside cabanas to continue festivities, to the hot tub, to the pool.

Fittingly as a member of the press, I found myself landlocked in the driest venue: the management suite. There, I shared awkward chat and the damp end of a joint with the band's manager Ryan Gentles (who carried himself in the manner of someone just a little too neurotically nerdy to be in the band itself), their Australian soundman, their UK press envoy Jakub and Ryan's assistant, Jules. All of the room's lights were on. We could hear laughter from the pool area, but we were discussing tour routing.

Suddenly, the door reverberated to a loud thumping. The handle wiggled and then clicked. The door swung open. Julian Casablancas stood in the hallway, legs apart. He slowly raised a middle finger.

'Fuck you!' he shouted.

The room laughed. He was not laughing along.

'Fuck YOU!'

'Come and have a joint, Julian,' called his PR.

'Fuck you!' he repeated, swaying.

'Jules,' he called, imploringly, '*please* come with me.'

She walked to the door and helped manoeuvre him drunkenly down the corridor towards the hot tub. In four years, they would be married. In fourteen they would be parents to two children, and in eighteen they would be divorced. At that moment, though, at 3 a.m. on 4 August 2001, they were going to join some friends in the spa.

I followed them down the corridor, out into the pool area, which was now filled with refugees from the Troubadour party lolling on loungers and lying on the grass in the warm LA night air, smoke billowing upwards through the soft lights.

This was no time to introduce myself to strangers. I removed my shirt and trousers, my shoes and my socks, then I climbed into the water next to Fab and Ewen, dipped beneath the surface and kicked off towards the deep end.

Back in London, I composed a follow-up email to my new friends at *Life*, the *Observer*'s magazine supplement. The subject line had the same two words in it as my previous email, sent just before I left for LA: The Strokes. This time I added a question mark: The Strokes?

In January, I'd pitched Billy Childish as a profile feature on a whim and the *Observer Magazine* had gone for it enthusiastically, the editor telling me that if I kept bringing them good music pitches we'd be in business. It was very encouraging. I was very encouraged. So I pitched them other feature ideas.

The relationship was nevertheless opaque. Some ideas stuck, others didn't, but I was never quite sure why. It was unpredictable. Unknowable. Sometimes, even being commissioned to write a piece was no guarantee of seeing the work appear.

I went down to Billy Childish's house in Chatham, shared some herbal tea and asked him to lay his mystical-punk philosophies all over me. Then I wrote 3,000 words as prescribed for the following week. Eighteen months later *Life* published them. I hadn't had to supply a single rewrite in that time. They were just waiting for the right moment to unleash it upon their readers, leaving me to field dozens of quizzical, increasingly enervated phone calls from Childish who'd agreed to the interview in order to publicise a particular release and exhibition.

In March, I got on a plane to Nassau at *Life*'s behest to spend a week hanging around beach resorts in the Bahamas with correspondents from the *Evening Standard* and *NME* – my old colleague John Mulvey – while I awaited a thirty-minute audience with Missy Elliott in Lenny Kravitz's house on Love Beach. Though the *Observer* had negotiated the access with the PR, they were distraught upon my return to learn about the presence of other members of the press. So they held the piece for several months as I desperately tried to get five minutes with Missy after her London show to add the bespoke material they required to run the article. There was a long moment when I thought my only payment for spending a week in the Caribbean was going to be spending a week in the Caribbean.

(I'm sorry, this tiny violin appears to be out of tune.)

The Strokes seemed like an easy win to me. There were other Sunday newspapers interested in them, but the band were signed to venerable indie label Rough Trade and everyone there wanted to start with *Life*, as at that time it was the most handsome supplement. It was printed A3 on heavy paper, unlike all the flimsier glossies. It had a bit of heft, even if it sold less.

I couldn't understand their hesitancy over the Strokes.

'I'm not sure,' said the features editor.

'About what?' I asked. 'They're the most exciting young band in years, your readers and their kids will be mad about them. They're silly and messy. They look fantastic. The album will be number one.'

'There's always a hot new band,' she replied, dismissively. 'This is the *Observer Magazine*. We can't just do the latest. What's so different about them?'

'They're joyous,' I explained. 'All under twenty-three, living every moment like it's their last. They're having sex and taking drugs and partying like they've just invented good times, but it isn't their motivation.' It was a by-product of their collective alchemy, I told her. They'd written eleven concise songs that had instantly connected with an enormous worldwide audience. Their lives were dreams coming true. Rock mythology was begging to be described in real time, I said.

'Sounds like a great music magazine story,' she replied. 'We'll keep our eyes on them.'

I told her I'd be in touch again about them. She sighed and hung up.

A week later, the Strokes appeared on the cover of *The Face*. That afternoon the *Observer Magazine* commissioned me to join the Strokes on tour in Philadelphia and then Pittsburgh on 15 and 16 November 2001.

The country had irreversibly darkened in the ten weeks since I'd last been in the USA, as had Julian Casablancas. There was no going back. It was a new era. He sat at the bar in Pittsburgh after their second show, his face on the counter, a beer by his head. He was no longer happy, carefree.

'I miss New York,' he said. 'I miss the life that created this album.'

Throughout those three days with the Strokes, the atmosphere was disjointed, fractious, tired. This was not the piece the *Observer* wanted me to write. They wanted the Rolling Stones on tour in 1965. They wanted mayhem, mischief. I'd witnessed all of that in Los Angeles: orgies, drunk-driving, a punch-up, some very goofy repartee. The story had now moved on, though.

On 11 September that year, the Strokes had been booked into their rehearsal room in Manhattan. Instead, they found themselves wandering through the same downtown streets and bars as my brothers that evening, similarly dazed.

They still had a long US tour lined up until the new year, but nothing would ever quite be the same again for them. The window had closed. They were suffocating in their success and the sudden rearrangement of their city, the approaching war.

Casablancas in particular appeared deflated, depressed. The other band members were upset about 9/11, but they were nevertheless getting on with the business of being single young men in a successful rock band on the road. For Julian, the game was up already. He looked broken.

'Right now in my head it's like living in a dirty room,' he explained. 'Once it's nice and clean again, I'll be able to think straight, but it's way short of being clean right now.'

He didn't want to be on tour any more. He'd fallen asleep the night before in his bunk on the bus to the sound of guitarist Albert Hammond Jnr and Fab watching porn at full whack through the stereo in the lounge just behind him. He was changing his mind about a lot of things.

'I never had the rock-star dream,' he said, with a swig of his beer, raising his finger to attract the barman for refills. 'I thought it would be cool to be a modern-day composer.' The reality of playing shows across the States, across Europe, was hardening his ambitions. 'I want to be one of those people,' he said sadly, 'be they writers, poets, musicians, who leaves clues for the next generation. That's my aspiration.'

He didn't think he could do that on an overnight bus to Cleveland, no matter how many girls would be waiting for him to climb down the steps at the other end.

When I eventually got back to London via the many new unsmiling security checks, a pioneer of paranoid transatlantic travel in the immediate post-9/11 moment, I tried to write two pieces in one. I wrote about the arrival of the most exciting young American band in a generation, and I also wrote about their end. Neither story rang entirely true. The most exciting young American band in a generation had already left the scene before I'd arrived in Philadelphia. Their time had been between the group's baby steps in England in January and that first plane hitting the North Tower. But they weren't over, either. The Strokes carried on for decades. They're still going. They've written some very good songs subsequently, as well as releasing some occasionally disappointing albums. There have been long tours, drug addictions overcome, marriages, divorces, children, too. But they wouldn't be any less loved, their influence smaller, if they'd split on 11 September 2001. Those first nine months in the public eye still define them.

When I left the full-time *NME* gig, I suddenly remembered that if you don't arrange to meet people then you drink alone.

At *NME*, you just walked out of the office into a social whirl, something that a lot of the time you tried to escape, but which was available on tap nonetheless. You were never lonely. You just chose to be alone.

Those rules were now different for me. I could always find entertainment in the week, a trip to the office, a gig, maybe a drink with a pal, but as a homeworker the weekend loomed.

I did not want to break from sending desperate pitching emails from the kitchen table in the week by instead standing in the bedroom, looking from the window at weekends. Everyone I knew had jobs, relationships, so at the weekend they combined a day away from an office with shopping, DIY, some kind of binge.

I had to get away from my flat. I too had a relationship, but it was not providing as much diversion as I required. Escape from home at the weekends became a key to my sanity.

So I went to every QPR game, home and away. When I'd first moved back to England in 1985, going to the football was the only link I had with my time before we'd moved to Paris. The stadium was still there, in the exact same space in Shepherd's Bush, down the same streets, past Shepherd's Bush market, along Uxbridge Road, on to Loftus Road, through the turnstile, up the steps, behind the goal: a literal journey down memory lane to an unchanged place of nevertheless unpredictable adventure. I didn't have a childhood home to return to and I hadn't stayed in touch with primary school friends, but what I had was Loftus Road, the QPR stadium. That felt like home, that was my ancestral base, the one thing that I had happily done with my dad and continued without him. When I returned to the city, I went every week, on my own but never alone. Since the mid-noughties I've gone to games with a tight group of friends, but for decades football was something I attended alone. I have never felt lonely at a football match.

That season, 2001–02, QPR were on a tour of the lower divisions, so on alternate Saturdays I found myself on trains to Bury, Peterborough, Colchester, Blackpool, Port Vale, Huddersfield, Northampton, Swindon, etc. with just a newspaper, a small green pocket radio and a light sense of adventure for company.

On Saturday, 15 December 2001, I climbed from the train at King's Cross in the early evening on my way home from Chesterfield. QPR had won a thriller 2–3 in front of a raucous away following, but the policing after the match had been more laid-back than the mood of the locals and I'd had to run from men in ropey jackets waiting in the shadows to kick departing cockneys on their way to the station. I was glad to be back in the smoke.

As I walked through the King's Cross concourse to the echoing cheers of fans similarly pleased to be home, I noticed the news-stand was filled with Sunday's papers.

There, splashed across the top band of the front page of the *Observer*, was the promise of the Strokes in the magazine, alongside my name.

I grabbed a copy and pulled the magazine supplement *Life* from its guts.

A black and white photo of the Strokes adorned its cover. There was nothing else. Just these words:

Post-Millennium Tension

The Strokes
On the road with the new gods of rock
By Ted Kessler

I laughed. I knew they'd come round.

One can easily mistake moments of great elation as the beginning of something, that hard-fought personal achievement marks a moment of lasting consequence. Really, though, this cover marked the end, a carriage clock for my youth. No story would prove to be as carefree, as joyous as that first adventure with the Strokes in LA in the summer of 2001 again. The *Observer* story was like the space capsule falling back towards Earth, watching the moon disappearing through the window.

Down below, the new era was already under way.

18.
Easy Come, Easy Go

One afternoon in 1991, when I was dropping an interview off in the *Lime Lizard* office on an industrial estate in Highbury New Park, a serious young man with short, thick hair and a tensed jaw introduced himself.

'Ted, hello,' he said. 'I'm Gareth Grundy.'

I recognised the name from bits and pieces in the magazine. Unlike the other *Lime Lizard* writers I met, he seemed personally relatable. He didn't immediately give off the air of someone who spent his days in a darkened Holloway Road bedsit writing in the first person without punctuation (or a concrete commission) about complex maths metal amidst piles of yellowing *Melody Maker*s. He was wearing contemporary trainers and a tidy polo shirt. I felt he was someone I might be able to talk with for a moment without being scolded for my relatively mainstream musical taste.

'I was wondering,' he asked in my ear, over the brutal thud of Godflesh being pumped from the stereo, 'how did you come to have reviews printed in *Select*?'

Gareth was a couple of years younger than me, it turned out, still at university. He'd just started to have work appear in *Lime Lizard* and understandably wanted to branch out. I suggested he send some photocopies of his work to editors on real magazines alongside a smart covering letter and that he develop a thick skin.

The advice must have worked out for him, because when I bumped into him at a show in 2003 he was the deputy editor of venerable music monthly *Q*. He asked me what I was up to. I said

I was freelancing for the *Observer* and some other places, but that I was still on a retainer with *NME*.

'If you ever want a change of scenery, I'm sure we'd be happy to have you write for *Q* instead,' he told me.

He was probably just making small talk, but it was the closest anybody had ever come to poaching me, other than James Brown when he was launching *Loaded* and hoovering up young writers to mould, so I took it as a transfer bid.

I couldn't afford to leave for *Q*, though. Shortly before my first year as senior writer was to end at *NME* in January 2002, I went to see Ben Knowles and suggested that he keep me on a much-reduced retainer. I realised they wouldn't continue my old full-time wage for a second year. I also knew, though, that Steven Wells was on a £600-a-month retainer, agreed many years before, back when the byline of the ferociously funny Swells (as he was known) had valuable commercial appeal. I wasn't in his league of brand recognition. But I could do the work. I was reliable. They probably wanted to keep me on board.

Ben agreed and signed off the £600. It wasn't much, but it covered my half of the mortgage on the flat in West Hampstead that I shared with my then-partner. It was one thing I could rely on.

So I had to thank Gareth but pass on his offer.

'Oh well,' he said, 'if you change your mind, drop me a line . . .'

A month or two later, the bank sent me a stern three-line letter. My mortgage payment had failed due to insufficient funds. I went into a branch and asked for a printed statement. There it was in black and white: my £600 from *NME* had not been deposited. I called Karen Walter, the long-term *NME* editor's secretary, a beacon of light who'd steered successive editors reliably away from the rocks of folly since time's dawn (the early 1980s).

'Karen,' I began, 'I don't appear to have been paid my retainer this month.'

'Oh dear,' she replied, her voice that typical shade of concerned care that made us all feel like we missed our mums. 'Why don't you come in and ask Conor about it? I'll look into it in the meantime for you.'

Conor McNicholas had taken over from Ben Knowles a few months earlier, his stated remit remarkably similar to that of Ben's incoming manifesto pledges in 2000. He was to revitalise the magazine with bright new writing talent and the biggest cover stars.

A few years earlier, when I was features editor, Conor had, unbidden, sent Steve Sutherland a thick document suggesting how he'd revolutionise *NME*, detailing what a terrible job we'd all been doing – Sutherland included, I presume. Don't worry, the document explained, Conor had a plan. Steve was very taken with it. He told John Mulvey and me all about the document in our weekly cover lines meeting to take our minds off the tortuous job in hand – or perhaps to provide focus.

'A lot of it is bollocks, of course,' admitted Steve, undeterred, one finger in his ear. 'Marketing speak. Pie-in-the-sky nonsense. It's not based in reality. But he's a very bright lad, he knows the paper inside out. I'm going to get him working on the news desk for a week, see what he's about. We can take a look at each other. He might shake things up.'

Editors love to 'shake things up', especially when times are tough. It draws attention away from them, injects some of the angst they're feeling back into the workplace. It's the print-world version of a culture war. Something silly that's just serious enough for everyone to get worked up about.

Occasionally, the addition of an ambitious, yapping puppy or two to the office just for the sake of 'shaking things up' without a role in mind will spark new life into the veterans who, fearful that their days are numbered, suddenly call on the old skills that got them there in the first place. It's risky. It tells staff that the editor otherwise relies upon exactly what he thinks of them. If the editor is weaker than he imagines with his bosses, it can provoke a mutiny. Losing one editor may be more cost-effective than an entire team for publishers. But it can pay off if it energises staffers.

Not this time.

Conor's week did not go well. The trial spanned two days, perhaps, before a bruised McNicholas left. He would probably say that the news desk staff made life purposely difficult for him, behaved in bad faith, dumped impossible tasks upon him without maps for success. The news desk no doubt resented his presence, and they did not hide this; he was not a news reporter by any stretch of the job description. He was an editorial marketing whizz – a genius at marketing 'Conor McNicholas' in particular. The news desk was made up of grizzled former local paper door-knockers who thought they alone on the paper were real journalists, so why should they wet-nurse this brown-nose?

I do not know the truth. I kept myself as far away as possible from both parties. I understood my place.

Conor, to his credit, did not shrink after the experience. I have never spoken to him about it, but I imagine it may well have motivated him even more – and as someone who'd sent an editor a long pitch for the recipient's job, he was already transparently ambitious. McNicholas worked at a bunch of magazines I can't be bothered to Google before resurfacing as editor at *NME*'s dance music sister title, *Muzik*. When Steve Sutherland regained editorial control of *NME* and sought to replace Ben Knowles – who'd been sidelined during a spell of ill health – he returned to Conor, who now had the workplace experience to step into the *NME* office and make his mark. The news desk was the first he attended to.

Each *NME* editor arrives believing they have the master plan to reinvent the paper positively. The truth, though, is that without an in-bloom music scene with a bedrock of young, exciting bands, the job is impossible even for the most gifted editorial team. If you have the acts, the personalities, the access, even a team of variable skills can profit. Just as I had during the musically fertile early- and mid-1990s.

Conor had taken over just after the Strokes resuscitated indie-rock in 2001–02 and in their wake a stream of new and ambitious off-centre rock bands piled in through the door, acts such as Kings of Leon, Yeah Yeah Yeahs, Interpol and the Vines. Even the White Stripes, who'd been around a little longer, only really set fire commercially in the wake of the Strokes. Having had no cover stars eighteen months earlier, *NME* suddenly had half a dozen reliable new big sellers, groups who appealed to a readership roughly the same age as the bands. The ideal mix.

Luckily for him, Conor did have that skilled editorial team, too. James Oldham had employed all his wiles to engineer his *NME* exit via a deal for a record label he launched with Universal Music's money, Loog. But Conor overcame this loss by leaning on two talented, experienced deputies in Alex Needham and Malik Meer to run the editorial of the magazine, while he fixated on the kind of hifalutin marketing hoo-ha editors always moan about not having time for. That Alex and Malik are now respected *Guardian* bigwigs underlines how fortunate he was to have them perform his heavy lifting.

But, perhaps most valuably, a parochial young British band that his readers were mad about had also turned up. He needed the Libertines, the Libertines needed *NME* and the readership couldn't get enough of these endearingly shambolic squat-shanties from the wise-cracking rapscallions with antique jackets and tea-stained teeth. They wrote about them so often that eventually even I had to have a go.

The Saturday before I arranged to meet Conor to unravel the mystery of my lost retainer, I spent the night trying to not look too much like a policeman at the back of the Hope and Anchor pub in Islington as it filled with drunk teenagers waiting for Pete Doherty to play a solo acoustic show. The Libertines' frontman's fondness for drug chaos and models had made his name tabloid chum in their waters so he was on a run of unannounced guerrilla gigs. Unfortunately, it sometimes seemed like they were a secret even to Doherty. I'd been to Northampton a few days earlier on a similar mission but he was the vital missing ingredient. He'd just enjoyed a brief spell in Wormwood Scrubs for some drugs malarkey, yet his reliability had not been reformed inside. As the clock approached midnight at the Hope, I feared I might be dealing with another no-show. The story I'd been commissioned to write was along the lines of 'the hunt for Pete Doherty', so I didn't necessarily need to find him. But having interviewed old associates and new friends about him I hoped for the pay-off of him turning up.

Just as we were about to be kicked out of the Hope and Anchor he arrived, looking a little untidy and sounding as hoarse as the undead, but he strummed a handful of songs on a battered guitar, the audience sang every word for him, then he jigged in the street alongside them. I headed home to write my piece.

As it turned out, it was the last thing I contributed to *NME*.

The following Tuesday, after I emailed the Pete Doherty story in, I took the Tube to King's Reach Tower to meet Conor in his new room at the other end of a remodelled *NME* office, the territorial cubby holes of old having been flattened into call-centre-styled long hubs of desks. Karen had put my name in his diary, but as Conor consulted it he said he was unsure why.

'What's on your mind, Ted?' he asked.

'I called Karen because my retainer didn't arrive this month. She didn't know why, so she suggested I ask you.'

He blanched.

'Oh God,' he said. 'Didn't we talk about it?'

'No?'

'I spoke to Swells. I'm so sorry. I thought I spoke to you too?'

'About what?'

'We've had to stop both your retainers. The budgets have been cut. I'm sure we spoke.'

I took a moment.

'Nobody told me before I received a letter from my bank,' I replied.

'I'm so sorry, Ted, but there's nothing I can do about it. We still want you to write for us, though.'

'I'm in the paper every week and Swells hasn't been in it for months. You told him but not me?'

'Sorry,' he repeated. 'Bad oversight on my behalf, there's just so much to take care of in this job. It's no excuse, but things slip sometimes.'

I thanked him for his time and left the office.

At home that afternoon I wrote two emails.

The first I sent to Gareth Grundy saying that I'd love to be considered for commissions in Q. The other I wrote to anybody still employed by IPC who I'd worked with at *NME* in any capacity. I gave the email the subject line of 'Off to pastures Q' and explained that after a decade on *NME* I was leaving to write for Q magazine. I thanked everyone for the best ten years of my life and wished them every success. All farewells should be sudden, as we know.

I received generous well-wishes from everyone in reply, even those I didn't expect to hear from. I think we could all afford to be magnanimous now. It was time. I'd overstayed my welcome.

Only Steve Sutherland failed to respond. I didn't hear from him. I still haven't, even though he had made me his staff writer, his live reviews editor and his features editor in successive years at *NME*. He gave me a salaried job when I believed I would never be a full-time employee ever again, so I don't hold any grudge. He was always very supportive and encouraging of me, and I'm fairly sure we didn't fall out. I certainly didn't read too much into that unanswered email. He hadn't responded to my clippings I'd sent to him all those years ago at *Melody Maker*, either. As Conor explained in our meeting, when you're very busy some things slip through the cracks.

Post-Millennium Tension

*

For many years, between the mid-nineties and the late noughties, I played football twice weekly with Steven Wells. He brought me into a Sunday seven-a-side game at Old Street where we on the blue team played a fairly competitive match against the whites: two teams made up from a large pool of mates of mates, from architects to members of eighties punk bands to waiters to adman creatives to bike couriers to political advisers and broadsheet journalists, all of whom stuck rigidly to their appointed team's colour.

Although it was just a weekly seven-a-side with no tangible prize, places were valuable and the result seemed to matter to all. Perhaps part of the reason for this seriousness was that Swells delivered some of his most caustically hilarious prose in his long weekly match reports that he sent out soon after the game. He was a brilliant stylist whose acerbic and overblown tone was most obviously an influence on *Black Mirror* writer Charlie Brooker. There were even conversations between players about whether we should publish a compilation of the reports commercially, such was their vintage Swells-isms. Like many musicians over the years, the Sunday players both feared and craved Swells' written appraisal.

We also played together between April and late September every year in Regent's Park on Thursday evenings, in a match that we and Johnny 'Cigarettes' Sharp organised out of any *NME* and *Loaded* journalists we could cobble together, mixed in with a handful of civilian friends. Turnout was often low. There were weeks when we played four-a-side. Sometimes, fewer. Other weeks, twenty-three people would turn up. We were adaptable.

Swells was not a natural footballer. He'd come to playing it very late, in his upper twenties, his earlier life having been too consumed by punk and politics for sport. He had rotten ball control and his pace was non-existent. Yet, I always wanted to be on his team. We formed a lead-footed but sturdy defence together.

'The team that shouts the most always wins,' he'd remind his team before kick-off.

If Swells was doing the shouting that was inevitably true. He'd cut his teeth reading his poetry at punk gigs in Yorkshire pubs so his gab was razor-sharp. He'd spend entire matches in Regent's Park ferociously roasting individual opposition team members at the top of his voice, sometimes so hilariously that we'd have to pause to stop laughing or to prevent players trying to fight him.

Some weeks, a group of young bucks training together for their actual league game near our jumpers-for-goalposts kickabout would take one look at the rabble of pot-bellied old soaks led by a loud-mouthed middle-aged skinhead wearing round spectacles and baggy tracksuit bottoms and challenge us to a game, sure of a confidence-boosting victory ahead of their real match at the weekend. Swells would destroy them. He'd pounce on one detail – an overheard nickname, a haircut, an imagined occupation – and relentlessly caricature it at the top of his voice, pounding the seam until they were too self-conscious to play freely.

At Swells' thronged memorial in an Islington pub in June 2009, when, not long after he'd achieved some kind of happy-ever-after by marrying and moving to America, he died of cancer, I thought of all the times he'd made me weep with laughter on football pitches over the years. I considered what a rare privilege it had been to play football mainly for the comedy rather than the exercise.

I remembered one conversation we'd had ahead of a Thursday match in 2003, too. We were alone, huddled beneath a tree together in the streaming rain waiting forlornly for anybody to play football with by the Outer Circle gate in Regent's Park.

'So,' I wondered, 'when did they tell you your *NME* retainer was finished?'

'You what?!'

I told him my story. He threw his head back laughing.

'Ted! My retainer?! I can't even remember having a retainer.'

He saw the look in my eyes.

'Look, you know the expression "easy come, easy go"? It's wrong for music journalists. It doesn't apply for any of us. It should be "hard come, easy go" for music journalists. Getting a regular wage from a music magazine is difficult. These cunts don't want to pay people. You had regular money from them for ages. Then one day, it's gone. Who cares why or who got rid of it? Easy go.'

Through the storm we could see Johnny Cigs and a few of his pals jogging down the sodden path with bags and papers held over their heads towards our tree. We were going to have a game after all.

19.
The Wallace Space

What really went on there? We only have this excerpt.
    – The Fall, 'Cruiser's Creek'

After I'd contributed a couple of features, the *Q* editor Paul Rees invited me in for a coffee.

There are going to be a few changes at the magazine, he explained in a café beneath their office on Winsley Street, by Oxford Circus. He'd been there a year or so having come over from *Kerrang!*, but had left on a honeymoon sabbatical soon after taking the job so he was only now really getting his feet under the table. Would I be interested in becoming the new reviews editor? he asked.

I was shocked as that implied the current reviews editor was leaving. Paul said he just wanted his own team in place. In that case I was surprised to be his choice – we didn't know each other, this was our first conversation – but I thanked him and asked if I could think it over.

I called my friends. Should I take this job?

Are you mad, they replied. Of course! You're an unemployed music journalist and this is one of the few decently paid jobs in music journalism.

Hmm. I paused.

Truth is, I didn't really like *Q* magazine. Whenever I flicked through it in WHSmith after it started in the mid-eighties it always had Phil Collins, Mark Knopfler, Annie Lennox or some other middle of the road nause on the cover. The writing was full of itself, smug, self-congratulatory, purposely fogey. When it wasn't like that it was unnecessarily cruel and judgemental, as with its Who the Hell regular, in which an unwitting interviewee was dismantled with extreme prejudice over 2,000 words. It was a feature constantly held up by successive publishers in later dressing-downs as an example of the kind of thing music journalism no longer had the guts for, heralded as such by people who'd never aimed a punch upwards in their lives.

Once Q had evolved into a more straightforward music magazine in the early 1990s it became a haven for some brilliant long-form writing. I'd tune in specifically to read the two masters of music profiling David Cavanagh and Adrian Deevoy, Phil Sutcliffe too, but the tonal smugness lingered elsewhere. My love of music was not arch, it wasn't wry, so I struggled with Q. Its pages also carried a whiff of BO. Where were the women writers?

More recently, since 2000, it had just seemed a little lost and dull. It was now an unashamedly mainstream music magazine, yet I found it a very quick flick in the newsagents. It squeezed a lot into its pages, but not much from its subjects.

So of course, I took the job.

I bought a brand-new pink Lacoste for my first day, 10 May 2004. The issue on sale before I joined was Q's 'Sex Issue'. I figured the only way was up.

I was surprised to discover a very austere working environment. It was the complete opposite of being on staff at NME. Everyone took the job incredibly seriously. Personalities were reined in, professional, quietly industrious. Everybody was getting shit done all day long, turning straightforward editing tasks into labyrinthine feats of shared responsibility.

The commissioning section editors also did everything that the sub-editors had done at NME. Once the edited copy was designed, it returned to section editors for cutting to fit and picture captioning on screen, for headlines and sells. The subs, mean-while, were micro-managing fact-checkers, as if it was the *New Yorker* or something serious rather than a playful celebration of music and its biggest, daftest characters. All of your designed copy for the section, once you yourself had edited and then cut 'n' captioned it, had to return to the deputy editor. He'd already read it on edited Word documents, but he'd then excruciatingly tweak every detail on his printout as you watched him scrawl across the page in thick red ink out of the corner of your eye. When he was ready, he'd wheel his chair along the floor and slowly go through the page note by note with you, watching you change the work on screen in front of him, while you both ran through dozens of new headline suggestions together for three out of five album reviews for Ash or Joss Stone.

After that, it went to the magazine's editor who, typing ex-clusively with his index fingers, would blast through each page of your work, changing every headline, every sell and picture caption you'd laboured collectively over so tortuously in about five minutes, without really reading the copy in front of him. His oft-stated mission was to make everything 'more pithy'.

Then the sub-editor's final role was to secretly undo all the editor's work and return the magazine to a recognisable form of English. The only thing they left untouched were the monthly editor's letters at the front of the mag, which read as if they'd been written by an Elizabethan guitar technician: they decided to preserve these unedited as evidence of who was committing most of the crimes against English across the rest of each issue.

On a day-to-day basis it was painful, laborious, insanely com-plicated and joyless. But I did learn a lot. I learned how to edit. I thought I knew this already but as it was revealed to me at *Q*, I knew nothing about editing. I became an editor.

Having now learned what being an editor entailed, I started to wonder if I wanted to be one. All that I'd loved about it had been sucked from the process at *Q*. I thought being a music magazine section editor meant you'd lucked out, you were a cavalier who'd been given the keys to the palace, but we were roundheads on *Q*. We were spartan, we aspired to purity. We weren't building glorious monuments to music and its makers. There were no hoots of collective joy at great schemes coming together, no madcap ideas that might just work out. There was no fun, no jokes. Nobody was late. Nobody went to the pub. Eyes on screens, only raised to watch the heads of the *Mojo* art and picture desk go bobbing down the corridor at 12.45 on their way to the Champion, returning flushed at 2.30 (ish). This would induce sharp comment amongst some *Q* staff, but Dave Everley, the hulking front section editor who'd joined shortly before I had from the weekly metal rag *Kerrang!*, would exchange hungover glances over the desk with me. The best ideas originate collectively in the pub, in the daytime. Everyone knows that. We still remembered it.

At *Q*, they instead scheduled meetings specifically to have ideas. They'd book their ideas meetings into stark white conference rooms at 9.45 am. Bring a notepad and lists of suggestions for these vacant content categories and afterwards we'll just agree to do a list issue about the 100 Greatest British Albums of All Time That You Must Own Before You Rust. There was a mad hunger for list features that I did not share. I just wasn't interested in making lists.

At first, and for quite some time, there was no writing to be done by staff. But there were meetings. Meetings every day, sometimes all day. I went to as many meetings in the first six months at *Q* as in the first six years at *NME*. Meetings about agendas for future meetings. Meetings with freelancers to see if they had any ideas. Meetings with section editors. Meetings with the marketing team, the events team, some guy from a chain of hi-fi stores who went to school with the CEO. Meetings about next month. Meetings about last month. Meetings with the deputy editor and the production editor wondering whether there was anything they could do to help speed up your copy delivery. Meetings about holidays. Meetings about holiday cover. Meetings about covers, planned out eighteen months ahead.

One-to-one meetings, too. The worst kind of meeting, but also the most regular. Every day, sometimes twice a day. A tap on the shoulder. Have you got two minutes?

It was a music magazine. I had to keep reminding myself that. It all felt so much more sensitive, difficult, dangerous.

Slowly, the repressed personalities did emerge, coaxed out by Christmas lunches, the Q Awards nights, leaving dos. Something had to give.

One bright morning, I arrived at work, swung into my chair and swivelled around to my desk, pressed on the computer. What's this? Just to my right, on the dividing patch between my desk and my neighbour's, was a fat, haphazard line of cocaine.

I was the last to have arrived on my four-person pod. Gareth Grundy was sitting at his immaculately tidy desk next to me. He must have seen this huge slug of gak sitting between us. Other than his keyboard and Moleskine diary it was the only item in his workspace.

Maybe it's a test. *Will Ted say anything?* If Ted just sweeps it away it's his cocaine. He probably knocked it out last night, the degenerate. March him down to HR, out of the building. Call the police.

'Hey!' I said, theatrically. 'Whose coke is this?! Have you seen it, Gareth?'

Gareth had not seen it. For a few minutes, everyone gathered around the line of cocaine and discussed its provenance. Nobody was admitting anything. There were some jokes about it. Eh, Dave, did you leave your coke on my desk? At it again, you nutter, Gareth? Steady now.

No, really, whose coke is it?

Could it be a cleaner? Unlikely. Maybe it was a passing *Mojo* or *Kerrang!* staffer, or someone from another floor searching for a quiet spot for some drug-taking, a cocaine sanctuary up on the top floor, in the music mags area with the good stereos. Imagine chopping out a line and forgetting about it, though.

It was, of course, my line of cocaine.

I was always coming back to the office after a night out. Sometimes you'd bump into another lost soul wandering around the floor, trying to get their act together, but there was no need for mutual acknowledgement, it went in the vault. There we were, right in the centre of London. A sanctuary in the early hours after a turn on the town: just sign yourself in. Take a breather before heading home.

With a flat hand, I swept the line of chang into the bin. Shame. What kind of dolt leaves a line on a work surface overnight?

The mood of the one-to-one meetings soured two or three years into the job. They became bitchier, more accusatory. The endless list covers and chin-stroking U2/Killers/Springsteen stories were no longer scoring quite as big. Sales were slipping. Not by much, but they were heading down. The magazine was boring. That pithy writing style was wearing thin, too. But it simply required small fixes. Some changes in tone, attitude – a much higher reliance on instinct and taste, two elements that were quashed in the office but, as far as I can tell, are absolute requisites for music journalism. Deliver a magazine that you might want to read, then at least you can look in the mirror. Make it for you and your circle and you will be halfway there as long as it's broad and inclusive. Trust in good music you love.

Paul Rees chose a different path.

Later that morning, after the cocaine had been discovered on my desk, he tapped me on my shoulder with a 'two minutes Ted?'. He took me into a nearby meeting room.

I was not mentally prepared. I was, in truth, extremely hungover. I thought he was going to hand me a written warning for the desk drugs, but instead he quizzed me about different personalities on the magazine. I just nodded along, barely able to speak. I'd been hoping to keep my head down all day, close to calling in sick.

'Thank you for your candour,' he said to me, bewilderingly, as we wrapped up.

Soon after our meeting, he made sweeping changes. Gareth and the art director left, sacrificed to allow the most radical redesign of a magazine imaginable. The *Observer* immediately snapped up Gareth, as soon as his redundancy hit his account. They knew a good editor when they read one.

We were gathered into a room and told that *Q* could no longer be simply a music magazine. *Q* would be 'about more than just music'. *Q* was going to be a music and lifestyle magazine. Practically, it meant there would be big interview features with the *Top Gear* presenters, footballers, actors and comedians, in amongst the usual U2, Coldplay and list features. There was one hairy moment when it was suggested that as a statement of our new direction, of our intent to 'cover anybody in the *Q*-style', we should commission Boris Johnson for the Cash for Questions feature, but we managed to talk the politburo down from that goose-chase.

A raft of fresh editors were hired for the new dawn specifically from non-music titles, from film, lads' and tech magazines. All men, of course. To any outsider it would've seemed that it wasn't the fields of expertise that needed changing in *Q* for the tone to become more inclusive, it was the gender balance. But *Q* remained resolutely male.

Still, the personality of the magazine was massively altered by the arrival of new art director (or creative mastermind or whatever demented title had been dreamed up) Ian Stevens from *Empire*. As soon as we witnessed him in action he became known as 'Maverick' to his new colleagues, in homage to Tom Cruise's *Top Gun* character, as Ian seemed also to be co-produced by Don Simpson and Jerry Bruckheimer. Rather than reject this jokey nickname, Ian embraced it. He answered to it. He became Maverick.

In months to come, he'd explain his early behaviour in the office as being influenced by 'the new guy who goes to jail and has to beat up the main man in there straight away to assert himself'. This meant that Ian set about destabilising Paul's authority from his first day. A tall, muscle-bound fellow who always wore tight T-shirts and a too-small suit jacket no matter the weather – typically, he came to work in moccasins without socks during 2009's Arctic snow week that shut down the capital – Ian would arrive in the office whenever suited him. Once in, he'd fling off his jacket, pick up a cue and shoot a few rounds on the pool table that Paul had bought the office to placate us (unsuccessfully) for firing some of our most hard-working, capable colleagues. Then he'd gather up a crew from their desks to go and get completely smashed in nearby bars for the rest of the day, wrecking the production schedule. It was a kind of beautiful anarchy, and great fun, except the redesign that was concurrently delivered was illegible. The fonts were too small, the drop-caps so big you couldn't read beneath them. None of the signposting made sense. And the content itself was batshit: who bought a music magazine for a six-page deep-dive on comedian and sometime TV host Ross Noble? It was commercially suicidal.

The first redesigned issue of Q that was about 'more than just music', featuring AC/DC on the cover, sold quite well, hitting a similar total to the magazine's previous sales. The next issue, with Razorlight, was down an unimaginable 25 per cent. I'd seen one disastrous redesign close-up on NME, a new look which lost a huge percentage of readers when the weekly went full colour and changed every font to wAcKy. But this Q redesign was an unprecedented disaster; it was so expensive the cover shoots alone cost what the entire words and picture budget would be in less than two years. Those twenty-odd thousand readers we'd scared off remained lost. When readers leave, they go for good.

Q persevered for a couple more issues along the 'more than just music' route before a panicked reverse ferret was ordained from on high. Before we knew it we were charged with turning Q into 'the music bible'.

Well, alrighty. Let's try this again. Except we didn't have the staff for this music bible steer now.

We did our best. The magazine wasn't very good. Sales continued to tumble. Staff drifted off into new jobs and new recruits joined, on much lower wages. I became features editor by default. I tried to commission some features that would be interesting to read, but was constantly being tugged from above towards painful conceptual lists. I did make Sylvia Patterson our main cover writer in an effort to change the locker-room vibe, and the addition of the gregariously straightforward and industrious Niall Doherty in my old reviews job helped puncture the office pomposity. He made fun of everyone. We all needed it.

But the sales kept dropping.

New publishing executives took over. They were not music people, nor obviously magazine people, but they were coldly ambitious and mean-spirited. They loved numbers, but they hated ours. They demanded a halt to the slide. This new publishing team were not fully aware of the magazine's schizophrenic recent history, however, and that ignorance presented a final opportunity for diversion for our editor, a way out from the tumbling numbers and the rotten, expensively built magazine. A chance to shift focus.

An email arrived in all the staff inboxes one morning in 2011. It told us this.

The magazine was going to be reimagined once more, top to bottom, to save it from its downward sales spiral. Failure was not an option. The work would be radical, forward-thinking, out-of-the-box. We will take two days to explore this, absorbing advice and wisdom from other geniuses throughout the wider Bauer business. Here's the schedule. See you on Monday at ten. We'll be doing the work in Covent Garden, at the Wallace Space.

*

There were many mad diversions on the way to rock bottom of the British music press, but when anybody asks me where it went most significantly wrong for *Q* magazine I am able to supply a two-word answer: Wallace Space.

An impressively repurposed warehouse building just off Newton Street, the Wallace Space (or wallacespace, as it styles itself) is one big breakout area hired out to companies so that their staff can blue-sky brainstorm to their hearts' content, either in beanbags or upon sofas in lounge areas, in more traditional meeting rooms, or perhaps over lunch.

I arrived early with a couple of colleagues, determined not to draw particular attention to ourselves. We wandered through the corridors searching for our room and took a couple of wrong turnings as is customary. One wrong turning led us straight into a meeting room where the editor, in conversation with our new publisher and marketing manager, was scrawling the finishing touches to a list on a large flipchart. The heading underlined at the top of the list simply read 'Conclusions' in big red letters.

Seeing us, Paul flushed, flipped the chart over and barked the meeting room name at us. We backed out with thumbs aloft, embarrassed to have ambushed him organising his ambush of us.

The meeting began on a bit of a downer. Paul delivered an impassioned speech about how he couldn't stand idly by as we continued to lose 10 per cent of the readers with every passing year, that the time for radical change was upon us.

Radical change is usually what is proposed when just being better is too difficult. It's a cop-out. At *NME* in the new millennium they proposed that they'd declare a new year zero and not cover any acts who had formed after the mid-nineties. Everything would be young and fresh. Within eighteen months they'd put Keith Richards, Ozzy Osbourne and the deceased Kurt Cobain on the cover and handed *NME* awards to Arthur Lee of Love and the 1970s staff writer Nick Kent for some historic service to rock. It's always hot air released to get out of a tight jam at that given moment.

The most radical concept for a monthly music magazine is to be a really good one. That's hard enough. Blowing everything up in a panic every three years was an unnecessary extravagance that the magazine couldn't afford. *Q* just needed to work with more skill at what it already did. People weren't bailing because they hoped to see the magazine embrace radical change instead. They wanted a really good monthly music magazine, perhaps with its cover CD back on it. They weren't getting that regularly enough. There was clear room for improvement.

A couple of issues earlier, *Q* had put Kasabian on the front. Struggling for a cover concept for this popular but already well-documented pair of indie-pop lads from Leicester, it had been decided that what was needed to move the story along was to position the band as decadent rock lords, like the Rolling Stones or Led Zeppelin in the late sixties, early seventies. Crushed velvet. Messy stately home. Naked women. (*Sorry, did you say naked women?!*)

The first shoot looked like *Razzle*. Semi-nude glamour models draped across tables as the two band members scratched their stubble awkwardly in the foreground. Paul asked the team what we thought. We said it was not fit to print, hoping he'd ditch the concept entirely. Instead they reshot it, upgrading the vibe minimally from porn mag to lads' mag with two naked models hanging from the band on the cover. It now looked like *FHM*, the one Bauer monthly magazine undergoing an even more determined sales tailspin than *Q*.

The Kasabian cover sold terribly and was received with understandable derision externally. It was the final straw internally as well. So here we were, back in the land of radical change.

The new publisher – a former advertising executive who'd unfathomably been given the entertainment magazines in a dramatic lane switch – picked up the meeting baton. She had three questions for the room.

'Who,' she asked, 'thinks *Q* is doing well?'

Don't be silly. Nobody raised their hand.

'Who thinks *Q* is doing OK, but there's room for improvement?'
That pretty much covered it. We all raised our hands.

'Who thinks *Q* is terrible?'

Only one person raised their hand: our new publisher. As she did so, she stared us all down, one by one. Next to her, Paul Rees queasily raised his hand too, as if this magazine she was describing was not the one he was editing.

The tone was set.

We were joined by people from events, from radio, from sales on *Grazia*. And we got into workshops, baby. Oh yeah. We workshopped it out.

There were some pretty ambitious ideas.

Q would be a members' club, a physical space where readers could come and hang out with the team. *Q* could put on gigs – 'Elbow at St Paul's Cathedral' as an example – and sell the tickets. *Q* could launch its own festival. *Q* could deliver a series of nationwide pop-up gigs. *Q* should open a record shop. Q: the record label, even – why not? *Q* should redesign the reviews section to allow readers to review the albums as well as, or perhaps instead of, the reviewers. Readers should be able to ring a premium number and rate gigs they'd seen. *Q* should operate a ticket swap shop, becoming a tout. Why doesn't *Q* host votes for set lists by big bands, like Foo Fighters? *Q* should pitch itself as a television show where readers, writers and artists review albums. *Q* could launch its own reality TV show, perhaps even as some augmented feature of the magazine (idea needs work) . . .

See those blue skies and watch us soar beyond them. We were reinventing the wheel as a supersonic instrument of space travel, yeah!

What about the magazine? asked some of the more fogeyish staffers, like me. Would we still be a magazine at the end of all this?

Yes, of course. But with a totally different, younger, more modern and tech-savvy readership. We will replace the old sods who've kept the magazine afloat for decades with a massive new readership of kids who are out there just waiting to spend four quid a month on a heavyweight print magazine if only we'd engage with them.

After the final break, Paul shamelessly flipped over his 'Conclusions' chart as if he'd just written it at the end of the session and not before its start. He then presented 'our learnings'.

Conclusions

Toplines

It's a conversation – talking with you about music

It's a 24-hour-a-day service

It delivers unique, shared experiences

It is now and new, not then and when

Aims

Faster editorial

Unsigned act on the cover

Reinvent the logo, reinvent the mag

New, younger writing and editorial talent

Everyone blogs and engages socially

Everyone uses Twitter

Introduce a tweets column in Q Mail

Readers tweet in picture captions

Q Tone: peer not authority

Be more spontaneous – mirroring the nature of the Internet

Q is:

A 360-degree service that introduces music fans to, tells the stories behind, and invites them to discuss new music

After the Wallace Space meetings, we returned to the office to prepare for the glorious 360-degree future, heads spinning in order to accomplish this feat. For the editor, that meant a series of ostentatious one-to-one meetings with the two young interns, the junior sub and the trusted deputy editor. No doubt at the end of each meeting he thanked them for their candour.

The rest of us noted these comings and goings and buckled up.

Things escalated quickly. The print magazine was converted to widely and ostentatiously incorporate tweets and hashtags, in an attempt to become some kind of hybrid social media–magazine. A modernisation which appeared dated as soon as it was designed. The interns and junior sub were empowered with wide-ranging but confusing writing roles, asked to fly just as they'd mastered walking. A Q Calendar was proposed, so everyone could announce the gigs we were going to, the nightclubs we'd visited, by writing our half-truths on a wall planner – but we also turned every Monday's meeting over to each staffer telling the room what we'd done over the weekend, so as to emphasise that we were a 24/7, 365-days-a-year no-time-off music-living-loving operation. Instead, it felt a bit like being in Year 2 at primary school.

Luckily, I soon stepped away for a two-week paternity break.

When I returned there was another momentous redesign under way, back in our old offices on Winsley Street. If in doubt, lock yourself away in a room and redesign. Every problem can be solved by radical change. All staff were periodically invited down Oxford Street to visit from our Shaftesbury Avenue office and inspect the damage. Everyone except me and the senior designer Salman who'd joined shortly before I had. We were not welcome.

We recognised straight away that we were to be the sacrificial lambs this time, as Gareth and the previous art director had been, offered to the gods of publishing so that our elderly flesh might bring forth thousands of new, much younger readers. We'd seen this happen in other people's lives and now it was happening in ours. My colleagues who were spared told me they had spied a new desk plan in the redesign room where my presence was erased. I googled constructive dismissal.

Presently, Paul brought his redesign before the publishing top table for blessing.

They wondered if he had lost his mind.

He returned to the drawing board.

Meanwhile, the core staff continued with the monthly magazine. Somebody had to.

Since the rejected redesign, however, external Bauer focus suddenly appeared on everyone's work. There was now a new committee for Q covers, to perfect them as they weren't selling. Maybe it needed more eyes on them. As many cooks as possible. Obviously, the staff weren't involved. The editor was joined by the publisher, the marketing man, some guy who'd worked on *Heat* bodging their cover lines and anyone else they could find in a position of influence who hadn't read a music magazine for pleasure in recent memory.

The committee gazed noisily at the latest cover, an interview with a new artist, Lana Del Rey. We were taking a chance on someone yet to release an album, which was good because her single was great and she had more where that came from, but worrying as the people who were writing the lines on the cover had neither heard her nor read the article. They stood around the art director's desk as his fingers hovered above the keys, ready to input their jewels. The cover photo of Lana featured her with blood coming from a wound above her eye, in homage to her recent 'Born to Die' video in which she's victim of a fatal car crash.

They all spoke at once for about twenty minutes. They wanted to say that Lana Del Rey was an exciting new artist, but they also wanted to mention the blood.

Wait! How about something that tied the two elements together?!

Half an hour later, they had it.

Everybody's Mad For . . .

LANA DEL REY
So What's So Bloody Good?

So what's so bloody good, eh? They were very happy with that. Send it to print.

Bauer soon started to notice how much money had been spent by *Q* in recent years on redesigns, cover shoots, blue-sky away-days. EMAP, our previous owners, had been less focused on individual bottom lines than Bauer. EMAP were worried about the overall share price. Bauer, privately owned, cared very much for each individual title's profit margin and spending. *Q* had blown tons of cash while making less money than previously. Mild panic seeped into our office from above.

Everyone on the staff, we were told, urgently had to start writing. Claw back some budget however you can. This was a huge culture shock to *Q*, which had always frowned upon the staff getting their fingers inky, but I was happy. I worked on magazines initially because I wanted to write. Now, I finally could again.

I went to Seattle to interview Florence Welch of Florence + the Machine for the cover soon after. Florence was a big job that nobody else wanted. Few of the staff or freelancers seemed to like her music, but I did, I loved it, always had. I'd interviewed her in her early days, before the first album, and I knew she was smarter than the average young pop singer, funnier and more eloquent too. I volunteered for the task.

Over a seafood lunch and strong Bloody Marys Florence described her current nervous exhaustion, saying her heart was broken, that her life was out of control. As she spoke, tears rolled down her face and dripped on to her shellfish bib. She was breaking up with her long-term boyfriend while also number one in both the UK and the USA with her cover of 'You've Got the Love', swinging between hedonism and despair. It was a perfect emotional storm.

It was also the dream story. I told it to the best of my ability, aware that it would be harder to make the guy writing eye-catching cover stories with number-one pop stars redundant, as that was still part of the redesign plan.

I needn't have worried.

The redesign went back to the board.

Once more, it was rejected.

The magazine quietly reverted to its more recognisable monthly music magazine form. Comfy joggers, Kings of Leon on the car stereo, a nice mild Cheddar. Woo-yeah, this sex is on fire.

The hashtags were scrubbed from the magazine. The new regular #YouAsk feature reverted to Cash for Questions. Just enough balance was being restored for us to continue rolling.

Soon, Paul stopped coming to work, instead sending oblique emails for us to carry on in his absence as he 'worked remotely'.

After a month we were invited to a meeting. Paul arrived and told us he was leaving. He thanked us for our efforts, but announced it was time for a change. There was a small smattering of applause, but no leaving do. He just left.

Later that same day, a new editor turned up. He was actually an old editor, Andrew Harrison, who'd edited *Select* and *Q* before leaving dramatically with a bunch of former *Q* eds to launch the rival *Word*. I knew him to be a meticulous copy-editor as well as a fine writer. His pummelling work ethic was renowned. He loved *Doctor Who* and Orbital, Saint Etienne and politics; he was anti-rock and any kind of long workplace meeting: as is usually the case, he was the polar opposite of his predecessor. The copy in the magazine was all that mattered to him.

He marched in, said a brief hello to everyone, pulled up a chair and started work immediately on the issue that was due to go to press in just a week.

He looked at the proposed cover.

'Oh no,' he said. 'No, no, no. We can't do the Black Keys.'

Instead, he suggested a cover based around the back stories to twenty great old albums. *Bummed* by Happy Mondays, *Back to Black* by Amy Winehouse, *Three Feet High* by De La Soul, etc. It would tell how these beloved long-players came to be despite some notable obstacles.

'Untold tales of twenty chaotic classics!' he described it excitedly, repurposing the entire issue in a few days around these stories of mayhem.

It definitely felt more like something I might read too, and I tucked into the work enthusiastically, but I couldn't help but wonder about the bewildered reader. Only a few months earlier we'd declared a new year zero. What had been written on that flipchart? *It is now and new, not then and when.*

Forget about that. We didn't mean it. Have you heard the one about the Smiths recording *Strangeways, Here We Come*?

On that first morning under the new reign, Salman and I bumped into each other in the kitchen and took a moment to shake hands. We had prevailed, despite the odds looking iffy for a while.

Little did we know that the madness was only now truly upon us all.

20.

Dickie

I was sitting at my desk minding my own business when the call came. It was from my brother Daniel and it began like this. 'Your mother has collapsed . . .' And then he paused for a good moment because my mother is also his mother and, despite our joint efforts not to imagine the worst, we both knew the worst was most likely to follow.

It was Wednesday, 4 September 2013. Three days earlier my heavily pregnant girlfriend, young daughter and I had moved across London to a new address, but now I was weighing up catching an immediate flight to Washington DC to visit my mum in hospital near the area of Maryland she'd made her home since 1985. On one hand, my mother Anne was seventy-three, she'd been found unconscious on the floor of her kitchen by her husband, Jim, and she was barely responding. On the other, my girlfriend Jean's nearest relative was in Australia and she was due to give birth in five days. I slept uneasily on it.

Jean reassured me that the twinges she was feeling were probably nothing as I left at dawn for Heathrow on 6 September. Not true, as it turned out. I was about to step on to the plane when Jean urged me to turn around quickly. Nine hours later I was in Homerton Hospital holding my newborn son, and three hours after that I was standing alone in a pub garden at last orders, raising a glass to the moon above. I had a son called Joseph and my mother, unfortunately, had a golf-ball-sized brain tumour.

We know how this story ends, don't we?

I made it to DC a fortnight later and travelled straight to the hospice where Mum was by now clinging silently on to life with my brother in attendance. When Daniel stepped out to make a call, he suggested I keep talking to her because Jim thought it might be of some comfort. I agreed, of course.

And then, alone with her, I paused, wondering where to begin. Since she'd married Jim in 1998, we spoke so infrequently: phone calls around birthdays and so forth, maybe a flying visit once a year or so. This was a reflection of the strength of her relationship with dependable Jim rather than our own. He gave her everything she needed and I had been in a different time zone since sixteen.

It hadn't always been thus, but distance had gently massaged away the confederacy we'd forged in my teens, if not our actual bond. In the end, we only had an outline traced between us. I sat by her bedside in the hospice flicking through my memory files wondering what I could tell her. How do we begin to catch up? Then I remembered Jean's suggestion that we donate my mum's maiden name to Joseph, an abbreviated version of which, Dickie, she'd been called by Su Strettell since their school days.

'Hey, Mum,' I began, 'I forgot to say we've given Joey a middle name of Dickson . . .'

Out of the blue she delivered a series of long, loud moans. Her arm raised, as did her head, ever so slightly, reaching from beyond somewhere. I'm ashamed to say I was so unsettled I backed away into the bathroom. I leaned against the sink in the damp, yellowy glow of a room that seemed to echo with historic misery and gathered my thoughts.

When I returned from her bathroom, Daniel was back and my mum was peacefully sleeping. We chatted across her bed about other domestic news but she didn't stir again.

The next morning at her house my brother took a call from Jim at the hospice. My mother had died in the night. We were in the kitchen where she'd collapsed, a place in which I'd never lived but which was nevertheless filled with belongings I could recall from my childhood. The mugs in the cupboard, the paintings on the wall. An old Snoopy spoon I remembered using as a kid and that she still kept in her cutlery drawer.

I thought guiltily of our last interaction the day before, and also of all the things we'd left unsaid over the years. I thought of my children at home with their mother in England, their lives flashing before me. I vowed to tell them to regularly and often check in with their mother, to not let it slip, no matter how secure they feel in their hearts. Pick up the phone. There may never be that final catch-up before the slate's wiped clean for good.

It was a warm, blue-skied morning in Maryland, a place where autumn does some of its very best work. If life is about anything, it's about finding somewhere you feel peacefully at home, and this was where she'd wanted to be. We called our brother Mark in Paris and broke the news to him too. And then we put our shoes on and stepped out into the sunlight, out into the streets where Dickie had lived without us for so long, wandering down the Capital Crescent Trail towards Georgetown, trying to her retrace her steps one last time.

21.
Beneath the Bright Lights

September 1990

A trip across the Atlantic in the early autumn to see my family, staying in my mother's apartment in Bethesda, Maryland, a leafy suburb of Washington DC. I'm sleeping in my middle brother Mark's bedroom while he shacks up next door with our youngest brother, Daniel. We are each separated from each other by three years and though I am now twenty-one years old, the occasionally violent tension between the three of us still simmers. This is entirely my fault. My brothers get on famously.

From my earliest memory of him, Mark and I fought physically, drawing blood from each other on many occasions. As the eldest, it's hard to escape the conclusion that I bullied him. He was merely sticking up for himself. Now, in this memory from 1990, even though I am an adult and he will soon be a student at New York University, I can still sense that he feels he owes me one. Which he does. The first time I visited my mother and brothers in 1986, the year after they moved to DC, we tussled and he smacked me one in the mouth, cutting my lip. That reduced the debt. Taught me a lesson, too.

I'm the one who escaped, ran away at sixteen to return to swinging London. I am an irredeemably anarchic element in this family unit. Mark is considerate, kind, selfless to a fault – in DC he assumed my old role of our mother's confidant, also acting as the de facto responsible adult, learning to drive early, taking care of administrative business. Daniel, meanwhile, is a gentle soul. He feels things. He is romantic. He has the sweetest, softest smile and the most sincere interest in any tale you tell him. He just wishes we could all get along. Like me, he has chosen music as his one true religion. He is constantly at worship, playing the guitar alongside nearly all that he does. He walks through the apartment with one hanging from his neck, repeatedly picking out the same riffs, whether he is making his breakfast or watching TV or talking on the phone to friends, the receiver resting on his shoulder while he strums identical abstract lines over and over and over and over . . .

'Sorry, am I bothering you?'

Yeah, Dan, I'm not really awake yet.

'Oh, OK.'

Dang-dang-dang-dang-de-dang . . .

May 2002

I have recently started a three-month stint back in the *NME* office where I'll be editing a one-shot magazine called *NME Originals*, about Oasis.

The work is easy – reprinting redesigned archive articles about the band – and the three-person team of designer Phil, picture ed Cate and sub Helen who have assembled to work on it are fun to be with. All freelancers love a three-month commission of easy work so the mood amongst us is good. We work lightly, socialise heavily. I do not know this yet, but I will be spending the rest of the summer here, as after this one-shot I'll be asked by editorial director Steve Sutherland to also take care of two other *NME Originals*, one about Happy Mondays/Stone Roses and one about Manic Street Preachers.

And yet, the experience is unsettling. I am back in the office where I felt so centrally involved in everything for so long, where my life made sense, but I'm on the periphery. For the first weeks, this is a literal placing. We have a row of desks at the rear of the redesigned office facing the backs of the editorial staff as they construct the weekly magazine: there are smart young gunslingers just beyond the divide, but turned away from us, telling their stories, losing their minds, having the time of their lives. I am both too close to and too far from the action for comfort.

That's when I hear it in public for the first time.

Pat Long, the new reviews editor, marches across the office holding a CD in his hand.

'I've got that Interpol EP,' he declares proudly to the gallery, as he opens the CD player.

Oh God.

The ambient office noise is extinguished as the room stops to listen in anticipation. This is the first official release by the latest hip name from New York and judgemental expectation is raised.

Pat presses play. I immediately recognise the guitar line, my brother's guitar line. 'PDA'. It was on the demo he sent me, a jagged cascade of melody that quickly unfurls into verse. It's intense, modern new wave. Just right for this room.

Pat turns it up and I involuntarily find myself rising from my desk. With an audible groan, I squeeze behind Helen and Phil's chairs, heading out of the swing doors towards the lifts before the chorus even arrives. I have to get out of here.

In Lizzy Goodman's tremendous oral history of the rebirth of rock and roll in NYC between 2001 and 2011, *Meet Me in the Bathroom*, my ex-colleague April Long remembers that I stormed out of the office saying something along the lines of 'oh no, not my brother's dumb band'. With respect to April's memory, that is not what happened. I would never call either of my brothers' endeavours dumb. That's my role in this family. I'm the dumb one.

If I groaned as I walked out it was with fear, not loathing or embarrassment. I was scared. I was too afraid to hear anybody in *NME* say they didn't like Interpol, that they thought the music was bad. I didn't want to witness mockery the like of which I'd heard so often in *NME*, that I'd dispensed routinely myself with great performative gusto. When Interpol play their first London show at the Monarch, I leave before the end of the final song as I can't bear to face anyone's opinion. That's how insecure and self-involved I am. In this long moment of professional uncertainty, I am afraid that Interpol will reflect badly on me.

That is quite a miscalculation.

Sitting on the floor amongst the debris of their hectic dressing room, after Interpol have played 93 Feet East on Brick Lane in late August 2002, Daniel and I have our first real conversation. I am thirty-three, he's twenty-seven. We've never truly spoken before.

In the months and years to come, whenever presented with a moral or professional dilemma, my two closest friends from that era, James Oldham and Andy Capper, who worked on *NME* with me before launching *Vice* in the UK, will pause to ask, 'What would Daniel Kessler do?' This is not a joke, nor mockery. They want to possess Daniel's mindset when faced with conundrums. They crave his ability to size up a situation, analyse a choice, see three steps ahead. Years after he becomes a successful musician with his own interests, former employers at record labels will still call asking for his guidance. He provides us all with calm pause for thought. He will serenely navigate many of us through divorce, grief, unemployment, talking us down from foolish impulses with a Yoda-like calmness for reading the pitfalls and advantages presented ahead.

I am an idiot for not realising this sooner.

When I left home, he was ten. He was just the kid. When I visited America, we'd play football, eat pizza and watch TV, but generally I'd hit the town with Mark as we were closer in age. Daniel visited London several times. Sometimes he stayed on my sofa. He wanted to connect, you could see it in him, but I was unavailable. I was always just too busy for this right now. Light's off, sorry, I'm just on my way home, mate.

Finally, in that dressing room, having witnessed the band live in its entirety for the first time, we connect. It helps that I am on the run from my marriage, in a prolonged state of high-pitched, hedonistic intensity. I am very in touch with my feelings. I've been like this for a few months and there is road ahead of me, too. Every reading on the dashboard is in the red. My lights are on. I am finally available.

Daniel asks how I am. And so I tell him.

In return, I receive sharp insight and constructive care.

By time I leave him an hour later, our lines of communication and connection are remade. I do not miss a note that Interpol play in London ever again.

In time, Interpol become my favourite modern guitar band. It doesn't happen immediately, for me nor any of my friends who are also a bit snobby about it. Ted Kessler's little brother?! Prrft! But it happens. The band are irresistible, inevitable. The best.

Takes a little while, though.

The hope of not wanting to hear any opinion about Interpol is comically forlorn as almost everyone wants to tell me what they think of them. Often, that's a surprisingly positive opinion. Oh, you love Interpol? Great. Oh, sorry, you *really* love them. Right, well . . . thumbs up. Glad you like them.

Then there are those moments when people need to let you know their ambivalence about Interpol, or far worse. That's OK. I get used to it quickly. At first, I'm not really sure how I feel about them either as I can't bring myself to listen to their record yet.

At Reading Festival in 2002, in the afternoon, one of the tents is filled with people who love them, including my brother Mark who is over to see them, while also checking on the status of my ongoing lost weekend. James Oldham and James Endeacott, the Strokes' A&R man, are also here with me, grudgingly. Sound like Joy Division and Magazine don't they? We'll stick with the originals, thanks. They hang around the back of the tent with me, sniggering. Not maliciously. It's just funny, isn't it? Your brother. That slow song though, 'NYC', the one about it being up to me now so turn on the bright lights, you know, that was good.

A few weeks later, I bump into Endeacott out on the drunk-in-pubs circuit. He grabs my shoulders. He's a big lad with a lot of corkscrew blond hair and a wildly enthusiastic manner at the best of times. He's evangelical.

'Fucking hell, man,' he says, wide-eyed. 'I get Interpol! I got them.'

'Oh . . . kay?'

'I was in Denmark last weekend and afterwards we all piled back to someone's hotel room, getting on it. Then, just as the sun is coming up, one of these girls says, "Let's listen to *Turn On the Bright Lights*." I'm like, no way, downer, but it's her room so . . . fucking hell. The sun is coming up through the windows, dawn streaming through red curtains, that first song "Untitled" comes on, the guitars and . . . wow!' His eyes are bulging. 'It's perfect. Amazing. Time and place. Just had to hear it properly.'

Daniel's glowing guitar lines blowing wired minds in foreign climes.

So it goes. Soon, people aren't coming with me to Interpol shows out of a sense of loyalty but because they want to. They're asking me for tickets, for ways in, for passes to the aftershow. Because the shows, though they are getting bigger, are also getting busier. Selling out the Astoria. Shepherd's Bush Empire. The Forum. Brixton Academy. Roundhouse. Alexandra Palace. Many times over.

In early 2003, *NME* finally stick Interpol on the cover, even though arguably less popular American bands have made it there sooner. What's the reverse of nepotism?

'We couldn't put it off any longer, they really deserve it,' the editor tells me, grudgingly, at a leaving do.

The pictures are terrible, but that's OK. They have bassist Carlos D. big at the front on the cover, singer Paul Banks small and hidden. Never mind. I read a long feature in *Q* magazine in which every possible biographical detail about Interpol is wrong. Doesn't matter. The band's progress is unaffected. They end up selling a million copies of their first two albums, going top twenty in the States with their second, and becoming their label Matador's biggest success. Their third album hits top five in both the US and UK. All of their subsequent albums are top ten in the UK. They headline festivals across the globe. David Bowie loves them. Every show sells out anywhere . . .

So, tell me Ted, what part did you play in Interpol's success?

I listened to them, in the end. I listened to them a lot, eventually. The floodgates opened and there are times, if going through an Interpol phase, when I wonder if I'll ever listen to anything else again.

I hear what everybody else hears: intensely romantic music allied to philosophical poetry. Heart and soul. The good stuff, if you like that kind of thing. When I listen, I don't hear my brother now, haven't for a long while. I hear my favourite band.

Took my time getting there, though.

Summer 2007

I am alerted to a blog posting on Myspace by one-time Creation Records supremo Alan McGee. It contains some strong opinions about the poverty of modern music, now that he's not centrally involved in its delivery, including far-fetched ideas about me and my brother. Oddly, only recently Daniel has told me about spending a good night out with McGee when Interpol played Mexico City. Nevertheless, I feel I must respond.

Here's what I email him.

Hi Alan,

I'm dropping you a line because I was quite surprised by some comments I chanced upon by you about me and my brother, Daniel. I quote:

Post-Millennium Tension

TED KESSLER [Q ALBUMS REVIEW EDITOR AND EX NME JOURNALIST] IS DANIEL KESSLERS BROTHER. DANIEL IS IN INTERPOL THEY HAVE ALWAYS HAD GREAT REVIEWS FROM DAY ONE . . . STITCH UP????

I just thought I'd clear up some facts for you.

1/ I was not on staff at either *NME* or *Q* (or anywhere) when Interpol's first album was released and had zero to do with its review commissioning. I started at *Q* the month that *Antics* was reviewed. So the only album I've commissioned a review of was the latest, *Our Love to Admire*. It was also the lead in *Uncut*, *Mojo* and *Observer Music Monthly*. I obviously had nothing to do with the commissioning on those magazines. There's no conspiracy. Interpol don't need the help anyway.

2/ I've never written a word about Interpol, nor have I attempted to convince anybody to write anything in particular about them.

3/ They've had plenty of bad reviews. I point you, ironically, in the direction of a recent *NME* review where Mark Beaumont suggested they were the worst band on earth and should be 'dragged into a ditch by their cocks and shot with a nail gun'.

Anyway, I just wanted to set you straight on those points. If you had any complaints about the way I or my brother conduct ourselves you could have easily called or emailed me, or called Daniel, who incidentally speaks very highly of you. Feel free to do so next time.

All the best,
Ted Kessler

Shortly afterwards, my email is shared online by McGee, along-side his brief reply:

Glad to hear it's not a stitch-up ted that would take away my faith in the music business. Still it's only rock'n'roll ted . . . alan

That draws our debate to a peaceful conclusion. I played no role in Interpol's success. I didn't – don't – have the power to positively shape careers anyway. I'm the person who put Terris and Campag Velocet on covers of the *NME*.

November 2008

A dinner at my mum's house in DC, alongside her inner circle. Barack Obama has just been elected president and my divorce is reaching a conclusion. Glad tidings. The horizon explodes with false dawns.

Afterwards, Mum suggests the group move to the living room for drinks. Sounds good. I'll have a brandy, please. Lovely.

We settle into sofas and armchairs. Mum extinguishes the lights. She lights candles. Well, OK. This is very moody. She walks to the stereo and puts a CD in, before sinking into a sofa, pressing play on the remote and closing her eyes.

'Next Exit' from the album *Antics* by Interpol starts playing at supersonic volume.

The guests side-eye each other. This is not the usual line-up you might run into at the 9.30 club on a night in town.

'Is this your son's band, Anne?' whisper-shouts one guest, but Anne doesn't say anything. She's lost in the music. So I wrinkle my nose and mouth an exaggerated 'yes' at him.

We then settle back into our seats and in excruciating deference listen to *Antics* at top volume in its entirety.

Ironically, in the summer of 2019 I do decide to put Interpol on the cover of *Q* Magazine and not a single person complains. There are no blog postings about it, nobody writes in to my employers at Bauer. Alan McGee doesn't ring. Nothing. It's fine.

Or is it?

I ask my colleagues, is this OK? Putting my brother's band on the cover?

They look at me like I'm insane. Well who else is there? they ask.

We go through the list of acts who have albums out that summer who are also headlining festivals. We cross out the names of those we've done already. We remove those whom we cannot interview because they will not do print media.

Interpol looks good, we agree.

Bands with fanatical supporters often sell better on magazine covers than those with wide commercial appeal. That's what we tell ourselves in those final five years or so, anyway. Go deep if you can't go big.

Interpol on the cover of *Q* sells fine. Better than some stadium acts of recent memory. In the bizarro news-stand reality, Interpol trumps Ed Sheeran. How about that?

A few weeks later, I'm sitting on the side of the stage with my girlfriend and our two children, aged eight and six. Interpol are headlining a main stage at All Points East Festival in Victoria Park, East London. It's a big gig, huge crowd. My kids have spent the last few minutes singing 'Uncle Daniel! Uncle Daniel!' between claps . . .

Then he's here, walking on stage with a salute to the crowd and, turning towards the kids, a little wave to them, too. He straps on, lifts his right arm and he's off, crazy legs Kessler striding across the stage towards the hysterical crowd.

My daughter leaps off her seat and starts to dance too as the music explodes next to us. My son sits on his flight case nodding along, poker-faced, until he starts to mouth something to me, but I can't hear him. It's too loud. What's that? The song ends. I lean in to him.

'Good drums,' he shouts in my ear.

Bathing in dry ice, on the stairs to the left of the stage, punching the smoke wafting through the Royal Albert Hall. Interpol are ushering 'Lights' towards its overwhelming conclusion and everyone present is standing, arms raised, dancing, singing as one, from the floor to the rafters.

That's why I hold you.
That is why I hold you dear

Afterwards, at the thronged aftershow, in a too-bright room beneath the venue, I hide the illegal cigarette behind my back and tell Daniel how much I thought Interpol's biggest fan, our departed mother, would've enjoyed tonight. We used to chase along nearby Kensington High Street and scrabble for goals in Hyde Park just across the road with her as kids so often. I felt her in the room. I imagined her here, singing along to 'Lights'. She'd have loved it.

He gives me his softest eyes. It's funny how much mental space you have when you're up there, playing songs you know well, in a groove and it feels good. 'I think about her every night on stage,' he says. 'I was thinking about her in "Lights" too. I think about conversations we had, her mannerisms. I think about it all.'

The morning after my mother's funeral a few years earlier, in 2013, during a thunderously wet Washington DC October, my brothers and I had sat in her living room awaiting our rides away. I was heading home to London, my brothers were off to New York together. My mother was a prolific photographer and she left behind not just several family photo albums, but also bags full of jumbled prints and Polaroids from the early sixties through to the late eighties. We had an hour or two on our hands that morning, so we began the impossible task of dividing them between us. The photos tumbled from brown manila envelopes and old pharmacy carrier bags on to her living room floor, the memorial evidence of long-forgotten joy strewn all around us.

A 1966 black and white of my dad unsmiling in white slacks, white shirt and wide-brimmed white hat standing on rocks by the sea in boat shoes, looking like a dude about to introduce the

Velvet Underground to some very heavy verse. A photo dated December 1971 taken from above of my old man and me, with a cowboy hat hanging from my shoulders, poised over my new baby brother Mark laughing in his rocker at us. Me, full-frontal naked on holiday in the early seventies, holding a snorkel beside my groin. My parents, before children, a pair of 1960s New York City hipsters laughing in Kodachrome by the harbour in some wintery beach town. My brothers and me in our mid-to-late teens on the balcony of Mum's apartment, lined up like an indie power trio heavily indebted to Hüsker Dü and Fugazi. A series of colourful mid-seventies summertime shots of the family larking around in Hyde Park, my mum in tight white flares and chocolate-brown vest, hanging from the Albert Memorial, just opposite where my brother and I now stood remembering her . . .

If someone were to ask me to describe the typical emotional punch of listening to Interpol's music without using musical references, dredging through highly evocative, previously unseen photos of loved ones taken by and of your recently deceased mother would probably cover it.

My brother and I chink glasses. 'I think about you too, bro!' he exclaims.

Laughing, we hug. I watch him drift off into the wall of eyes trying to catch his for a quick chat, the myriad *oh hi Daniel* moments that fill the rest of his time before hotel call.

I step outside. The moon is high, the streets are clear. It's a calm, unseasonably warm night. For old times' sake, I decide to walk by where I grew up, as I rarely make it near that triangle of London nowadays. I head alongside Hyde Park, up past floodlit Marble Arch, towards Paddington, along my old paper-round route. I'm hunting ghosts, following their steps in the square grey paving stones by Edgware Road and Star Street, down Sussex Gardens, turning left by the Monkey Puzzle. Mapping their imprints in concrete, alongside my own.

That's why I hold you. That is why I hold you dear.

22.
Janet

It is January 2008. I have recently moved out of my matrimonial home for good. My wife and I have been breaking up carefully for the past twenty months or so officially, but for much, much longer in reality, for many years without acknowledging it, only reading the control panel correctly when the nose was already pointing earthwards in a dive no pilot could avert. We crashed. My spouse spent six months out of our home, then she returned, both of us shell-shocked and in need of familiar comfort from the only person who understood what the other was going through. But now it is my turn to be out, walking down new streets, resigned despair turning surprisingly quickly into manic hopefulness. This time, it's over. I know that and I have been drinking heavily for weeks. I have never felt more alive.

When you're drunk and more alive than ever you find yourself open to possibilities you may not have otherwise considered. I am the bank that likes to say yes and I say yes to everything, always.

One cold night at the start of this year I say yes to free cocktails at some bullshit *Q* magazine Hard Rock Café party with mini patties, chicken wings and a grasping indie-rock band trying to woo drunks. I don't remember the music, but I remember the drinks. I arrive ruddy-faced around show time, simmering after a few after-office lager looseners in the Social, and demand a premium wristband that allows access not just to the complimentary beer and wine, but to cocktails. I get the wristband. I get the cocktails. I talk to a girl serving chicken wings about why she pierced her tongue. I drop and smash a tumbler on the dance floor. I shovel a line up my hooter in the toilet and upon my return to the fray I slip down three stairs, regain my balance and make a fabulous joke about the tumble to my fellow revellers. Turn the ambient sound down, overlay with some minor-key synths and you are watching a government infomercial about the perils of binge drinking at Christmas on public transport. Always use the handrail when using the moving escalator, please.

Later, I find myself in a fancy hotel bar full of candles and marble. I am holding the floor back from colliding into my face by leaning hard with my palms on a glass table. I have already stolen a packet of Marlboro Lights from the bar top and described my career as a 'natural thief' in detail to surprised, teetotal work acquaintances.

I turn to my right and – what's this? I'm kissing someone. Or am I? I fade out and in and out and in and out of the embrace, the face of the person I am kissing morphing into a dozen different shapes and personalities, until I am lost in some kind of dreamy reverie about all the people I am kissing: friends past and present, old lovers, new lovers, imaginary lovers, a former schoolteacher, perhaps, and then . . . and then I start to drift off. I wonder if I'm actually at home, asleep. Could be. I pull back. Dizzy, I look hard at the bemused face in front of me. Oh, it's Janet, who I know on a cordial basis. She works on another floor in my building and we have no history beyond casual, convivial chat when our paths cross on stairs, in lifts, by desks. There is no chemistry between us that I have ever previously been aware of.

Yet, I say that there is chemistry. There's chemistry, Janet. You must know that. You must. She doesn't know that, she says. She's never known that. How could she? We barely know each other, let alone our feelings for each other. Oh my God, she says. Are you sure? Her bemusement levels are breaching the levee, but I just nod sadly, seriously. It's true, Janet. There's something between us. Something real. It's very dark in here, I then think.

Who am I speaking to? Oh, it's Janet. Janet. Ah. I've always liked you, Janet. Shall we leave?

We leave. Janet climbs into a cab, wisely closing the door sharply behind her. I smile. I wave. I take a little tumble backwards into a man with big hands. I ask him, the doorman, for a light for the first of my stolen Marlboro Lights. He gives me a whole box of matches and I do my best to thank him. He tells me to watch my step and I give him a punchy little salute. I think I call him sarge. And then I move off into the early, crisp Tuesday morning, the week stretching deliciously out in front of me.

I walk in a general westerly direction, striding as if starring in a movie focused on the trials of a sailor on twenty-four-hour shore leave. I slalom. I clutch on to railings and scaffolding. I rest for a moment against walls and in doorways as the undulating world takes shape before me, wishing I had the power and persuasion to hail a cab, but that may take another thirty minutes of this faltering homeward passage to master. And then I text Janet. You know, to smooth things over.

Nice to see you to see you nice Janet.

That's what I text into the void. *'Nice to see you to see you nice Janet.'* That should cover it. I march onwards into the enveloping orange-blackness of the city's night . . .

Three weeks later I am standing at the bar in the Social, sucking down a fresh brew with friends. My phone buzzes in my pocket and I pull it out to see the name *Janet* flashing menacingly on its face. I put the phone back in my pocket and allow it to finish buzzing. Moments later, a double buzz. A message.

'Oh hello, Ted.'

The gentle pause. The drawing of breath. That doesn't sound like the Janet of Cumbria I know. That is Home Counties Janet: pony trials and the WI and a hand on the shoulder in the waiting room when the diagnosis is bad, very bad. It's a recognisable tone, however. Who is this, I wonder?

'This is Janet Cleese-Stenley.'

Oh yes, that's who it is. Excellent.

'You left a message, I think, on my home phone recently. You may have sent it as a text because it was delivered by an automated machine? Anyway, I'm sorry it's taken me this long to work out it was you, but if you ever wish to see me please feel free to get in touch again. OK? All right then, Ted. All the best and *do take care*.'

Janet Cleese-Stenley, great to hear from you, you, my former therapist, who clearly proved so useful in resolving all those issues during the course of our five meetings in 2002, back when I first left my wife. So that's where the message arrived: I'd sent a text message to my ex-therapist's home phone, at 3 a.m. And the message that would've been read out in disjointed electronic speech, as Janet Cleese-Stenley slept soundly by her husband's side in their well-appointed terrace house, perhaps ringing out on the answerphone machine to jog them awake? It was this: Nice-to-see-you-to-see-you-nice-Janet.

I decide not to return her call.

And we slide the vault's lid shut once more.

23.
Experiments in Democracy

There was a brief moment towards the end of *Q*'s long history, just after Andrew Harrison became editor in 2012, when the written word was all that mattered in the magazine.

His focus was only on the page, how the words fit together, how they could be improved after delivery. Nothing else measured up. Words strung together in sentences to deliver a story was all he really cared about and you either bought into that or you were sidelined. We learned more about editing copy, about shining the work of others each day under him than any of us had understood in many years. It felt like a gift. He was determined to make us readable after a long intermission, to become more like his previous, now defunct magazine. He was going to turn us into *The Word*, but we'd be successful.

It was a beautiful red-ink moment that lasted a handful of issues, then our paymasters put a stop to all that nonsense.

Andrew was cramming as many good words into the magazine as he possibly could, commissioning expensive illustrations to run in small spaces alongside them. The magazine was singing a beautiful song, tickling new tunes from its expanded writing workforce, music the like of which *Q* hadn't performed in decades, but Bauer was deaf to it. They could not absorb the wonderful melodies we were delivering. They could only hear the alarm bells sounding as every page budget was busted over and over again.

The magazine wasn't selling significantly better than before, but it was much more expensive to produce. That's the kind of equation that trips code red in twenty-first-century publishing houses. Surprisingly, the way our publishers went about tackling this overspend was by hurling an enormous amount of money at us. We didn't know this at the time, but it was their final roll of the dice. Soon enough, we were sitting on one side of a two-way mirror gnawing on biscuits as readers and non-readers alike discussed *Q* in focus groups.

Alarmingly for our bosses, most of those questioned said they really liked the recent issues of *Q*. Great writing. Good stories. Nice design. Some of the artists we covered were a bit off, they felt; it was a shame we didn't feature more modern acts that they were into, but otherwise it was a really decent magazine. The subscribers present actually said that this new version had restored their faith in *Q*. It had gone mad for a while before, hadn't it?

We took a few more days out of the office to sit in hired external meeting rooms with our bosses listening to more professional opinion about music magazines generally, *Q* specifically. Journalists, editors from other publications, record label people rolled in to chat about us, to us. Mostly, they wondered why our Internet presence was so terrible. Site under construction, we lied, hoping they'd be able to read from our coded eyelid blinks that it was really because investment in it had been axed. You should sort that, they advised. It might save you in the end.

Yeah, whatever.

BBC 6 Music came by to explain how they'd escaped their own likely extinction at the last moment, instead becoming a ratings smash hit. They did it, they said, by harnessing the goodwill of their core loyal listeners, hearing what they told them about the station and giving them more of what they liked.

That sounded like really sensible advice. We ignored it, of course. It wasn't the radical change that was expected. The old staffers sensed from all this external consultation that ill winds were on their way again, removing choices about the direction of editorial travel from us. Andrew was being told to sort out his word costs and he was telling us not to worry about that. Keep commissioning.

Our recent experience told us this was a political miscalculation. The new wave of radical change soon arrived in the shape of two very friendly former tabloid and celebrity mag editors. They joined as brand consultants at the behest of our overlords to finesse *Q*'s work, hone our commerciality. They were very sympathetic, often funny women who nevertheless were completely ruthless in temperament, as you must be when rising high in Murdoch's red-top empire. They were joined by the guy from *Heat* for a while, the one who'd been floating around randomly dicking up our cover lines at the end of Paul Rees's time. The tabloid hacks brought a couple of other younger tabloid freelancers to help them, and they all sat around in a shuttered meeting room brainstorming together about big-picture *Q* – a magazine none of them had apparently read before – while we continued the day-to-day work of producing the publication.

Their task was to imagine how to make *Q* more commercially viable, all the while being paid day rates that must have dwarfed the editorial budget. It appeared jarring to us, logically, that while we were being told to rein in costs at one end of the floor, we also had this bonfire of cash taking place in our name down the other. We kept our heads focused on daily work.

Their brainstorming went on for weeks and weeks. So long that I managed to have a child born, to have my mother die and to attend her funeral in the US, and when I returned a fortnight later they were still debating the same regular feature line-up conundrum I'd left them discussing.

Occasionally, we'd be called in to talk through some of their ideas. One day we entered the lair where the consultants were tossing ideas back and forth. Andrew was in a swivel chair by the window, arms crossed, face thunderous.

The guy from *Heat* revealed his favourite idea.

'Why don't we ask David Cameron to interview Morrissey? The Prime Minister's a huge Smiths fan. Could be fun! We'd get loads of press.'

Andrew exploded. He couldn't suck it up any longer.

'You have more chance of getting John Lennon to interview Jesus!' he shouted.

Shortly after, Andrew stopped coming to the office. Like Paul Rees before him, he sent us an oblique email saying he was 'working remotely' and we were to carry on as normal.

We'd seen this film already.

After it was announced that Andrew was stepping down, the outside tabloid workforce also reduced to just the two principal leads. The duo retreated to their ideas cave with printouts of *Q*'s flatplan and remapped the magazine's flow, page by page.

They emerged a few days later with a much-improved magazine page-plan that included several new regulars that the staff had come up with under duress. On one hand, the tabloid consultants had kept making us put embarrassing lines on the cover (for example, I reluctantly undertook weeks of negotiations to have Liam Gallagher dressed as an astronaut on the front just so we could accommodate their line: Liam's on a mission!), but on the other they had definitely improved the pace of the mag. Score draw.

Presumably, either they thought their work was now done or the money dried up, as they decamped soon after, leaving us to clear up both figuratively and literally after them. They then tore through some of the celebrity weeklies upstairs in the building, from where we'd hear tales of senior editors also mysteriously leaving in the months to come.

While clearing the *Heat* guy's desk we found his notepad of 'ideas for *Q* features' open. He'd left it, but we couldn't. We read them out aloud. Once we'd have had to handle these unfiltered thoughts with extreme care, lest one of them landed in the magazine and killed dozens of readers. But stripped from their author, we could enjoy them. They were defused. They no longer carried any hazard to us. There were some beauties, mostly based around daytime TV shows. Ready Steady Q: pop stars cook us their favourite dish; Through the Q-Hole: pop stars let us into their homes and readers have to guess who would live in a house like this; Who Are *You*: Pete Townshend fires twenty questions at a different pop star every month; Q's Style Challenge: we ask pop stars to make-over their rivals in a brand-new stage outfit!

That kind of thing, but also just some buzzwords like 'Bats', 'Milkshakes! Mmm', 'Moyles', or oblique catchphrases such as 'Little Britain, but NOW' and 'Pop star *Archers*'.

In the middle of the pad, ringed and underlined in red, were the words WHY AM I SO TIRED?

We never found out if that was a confession or a feature idea.

We waited for a new editor.

Nobody turned up.

We asked when a new editor might be appointed.

Don't you worry about that, just carry on with the magazine now that's been reorganised for you.

We drifted along like this for a while. It might have been a long time. It was definitely a few months. It's hard to be certain of the passing of time during this era, the linear calendar became elastic. What is it that Massive Attack sang about inertia creeping?

One day, a rumour swept into the office. They were about to announce a new editor.

We gathered in a meeting room with the publisher. She was pleased to announce that after a long search they'd found the perfect candidate to edit Q. The answer had been under their noses all along. We thought that meant that Matt Mason, the senior editor, was going to be promoted.

No.

The new editor of *Q* is Phil Alexander, the editor of *Mojo*.

You what?

Yes, Phil Alexander is going to be the new editor of *Q*. He'll remain the editor of *Mojo* though. He's going to edit both magazines.

This was unprecedented. A whole new ball game. Never been attempted before. The guy who edited one of our rivals was also going to edit us. Two magazines at once. How would this work, practically?

'Well,' said Phil, tucking his chair in after he joined the meeting. 'This is all a bit odd, isn't it?'

A tall, thick-set rocker who looks somewhat like his childhood idol Phil Lynott of Thin Lizzy, Francophile Phil had edited *Kerrang!* before *Mojo* and knew his music magazine craft. He was brilliant at meetings. He had good editorial ideas. His office politics were second to none – everyone thought he was batting for them. His only weakness, his Achilles heel, was that he thought that any blank space on a cover was begging to be filled with more words. His editing was otherwise exemplary. But would even he be able to edit two magazines at once?

We didn't have to wait long to find out.

In truth, he wouldn't be editing in the traditional sense. He'd keep an eye on us from his desk in the *Mojo* office down the corridor, making sure we weren't entering *Mojo*'s editorial lane as we had done increasingly over recent time. He'd come to meetings. We could run ideas by him. He'd keep a close eye on our budget. That was about the extent of it.

This was the signal that Bauer had done their best to bring peace and stability to *Q*, but they were now gathering all but the most essential troops and pulling out. They'd poured their money into *Q* to try and grow the brand; now that plug was pulled. No more expensive consultants or fancy away days. No more showy redesigns. No more radical change. Phil's job was to make sure we remained in profit, kept ticking over, didn't embarrass anyone. They certainly wouldn't be blowing any wedge on hiring a new editor.

All of that sounded fine to me, except magazines need editors. Football teams need managers. Policemen need sergeants. Pilots need air traffic control. Pubs need landlords. We can all muddle along for a while in a form of democratic anarchy, but every team needs to be told what to do, where to go, how. Policy, philosophy, tactics, authority must be designed by someone.

Bauer disagreed. No, you don't need an editor, they insisted. Then they decided that not only do you not need an editor, but you don't need an online editor, a senior editor, a chief designer, a picture researcher, a picture editor or a senior sub either.

One brutal morning, we were all called into a meeting room one by one. Only half the team left with their jobs. The rest were made redundant.

I was taken into the room for my chat with Phil and our new publisher. You're staying, they said. You're the most senior, experienced journalist now. We'll need you to be the link between Phil and the team. Run the magazine as you see fit and Phil will keep his eye on your work, giving you any advice you may need.

'So,' I replied, 'I'll be like the editor?'

'Well, sort of. Acting editor, unofficially. Phil will still do the cover and cover lines with you all, take a weekly editorial meeting.'

I didn't mind. I was relieved to have survived the cull. I was glad of the extra responsibility: as I was commissioning the features and negotiating covers I liked to have an overview of the magazine anyway. The dirtier I could get my hands, the more job satisfaction I enjoyed. I also felt that Phil was the best candidate to be remote controlling us from a rival magazine, as he was just about the only person who'd ever had a good idea for the magazine in the whole company.

During that first introductory meeting with us, Phil Alexander had said something profound to the Q staff, something that nobody in authority had ever suggested before. It blew our minds.

'Have you ever thought,' he wondered, 'of just covering good music that you like and ignoring the stuff you don't?'

Of course, I had thought of this. But I'd never imagined that we'd be allowed to do it. My experience up to this point had been the opposite, it had been to second-guess the readership.

So in 2015 we started to base the magazine around good music that we liked. And since there was no longer any significant budget, we did most of the writing about the music that we liked as well. It was very enjoyable work.

After a couple of years of this weird autonomy, of putting out a magazine without an editor, I went to see Phil Alexander.

It was late 2016. That summer, I'd scored an exclusive interview with Liam Gallagher, who'd been silent for three years or so since Beady Eye had split up. The piece made a big noise with his fans and external media, and it sold really well, 28,000 on the news-stand alone, nearly twice as many copies as we normally shifted beyond subscriptions (which gives an indication of how few copies *Q* was selling on the news-stand by then). I felt my stock was high. The CEO of Bauer UK Publishing – like all British publisher bigwigs, a guy who smelt like a Range Rover and looked as if he sold country estates for Savills – had grabbed one of my colleagues when I was out for lunch and said, 'Well done, Ted on that Liam Gallagher sale!'

'Phil,' I said, 'do you think it's time I was officially made editor? I've been editing the magazine in secret for two years now. I want the world to know. I'm tired of being our dirty secret. Put a ring on it, baby.'

Surprisingly, Phil agreed. He told me to compile a document answering some questions he'd fire my way, something he could take to the board to make my case for me.

I answered his questions as fully as I could. He thanked me for my input.

Q's publisher took me into a room and also had a good chat with me, saying he was happy to make me the editor now. He asked me if there was anything at all about the job, knowing what I did about it, knowing all that *Q* was up against, that worried me.

I said I didn't want to be *Q*'s last editor.

He laughed. 'Don't be silly,' he said. 'There are many other magazines that are much more vulnerable than *Q*. Keep doing what you're doing.'

Phil took me back into his room and congratulated me. Were there any final thoughts on my mind, anything in particular that worried me, he wondered?

I said I didn't want to be *Q*'s last editor.

He too laughed. 'Don't be ridiculous. *Q*'s a long, long way from folding now that we've stabilised costs.'

Shortly after, it was announced that after several decades working at EMAP and then Bauer, Phil Alexander would be leaving to join the start-up publisher who'd bought *Mixmag* and now *Kerrang!* from them.

My new role was also revealed externally.

I was to be *Q*'s new editor, its last as it turned out. Every day thereafter was a journey of ever-brightening enlightenment and joyful satisfaction, until suddenly the lights were switched off.

24.
The Beautiful Paul

I thought of all the writers to whom we'd given satisfying, regular work in recent years.

I thought of all those photographers whom we'd thrust into high-pressure situations at often short notice but who always delivered what we wanted.

I thought of the events team who had been made redundant years earlier, but who'd re-formed to organise our Q Awards every October, trying to get their own business together.

I thought of all the freelance subs and designers, the freelance picture editor, those marks in their diaries for the months ahead. All rubbed out now.

I thought about how in one swoop that solitary chunk of reliable, sturdy work had been whipped away from everyone with the closure of *Q*, at the very worst time, in the teeth of a locked-down pandemic.

With *Q* gone, there wouldn't be many alternative openings for the writers or the photographers, somewhere that paid a decent rate and offered a meaty regular income documenting contemporary music at length. Everywhere else was either engaged in reporting extinct music or was an independent periodical made on the fly with tiny budgets. Newspapers are a closed shop for music writers. Online a fool's errand.

All that work, gone. No redundancy payments for freelancers.

Then I thought about Paul Heaton's offer to donate £35,000 to us, a grand for each year of *Q*'s existence. I could split it into £500 packages, share it between everyone on the masthead, as well as those people toiling on the production of the mag and the awards. It might pay a few bills, provide a moment's breathing space.

I picked up the phone.

'Hi Ted,' I said, 'it's Ted here. I've decided to accept Paul's kind offer, the staff will split it with all the freelancers.'

'Oh great,' replied Ted. 'Paul will be very happy. He really wanted you guys to have it.'

'It's an incredible act of generosity,' I replied. And it really was.

A few months later we tracked down one of our Q Awards and engraved it with the legend:

PAUL HEATON
Q's ALL-TIME CLASSIC SONGWRITER
THANK YOU FOR EVERYTHING

He was going to finally win an award. In fact, he'd be the only Q Award winner of 2020. Our final award winner. I praised Paul Heaton on social media too, and he showed off his award in return. He was going to display it in his daughter's room, on a shelf in amongst her teddy bears and soft toys.

I wondered whether I would do the same in Paul Heaton's place, whether I'd donate such a significant chunk of money to those in need. And I thought I probably wouldn't. I'm just not as kind a man as he is, as perhaps can be deduced from this book.

But, then again, I couldn't even be sure about that, because I've never actually met Paul Heaton. We've never even spoken, before or since his donation. He didn't want anything in exchange, made no requests for publicity about it. He didn't want a fuss made, he explained to Ted Cummings. He couldn't bear the thought of the Q staff suffering, that's all.

He just gave us the money.

25.
Tell Me When My Light Turns Green

While I hung in a state of suspended anxiety between being informed that my job was in consultation and delivering *Q*'s final issue, I received an interesting email at home from Tim Vigon, an enthusiastic former PR from Macclesfield I'd known since the nineties. He was the guy who'd first brought that Strokes demo into *NME*. He now managed acts from his new base in Los Angeles, notably two singular artists I'd written about several times: Mike Skinner of the Streets and Kevin Rowland of Dexys Midnight Runners.

I'd interviewed both of them fairly recently. In fact, the latest Kevin Rowland interview had just run in *Q*'s penultimate issue. I'd visited him at his home in Clapton, a swish new-build apartment overlooking the River Lea and Walthamstow Marshes. We were to talk specifically about the reissue of his much-maligned 1999 solo covers album, *My Beauty*.

I was much less nervous than the first time I met him to talk about *My Beauty*, back in '99, when I turned up to a café in Primrose Hill the week before the album was released.

I'd done a lot of research that first time. I knew his story, the sincere passion of his music inside out. He was, after all, one of my favourite ever singers and songwriters. In that crowded field of idiosyncratic voices who'd emerged in the aftermath of punk, Rowland had released three of its most powerful and distinctive albums between 1980 and '85 with Dexys Midnight Runners, drastically changing the sound, the look and even the band members each time, yet maintaining one transfixing constant: himself. He was the musical visionary who'd delivered theatrical Stax soul sounds and Celtic folk mysticism to mainstream radio airwaves. An incredible lyricist, too, combining moods of withering defiance with personal vulnerability. I knew every word of his by heart.

Yet I was unsure about who I would encounter in that café. I had heard the tales from his youth, how he'd been arrested many times for theft and violence – he'd even written one of my favourite Dexys' songs about it called 'Kevin Rowland's 13th Time'. I knew that though he'd been born in Ireland, he'd grown up in the Black Country and had arrived as a teen in north-west London prepared to fight back whenever bullied about his Midlands accent. Once he attacked a group of men outside a pub with a length of scaffolding.

I knew he was intense. I knew he was thin-skinned, hated criticism. In the eighties, he'd tracked down and punched a *Melody Maker* journalist, Barry McIlheney, in Covent Garden after McIlheney had written something about Dexys that upset him. Rowland had been confrontational, self-destructive, prone to dramatic impulse, such as when Dexys stole back their master tapes from EMI in a daring heist, holding their debut album for ransom, hiding the tapes under his mum's bed.

I knew he was difficult. Several of his bands had quit on him or been fired in heated circumstances. I knew how many times he'd sabotaged his career because he felt unworthy, how the commercial failure in 1985 of his key album with Dexys, *Don't Stand Me Down*, had sent him on a spiral that he still hadn't recovered from – and that deep down he felt he was responsible for that failure because he refused to release a single or an edit from the album. For not playing the game, as usual, itself an act of subconscious self-harm.

I knew that he'd been a chronic cocaine addict. That he'd snort five grams a night at the addiction's peak, hiding under his covers in bed because he could hear voices talking about him from his fridge. That he lost his home to the Inland Revenue. That he spent months in residential rehab, had joined a religious cult, lived in squats because he'd blown all his money, a man who'd had number one records in the UK, Europe and the US adrift in the realm of hijacked electricity and stolen mattresses . . .

I knew all of that when I first met him in those tea rooms by Primrose Hill. And I knew that, despite all the therapy he'd been through and was still undertaking, he was opening another deep trench of future anguish for himself.

I knew – even if he didn't – that he was in the process of sabotaging his new album *My Beauty* by insisting on posing on its cover in women's lingerie and a dress that he hitched up to display his crotch. He was doing that despite the protests from his label Creation, the people he was relying on to sell his record. I knew the world of pain he'd engineered for himself.

So I wasn't sure who I was going to meet. What was he going to be like?

He turned up in the café in a long black dress, a pencil skirt. It looked cool, natural. Nobody gave it a second glance in the crowded room. I could see how he'd arrived at the style; he'd always been obsessed with clothes, being ahead of a look before it landed in the high street. I could see how a tall, slim man came to wear a long black skirt and sandals in the late nineties. I could imagine seeing it on runways, in nightclubs, on footballers papped in Mykonos.

The cover of *My Beauty* didn't look like that though. Here are my bollocks in lacy underwear. It appeared confrontational and confrontation was exactly what it received. I'm wearing stockings, a pearl necklace and red lipstick. My dress is hanging off me, my chest is bare. I'm Kevin Rowland. You may remember me from Dexys Midnight Runners: NY dockers coats; dungarees; Brooks Brothers' suits. Yeah, well, this is me now. Balls out in black pants. What do you think of that?

What people thought of it was relayed in widespread ridicule. Critics hated the cover, his label hated the cover and, actually, we don't want to hear your MOR cover version of 'You'll Never Walk Alone' or 'Daydream Believer'.

Once, the Kevin Rowland of Dexys would have taken that rejection on, punched back harder. But this recovering Kevin Rowland was not strong enough for it. He didn't have it in him any more.

So that's who turned up at the café. He was fragile. His emotions were raw, on the watery surface of the conversation we had. He appeared oblivious to the derision he was walking into, just when he was most open to sharing with the public who he really was, where he'd come from.

I loved *My Beauty*, the narrative journey it undertook in explaining via well-known cover versions his own autobiography, the richness of its sound, his voice, but I feared for him. I imagined the reaction it would receive and, upon meeting him, I could see how vulnerable he was to criticism. It did not bode well.

The final thing he asked before we left that day was about a review I'd written of the reissue of *Don't Stand Me Down*, the lyrical, mystical, confessional funk that had capped Dexys' recorded journey in 1985. I'd described it as his defining work and given it nine out of ten in *NME*.

'I read your review,' said Kevin. 'Can I ask you something personal?'

'Of course.'

'What was wrong with it? Why did you only give it nine out of ten?'

He held my gaze, his eyes filling with tears, as I told him nothing was wrong with it. It was nine out of ten.

He shook his head, with a rueful chuckle. 'See? That's what I'm like. That's my head. I get nine out of ten and torture myself about what's missing. It's hard being like that at times.'

When we met in his flat in 2020, he told me the ridicule that *My Beauty* had subsequently received had made him physically ill. He'd needed medical attention and eventually an operation for a stomach ailment caused, he believes, by the distress.

He'd thought afterwards that the reaction would finish music for him. He didn't need it. It was too much stress. For several years he stayed completely away from writing, performing, recording. But he returned with Dexys in the mid-noughties and early 2010s with revue-style shows and a couple of well-received albums. Nobody would have complained if he'd made a Dexys album every few years for the rest of his life, played a dozen theatres, did an occasional festival. There'd always be an audience for it because his songs, the brassy fire and brimstone of the first album, the Celtic soul stirrings of the smash hit second, had a fundamental connection with an audience. *Don't Stand Me Down* was now an acknowledged lost classic. The large band he'd brought together to deliver the shows were probably the best version of Dexys and they'd reimagined his catalogue so that stylistically it stitched together across his career. Those songs meant something to people. When he now played the slower-paced but much longer modern version of the first song he'd written with Dexys in 1978, 'Tell Me When My Light Turns Green', the whole room sang the soulful horn refrain a cappella along with him for a few minutes, joining Kevin Rowland down a path towards his desperate beginning.

He hadn't made any music for a few years, though. When I asked about it in 2020 he said he thought that side of his life was now finished. He had nothing more to add. The music's over.

I pushed him gently, encouragingly, saying that would be a massive shame for fans to hear. He demurred, gratefully. He'd moved on from music. That was that. The matter was closed.

We finished our interview looking back at *My Beauty*. He was much more at peace with both the record and the sleeve now. That's who he was then. If people didn't like it, fuck them. That's their problem. He was in a new place now, but he still wanted *My Beauty* to finally get its critical due. He'd put everything into it. It deserved better, he said.

This is the Kevin Rowland I'd expected to meet the first time, I thought. He seemed in good nick.

As we said goodbye to each other in his hallway, we chatted about my coat, about his wardrobe, about his plans to perhaps move to California. We'd given him a Q Award in 2019 to help with his residency application, to prove he was a valuable musician worthy of living in the USA.

It was amiable chit-chat. I'd bunked off school to see Dexys play live in 1983, climbed from the school bus in the Parisian suburbs a few stops after I'd got on, walked to the RER station and spent the day window shopping in Les Halles before they played that night, so I was just getting a kick out of making small talk with Kevin Rowland in his flat thirty-seven years later. It was one of the first concerts I'd been to and I'd received two weeks detention for it. I didn't regret it, even on day ten. It was the kind of thing he might have done to see his favourite group as well I imagined.

We shook hands and I wished him well. Suddenly, he put his hand on the front door as I opened it and said he had something he wanted to explain to me. He paused.

'You know how I said I didn't want to do music any more?'

'Yes.'

'There's just other things I want to do. That music persona, that Kevin Rowland we were talking about, that's another person. I'm sixty-six. I'm not getting any younger, you know. I've got other ideas to explore.'

'Of course.'

'I was working on a clothing line with someone for a while, but we ended up having a few disagreements about direction, so that ended.'

'Right.'

'Now, though, I'm working on a range of lingerie for men.' He held my stare for a few moments. 'So, that's what I'm doing. It's my main focus. I've moved on from music. I really want to do the male lingerie.'

I wished him well.

The email from Tim Vigon said that Kevin Rowland had really enjoyed my profile of him. Would I be interested in writing a book about him?

The timing could not have been better. *Q* was about to fold, so suddenly I was going to have a lot of time on my hands: this sounded like a brilliant opportunity. As I'd transcribed our recent interview I'd even had a passing thought that this would make a great book, writing it in the same tone that Kevin spoke about his past. He was very analytical, thoughtful. He told his story in clear detail, but always from his particular perspective. I could imagine it on the page.

I told Tim I'd love to, thanks for thinking of me.

Tim replied there was one caveat, as there often is with Kevin Rowland. Kevin just wants the book to be about Dexys, from 1978 until 1986, after *Don't Stand Me Down* came out, right up to the dissolution of that version of the band.

I said that wouldn't be a problem. It'd probably be tidier to have this story wrapped up chronologically like that.

Kevin Rowland then left a long voice note for me on WhatsApp. This is his preferred method of communication.

He was happy that I wanted to write the book. As there was a lockdown at that moment, we should get on the Zoom soon and talk about it. Once this lockdown was over, perhaps we could meet and get to work on it?

I absolutely wanted to do that and was very pleased with the offer. I just had to see out the end of *Q* first, see how the chips landed.

No problem.

'Oh, one other thing Ted you should know,' he said in his message. 'About twenty years ago I started a book with another writer. He even got an advance but, well, he interviewed lots of minor members of Dexys for it and their stories, their stories were all over the place. It wasn't right. It didn't sit well with me. I couldn't read their shit, they didn't know what was really going on, some of them were probably intoxicated at the time, you know. I pulled out. He had to give the advance back. So, I just thought you should know.'

I told Kevin that that was all fine with me. This would just be his version of Dexys, as he was the only constant member of the group. I would map his journey in the band between 1978 and 1986, his point of view of events.

'Great,' said Kevin Rowland. 'Sounds good, man.'

I agreed.

When the lockdown ended, I went around to Kevin Rowland's flat again to begin work on his book. He'd recently recovered from Covid and, since the weather was bright, he suggested we go for a walk around the marshes, to keep the air flowing between us. He knew a couple of good benches that might make decent candidates for me to interview him on.

So we set off towards the marshes, him in his smart post-war vintage baggies and me in my all-black mohair suit. Because that's what we both always wear, even when we're going for a walk through Walthamstow Marshes.

We tried his first bench. He was a bit worried about the sun because he was shooting a video the next day to promote the *My Beauty* reissue and didn't want to be burned. But we settled there anyway.

'You just start wherever you want, man,' he said to me, amiably. 'It's entirely your show. I'll do this however you want, I have total trust in you.'

I replied that we should begin with the first time he met guitarist Kevin Archer, then, the man he'd formed Dexys Midnight Runners with in Birmingham, in 1978.

So that's what we did. There was very little prompting necessary from me. It was like a dam bursting. He wanted to share the story of how this great soul band came to be, how he needed to share the credit for its design with Kevin Archer, the kind of person he was then (conflicted; repressed; insecure). More than anything, though, he wanted to tell me about the clothes. Dexys Midnight Runners were going to be the first New Romantic band; their look was miles ahead of Duran Duran, Spandau Ballet, all those guys, but he'd been talked out of it. Kevin still thought about that every day. His whole life would've been different if he'd stuck to his guns, but he was too weak. He still kicks himself about it, every single day. Why did he change the look?

We spoke about this for a very long time. Eventually, the sun started beating down upon the bench so we moved off and found shade, leaning on a gate on the edge of the marshes, by a car park. Every time a dog walker or a pram came by, we had to move off the gate to let them through. Just a couple of guys in bespoke suits and high-waisted slacks leaning on a gate in a car park by marshland in East London having a very intense conversation about the Rum Runner nightclub in Birmingham in 1979. So what? What are you staring at?

Kevin spoke about Dexys for two hours straight.

Eventually, we paused. He was exhausted. I needed to regroup too. There would be a lot of transcription.

Often over the next few weeks, Kevin left me a voice note. He'd be out in his car, thinking about it, and he'd have to pull over. You know, the more he considered his behaviour in Dexys, the more he felt I needed to know about his background. His father. His mother. His brothers and sisters. Growing up.

'Look, it's not part of the book. But maybe it is? Who knows, it's your book, man. I'm just gonna tell you this stuff and you do with it whatever you want. It might not be relevant. That's up to you, Ted.'

And then he'd tell me about his family, where they'd come from in Ireland, where they arrived in Wolverhampton, his extremely complicated relationship with his dad. Everything.

Some days I'd wake at 7 a.m. and there'd be a new message waiting from Kevin Rowland.

Oh aye?

'Ted, so, I was just walking and as I did, I started thinking about my dad . . .'

You could hear his feet on the path by the marshes, rushing through his memories at dawn.

It was overwhelming, but very exciting. I could feel the book forming in front of my eyes. It would be his inner monologue, Kevin Rowland telling the story of his journey through Dexys in the same voice of these messages and our conversations. That intensity. I started to write it, just so I could have something to show him, to see if he felt I was on the right track.

Before we met again, I sent him a 10,000-word chunk.

He left me a voice message in return a few days later.

'Ted, I've not had a chance to read what you sent me yet. I'm sure it's great. And whatever's not working, I know we can fix it. I'm really enjoying talking to you. I just wanted to clarify one thing in the meantime . . .'

Then he left me a series of long messages about something that happened on tour in 1979.

It was all gold.

I returned to his flat and once again we went for an inappropriately dressed walk through Walthamstow Marshes.

He'd read the chunk of work I'd sent him. It had taken him a moment to get his head around it, the style. Some of the voice wasn't quite right, but we could tweak that. Couple of dates might be wrong. He was certain I'd misspelled his old manager's name (I hadn't; this became tricky as he nevertheless kept correcting it incorrectly on the document). He'd shown the work to a couple of people he trusted and they were encouraging. They quite liked it. They could see the potential.

'Look, man,' he said. 'It's your book. I trust you. I know you have a vision for it. Just do it. It'll be great.'

He was very creatively encouraging. I had a real feeling of freedom about the project.

We spoke for another two hours. It was emotional. At one point, as we were sitting there on that bench on the marshes by the River Lea, he started crying while he described a conversation he had had with his mother after watching himself on *Top of the Pops* in his parents' house. Tears rolling down his face. Not sobbing, no loss of eloquence. Just tears.

It was a breakthrough. I knew I had something here that no other writer had access to. I left him two hours later feeling enthused. I walked the four miles home to Wanstead listening to a deep cuts Dexys playlist I'd made, filled with B-sides and live versions. I skipped through Leytonstone.

He was feeling good, too. He left me a series of voice messages over the coming days and weeks as I wrote more of the book. He was telling me stories, elaborating, fixing minor inaccuracies that he'd remembered along the way.

'I hope you're OK with me leaving you these messages,' he said. 'I'm just going to keep talking. I have a very good instinct about this book. I feel very strongly that you are the guy to write it, the guy I've been waiting for. I know that any problems we have we can fix. I feel very good about you, man. Just wanted to let you know. You're the one.'

Then he told me some heavy-duty tales about his brother and what his father had once judged him to be.

I wrote another 10,000 words and sent it off to him. At the same time, I sent what I'd written to a publisher who I thought might be receptive to an impressionistic official biography of Kevin Rowland. They were and said they'd take it to the next acquisition meeting so they could formalise an offer. Somehow other publishers got wind of the book and also got in touch, wanting to talk, but I had someone in mind in particular.

It was exhilarating. I knew this book had real potential. I was working every day on it. To have this rhythm of new work so soon after losing my job, my career? That was the dream.

Kevin left a message. He hadn't had a chance to read my latest work, but he wondered if I might like to read what one of his most trusted colleagues in the band had written about their time with him? It covered the period that we hadn't reached yet in our own conversations. I might want it as research for our next meeting.

What he sent me was incredible, full of unknown personal detail and band anecdote. There was so much to go on.

Then, after I thanked him for this gold mine of research, he asked if I might want to see some of his own writing about his early life? I told him I definitely would. So he forwarded several thousand words that he'd written about his childhood. It contained mind-blowing stories, as well as very avant-garde grammar. I thanked him profusely. On the back of these contributions, I wrote a load of notes and questions for our next interview.

In the meantime, both of our fathers were hospitalised. Mine with Covid and his with something unspecified in the voice notes (he was in his nineties so anything's possible). In the end, my dad spent nearly three months in hospital in New York, several weeks of that in intensive care. It was very distracting. He caught the virus from his barber, who had refused to wear a mask while giving him his first haircut of the year. Amazingly, at eighty-seven years old, my dad walked out of the hospital cured. Sadly, Kevin's did not.

During this period, Britain re-entered a period of national lockdown to curb the spread of the virus. So there were no more walks for Kevin and me along the River Lea. That was OK. We had a lot on our minds and we could pick the story up in the spring.

The publishing wheels were turning, however. There was a date for an acquisition meeting to discuss an offer for my im-pressionistic biography of Kevin Rowland. I was advised to agree a split with Kevin ahead of it, which we did very quickly. The money wasn't important to him. The story was.

The publisher's acquisition meeting was due to take place on Monday 16 November. On Friday 13 November, Kevin Rowland left a message for me. He needed to give me a ring about some-thing. Was I around?

I was.

'Look, Ted,' he began, 'there's no easy way of saying this so I'll just come out with it. I don't want to do the book any more. It doesn't feel right. I think I need to try and write it in my own voice.'

'Well, this is a blow.'

'I know, I'm sorry.'

'Are you sure we can't work this out?'

'No, I've thought about this a lot. The chemistry isn't right between us, I don't believe.'

(THE CHEMISTRY ISN'T RIGHT BETWEEN US? Was Kevin Rowland of Dexys Midnight Runners breaking up with me?)

'But Kevin,' I replied. 'You left me those long voice messages saying that you felt very strongly that I was the guy for this, that whatever was wrong in the copy you knew we could fix it.'

'I know I did.'

'Hmm. I don't know what to say.'

'I'm sorry, Ted, I really am. I'll ask Tim to discuss some kind of compensation as I know how hard you've worked on this.'

'That's not important, Kevin. I thought I was writing a good book.'

'I know, man. I know. And it is good. But it's not right for me right now. I need to step away.'

'Doesn't sound like I might change your mind.'

'No.'

'OK, well. Good luck with everything.'

'Thank you, Ted. Take care.'

We hung up.

I felt pretty gloomy for half an hour or so. I sat in the armchair in the bedroom where I normally throw my clothes off in the dark, sipping a large gin and tonic. I sent a couple of panicked text messages, stewing. Then I turned off my phone.

Soon enough, the misery lifted. It hadn't been a total waste of time, I decided. I'd spent a lot of quality time with one of my all-time favourite singer-songwriters. I'd heard some amazing stories from him – and I had plenty of anecdotes of my own from the experience to keep me busy in the pub for half an hour or so. It had been quite an adventure, for a music writer.

I went downstairs and joined my kids in front of their Friday night TV.

'Kevin Rowland has just dumped me on the phone,' I told my girlfriend as she offered to refresh my drink. 'It was weird, it was as if we'd had a love affair and he was breaking up with me.'

'Oh dear,' said Jean. 'Are you all right about it?'

I stared at the screen. It was a film about a talking dog who was having a stressful time getting home.

'Yeah,' I replied. 'I'm OK. There's something else I need to write first, anyway.'

Epilogue

When people ask me what school I went to, I often say the *New Musical Express*. Usually they think I'm joking, but I'm not, not really. *NME* built me. It occupied my teenage vacuum. I grew up with it. It became a part of me.

As a young reader, *NME* was the primary influence on my cultural preferences, my school of thought. I cannot remember a time that I wasn't entirely governed by the music I consumed. Music enabled me to navigate my emotions, choose my friends, my wardrobe. I knew it would be my religion before I was even a double digit, watching mouth agape as Elvis Costello demanded with menace that we pump it up while dressed in red Teddy Boy drapes and a polka-dot button-down shirt on *Top of the Pops*. But it wasn't until reading my first *NME* around eleven years old that I had a map for the journey.

NME refined the new sounds I listened to, opening my ears and mind to records beyond the immediate mainstream, as well as telling me incredible fables around its creators. In doing so, it coined a particular musical vernacular and massively expanded my vocabulary. As much as I enjoyed listening to music, I now discovered I loved to read about it, to pore over its iconography.

The photos I absorbed in my first years as a devoted reader are as evocative as any album sleeve for me – more so in some cases. I didn't always have the records, I may have just taped something from the radio. These photos allowed me to imagine the distant worlds that created them. This is where I wanted to exist.

Epilogue

I'll rip them down from my mind's eye so you can see them too.

The Clash on tour in the USA, 1979, in a photo by Pennie Smith of Paul Simonon, Mick Jones, Topper Headon and Joe Strummer huddled close together in front of Niagara Falls; handsome, roguish-looking men in stylish, dishevelled threads, all bar Jones wearing cocked hats: at that moment the epitome of how a white rock band should present themselves. Another Pennie Smith black and white shot, of Ranking Roger of the Beat, my favourite band in March of 1980, standing on the cover in front of a mural of a lion in Handsworth, Birmingham. Joy Division, in the week after singer Ian Curtis's suicide in May 1980, pictured by Anton Corbijn at the top of a Tube station staircase on the cover, Curtis turning back to look over his shoulder, his final glance at all of us.

For a time in the early eighties, at the start of my *NME* subscription, Anton Corbijn seemed to be providing iconic photography to *NME* each week. I came to believe that these momentous visions defined how music should present itself. Siouxsie Sioux naked on the front, her back to Corbijn's lens, a cap pulled over her face, Ian McCulloch of Echo and the Bunnymen, back-brushed hair, head bowed, a white horse looming behind him; Kevin Rowland's return in 1982 for his first interview after two years of self-imposed silence and he's no longer constrained by tight NYC docker coats and woolly hats: Corbijn frames his new denim dungarees and wild black curly hair with masterful gravitas; Bernard Sumner of New Order topless in the long hot New York summer of '82 on the cover, Stephen Morris wearing googly false eyes inside, leering like a premonition of acid house's euphoric, steamy madness coming six years down the track.

There were even occasions when the photos and words were such a perfect marriage that they rank as fondly in memory as a one-off hit single.

I vividly recall pulling *NME* from its mailer when the issue with Paul Weller looking serious and suited in black and white on the front fell on to the kitchen table in March 1984. I tore through its pages in heart-fluttering anticipation. Its insides revealed photos by Derek Ridgers of Weller and Mick Talbot from the Style Council in immaculate tailoring sitting across a boardroom table from journalists Tony Parsons and X Moore, all four locked in sullen, angry debate beneath the headline Long Hot Summit. This was heavy-duty music journalism!

I have all these images and dozens more burnt into my memory, as fundamental to the music I mythologise and adore as any performance I've seen. The interviews, the photos, the headlines, the covers, the reviews, the sarcasm, the passion, the captions: it's all integral to the journey I've been on with the music I love (as well as the music I hate). Later, when I became a music writer, those images inspired the kind of stories I wanted to tell.

NME also shaped my politics. Would I have worn a 'coal not dole' sticker on my school bag as a fourteen-year-old kid living in the Parisian suburbs without my *NME* subscription? Unlikely. It revealed to me worlds of outsider film, literature and television that were not on the O-level curriculum. I absorbed and trusted its evangelism for contemporary youth culture implicitly, seeing the world through its lens, until I left home and had to take a look for myself. Even then *NME* remained my homing device, a cultural compass.

Later, as a doofus delinquent adrift in adulthood, *NME* literally saved my life. I was seemingly unemployable when *NME* took a chance on me, brought me in from the cold, threw me a line. Before, the world had not really made sense. I was bluffing my way through the day-to-day. *NME* fixed me. It fit me.

I was – and remain – evangelical about contemporary music. That's what excites me most. I always want to share news of new sounds. At *NME*, they asked their writers, photographers and editors to build narrative worlds around contemporary music so that readers felt compelled to join us in exploring. I was the man for that. It's the *New Musical Express*: the clue is in the name. The brief was to sketch the first draft of musical history each week, and telling an unknown story is always more satisfying work than nostalgia (though writing this book has contradicted that somewhat).

NME designed a musical culture. It made sense of the artists, joined the dots between them, dramatised their scenarios. We provided context, added hyperbole, poked fun at it all. Build it up, tear it down, rebuild. Fifty-one issues a year, hundreds of new stories to tell and the weekly readership – 100,000 strong – were integral members of the crew. They were our friends, our followers, our confidants, our advisers and, sometimes, our adversaries, heckling and turning their backs when our steers were bum.

The first two years working at *NME* were an eye-popping high of collaborative creative joy the like of which I will never taste again; the rest of the time was spent chasing that buzz with ever-diminishing returns. Then, one day eight years later, you wonder what you're doing there. Who are all these kids?

Staff, contributors and subscribers of defunct rivals reading this greased-lens *NME* fable are now no doubt rolling their eyes, tongues out. Understandable. As former Arsenal manager Arsène Wenger once said mockingly to a crowing rival, everyone thinks they have the prettiest wife at home.

There were, of course, other British weeklies and monthlies devoted to telling their story of contemporary music, each with its own sizeable cult following, distinctive personality, its own language of love and laughter. *Sounds, Melody Maker, Select*: the mourning at each of their respective closures in 1991, 2000 and '01 was profound and sincere. That intense, poetically self-righteous championing of new underground music that *Melody Maker* practised so powerfully still influences a lot of what can be found on websites now, but it's one-dimensional in comparison. As for *Smash Hits*, which left this world in 2006 . . . *Smash Hits* invented a manner to deal with sparkly pop stars and po-faced musicians that was uniformly riveting. It was punchy, irreverent, hilarious but always heartfelt. At its peak throughout the 1980s and early nineties its humour, its lightness of touch, its innovative interviewing techniques brought pop stars into its universe in a way that no other media has really managed. Opening a biscuit tin and asking Elton John or Janet Jackson to pull out a random question is one of the great editorial devices.

It also gave birth to writers such as Chris Heath, Miranda Sawyer, Tom Hibbert, Sylvia Patterson and many other voices so commanding, confident and distinctive that when they grew too mature for sparky pop-star Q&As and pithy single reviews, new publications had to be built for them to populate and edit, dragging hundreds of thousands of readers along with them.

Q, and later to a lesser degree *Select*, then patented a new form of music journalism to deal with mainstream album makers that drew on *Smash Hits'* lightness of touch, but could go in deeper than anywhere else since 1970s *Rolling Stone* on international superstars (not that anyone ever managed to finish a dry old *Rolling Stone* piece, but that was the inspiration). *Q*'s niche became the 4,000-word, multiple-meeting profile with a household name: dig out Adrian Deevoy's raised eyebrow, boiled sweet sucking encounters with Prince, Madonna, George Michael or Bob Dylan for an illustration of how delicious an interview with a superstar can be. It'll have been a long while since you've tasted anything like it.

Those were also all good schools. I even attended some of them. But I was an *NME* student, through and through. I still wear that old tie.

There's a cliché that decrees that former *NME* staff always hate what follows their departure. That, in their opinion, subsequent versions of the paper are invariably worse than their own era. Not so in my case. I think *NME* improved for a good while after I left. They had a healthy crop of classic domestic *NME* acts in the early-mid noughties, like the Libertines, Franz Ferdinand, the Cribs and, in particular, Arctic Monkeys, and their readers and writers all seemed to be largely the same age as these acts. The classic formula for a healthy music weekly. They sabotaged that by chasing brand power at the cost of their central proposition, foolishly believing they were like Virgin – a brand name that could diversify into anything. Eventually they determined that advertisers rather than readers would save them, so they went for the reach of giving their paper issues away for free in train stations during the mid-2010s until they discovered the limits to the appetite for a music weekly from non-music fan commuters; huge piles of mashed-up *NME*s littered the London Underground, the advertisers withdrew and *NME* became simply an online proposition. Every now and then I'll come across a pop-up plug for their weekly online 'cover story' and I grind my teeth to dust.

I didn't read *NME* much after I left, however, as I had my own mission navigating the more stately and uptight monthly process at *Q*. I'd finally nailed it fifteen years later and was filling the magazine with the kind of long-form music journalism and story-telling I'd always dreamed of producing, until they then decided that enough was enough and pulled the plug there as well. And that was the end of contemporary music journalism in periodic form for mass audiences in the UK. Night night.

A music writer friend recently messaged me in distress. Though considerably younger than I am, she's still a music mag veteran, someone who grew up writing as a freelancer for some of the periodicals mentioned above. She can turn a trick for *Mojo* or *Uncut* if needs be, tell an old story from the 1960s, seventies, eighties or nineties when commissioned to do so. But what she really wants to do is write a story about the artists of today who are dreaming up incredible sounds, getting into scrapes, fighting their own demons, who are connected by undocumented scenes and evolving dramas. The many fans of these artists would no doubt love to hear such tales. My friend finds it very hard to pitch these ideas, though, because there's nowhere to print them.

The options seem to be to donate them to the noble indie web-sites or small-run print zines who'll pour all their coins on to the kitchen table and pay something symbolic for the labour. Or, if it's a living you crave, you contact one of the newspapers who still cover music in their arts sections. This is what she texted about.

'I very much resent having to play nice and sucky with these eunuchs,' she wrote to me.

There is a breed of well-educated young British men and women who pass all their exams, enter a graduate training scheme at national newspapers, progress through various desks, trying a bit of news, a bit of sport, maybe features, until they settle on arts. They've always enjoyed music. They put on some gigs at their union back in the day. Before you know it, they're commissioning all the music reviews and features at the *Guardian*, *Times*, *Independent* or *FT*. How about that? Sometimes, if it's a nice job with one of their favourites, they'll commission themselves to write the story, but mostly they order in. They'll have their star contracted reviewer, usually as old as I am, who has to dredge up an opinion every week about the latest blockbuster album and tour regardless of original insight, who is always poised with an obituary or op-ed about a music news item, and who can turn their hand to the forty-five-minute hotel interview junket every fortnight or so.

For the other story or two each week, plus the handful of small reviews, the commissioning editor will turn to their bulging inbox and pluck a freelancer. There are a lot of freelancers to choose from. The commissioner doesn't want to hear pitches about the big stars releasing records that month, they'll already have their bids in for those forty-five-minute hotel junkets. The commissioning editor will have one or two further stories to choose a week for the music section from dozens of strong ideas pitched. There's no music policy on a national newspaper. Just make it interesting, comes the instruction from on high. It's a tough choice, and it must be wearing delivering so much disappointment to desperate writers. In the end, the paper will probably go for an esoteric or underground artist, or perhaps a trend-based story. The commissioning editor will be governed by their own taste in terms of artist profile, naturally.

In normal circumstances, with a robust music press, none of this is a problem. It's a necessary differential. But when it amounts almost entirely to the large-scale print journalism around contemporary music in Britain it is desperate. The heritage music magazines will produce one or two features about contemporary artists that fit their mature demographic every month, they'll have excellent review sections too, but there's a vast number of good music stories that are unreported, especially from the middle market. Band on decent third album, selling out a three-week tour of one- or two-thousand ticket venues? Not a story that's ever covered, even though the real tale can only ever be unpeeled by investigation and there's a big constituency hungry for it. American singer-songwriter, over to perform songs from her sixth solo album on Jools Holland and headline a few theatres in the big cities? We'll never know the devastating provenance of those songs, the personal tale behind it. Say there's a British rapper who, after years of not having hits, has now broken through with a landmark single and accompanying album – there's no way he's going to speak with newspaper journalists, or any journalists, as he has no relationship with the press. They haven't been interested before now. He can just speak directly via his social media instead, maybe give an interview to Radio 1.

Where's the context, the drama, the myths and fables around these and other modern artists? How can anyone love them properly, engage with their musical journey, take the piss out of them, if we don't know who they really are? Where's the iconography? If Pennie Smith didn't take a photo of you wearing that incredible hat, did you ever really put it on?

New music is not less popular nor is it diminishing in quality. Every year when filling in my albums of the year vote for *NME* or *Q* I'd always dad-joke in the office that it was 'the best year for music'. I'd mean it too (apart from in 1999). This year is no different. I recently filled in my top twenty list for *Mojo*, and could have filled it twice over. As I read it back, though, I realised that the only back stories I knew behind all the records came from the press releases that accompanied them, from some reviews I'd read or from my imagination.

Considering this, I wondered how heritage magazines will function in thirty years if all the juicy music stories after 2020 are no longer properly witnessed, described and illustrated? Where will they look up the history of the 2020s? As Mark E. Smith pointed out in the Fall's 'Putta Block' way back in 1981, 'The only reason you know this is because it was well documented.'

All is not lost. In fact, the destruction of the music press may present an opportunity to the budding music writer. Better that the old structure be gone entirely rather than some remnants are kept alive to provide false hope of gathering crumbs tossed from the table. It's year zero for music journalism. Let's start again from the bottom up.

Document music culture. It's yours.

The unemployable twenty-one-year-old delinquent doofus is faced with the same choices that I was thirty-odd years ago in their position. I loved music, I wanted to write and I had nothing else to do. I didn't do it for money, for a career in journalism. That seemed as likely as becoming a pilot. I just wanted to do something other than stare out of the window. I did it for free, I did it for fun.

Then, we contributed to fanzines. Now technology has evolved. Email newsletters provide a direct route to potential like-minded readers and communities; instead of standing outside venues waving photocopies around, we have social media to signal what we like, who we are. Who needs big international publishing houses with their printing presses, marketing budgets, distribution

networks, fancy offices and free pastries, their armies of accountants and sales teams? We have the Internet! We have broadband.

I started a newsletter on the Substack platform after *Q* closed
with a couple of colleagues, Niall Doherty and Chris Catchpole.
Hilariously, we called it *The New Cue*. Do you get it? We now produce three newsletters a week for around 7,000 email sign-ups
and near enough 1,000 subscribers. We provide interviews with
interesting music makers, recommendations for tracks, albums,
playlists, books – you name it. We get people to tell us the story
behind the song they wrote that you love; we ask your favourite
musician to blow our minds with an offbeat album choice. That
kind of thing. It's twentieth-century-style editorial content delivered on twenty-first-century platforms: a music paper you can
read on your phone, on your laptop, taking care of other business.
We're going straight to the reader, cutting out the middleman.

The photos we run are always selfies provided by the interviewee, which is a long way from an Anton Corbijn or Kevin
Cummins portrait, but nevertheless adds a bespoke immediacy
to the publication (I like to think). *The New Cue* keeps us busy
and it's satisfying work because it doesn't really feel like work,
which is what music journalism was like when I first started
producing it, long before I was invited to publishing meetings
in air-conditioned meeting rooms with marketeers, accountants
and advertising dynamos. It has given me an insight, I believe,
into a future for music journalism in the 2020s and how that gap
may be plugged by music-mad kids who like reading and writing,
making their way beyond the editorial gatekeepers, connecting
with like minds.

First of all, be young. This is important. You can be old too,
but that market is over-subscribed and very competitive. If you're
young (and there's no pandemic raging) go to gigs, go to raves,
get amongst it as much as possible. Listen to music radio whenever you can. Share music, stream it, buy it if at all possible but
don't feel guilty if you can't – just remember that you definitely

will buy it when able to. And read everything old and new that you can lay your eyes upon.

Right, you're ready.

Open a newsletter account with one of the platform providers. Doesn't matter which yet. It's free. Mess about with its design. It's easy, isn't it? Any idiot can do this. Think of a name. Go on. Anything will do. How about Cloak & Dagger? It's meaningless but we need something.

Now, decide what you're going to produce for Cloak & Dagger. Let's say you're going to pick one of your favourite current music-makers to interview, Q&A style, every week. Maybe you'll throw in a gig review of something you saw, make a playlist of your favourite new tunes, recommend an album. (This all sounds very familiar. Have your own ideas, please: they'll be better.) I'd take pictures of people I see at gigs or clubs that I like the look of and run those (with permission), but that's just me. You could stick those on your Instagram to lure people over. Just an idea.

Now, you ask, how do I get to interview my favourite rappers, singers and players? Make a list of them. Google each press representative, making a particular note of their digital PR. These people are your friends. They need you, you need them. Together, you can make each other's dreams come true. Email one, state your business, ask if you could possibly interview their charges for your music newsletter, please. Be friendly, be polite. Tell them Ted Kessler sent you. If they don't reply, try another in a few days. You'll be surprised how happy they are to furnish you with interview time on the whole, though. Everyone wants to feel wanted, so the PRs will do their best to put you together with newer artists as they need to fill those allocated hours of promo. There's nobody else taking up that time. Once you've had a few of these interviews released into the wild, the PRs will start contacting you. Like I said, you need each other.

Doing these first interviews with newer artists means that you're building relationships with them. They'll remember that you were there at the start when that dickhead from the *Standard* couldn't be bothered to even open the link to play his promo releases. Who does Stormzy trust now, who does Florence Welch or Alex Turner let in? By and large, they'll only talk to those people who were always there, who they know won't do them wrong, who aren't jumping upon a bandwagon. Get there early. You spotted them first and you're both at the beginning of your journeys. Show them your worth. That could be you in the role of trusted confidant when you're both peaking in five years.

Start gathering material and, when you're ready, publish. Make sure you always publish at the same time on the same day each week. Don't over-commit, but stick with your plan no matter what – that's how you'll gather readers. Be reliable. Listen to criticism and advice, but stay true to your instincts. Let fans of the artists you cover know via social media what you have done, ask them to spread the word. You should encourage comments on your posts so that you build a community.

Collaborate with other writers and photographers or graphic artists, reach out to them, don't be aloof: nothing beats making ideas happen with kindred spirits, even if they are very different from you in many ways. You learn about yourself and people in doing so. Slowly, your publication will bloom, as will you. Congratulations. You are now a publisher.

From these seeds a new music journalism will grow. We'll have to see what shape it assumes, how it connects and mutates. I can't guarantee everyone will be successful, but it'll be a caper, it'll be enriching. Who knows where it may lead? And if there's any money in it, well, maybe you'll see some of that. If you don't, that's OK. We had a good craic. We learned something.

There will be successes, there will be glorious failure, there will be tales to tell. In thirty years' time I hope to be opening your book upon my deathbed, learning all about the adventure you've been on, about the worlds you created, the future you imagined, the past you saved.

Afterword

It was on Primrose Hill, drunk on my final day as editor of *Q*, eating an ice cream with a friend, that I decided I was going to write a book about my experiences. I had quite a set idea for it. I wanted to deliver a series of short stories from across my working life. The tales would all be very tight and punchy, each about a specific incident. The focus would be narrow. Invariably, I would be the only fall guy in the story, the butt of the joke. I wanted to convey the career and lifestyle arc of someone arrested in their place of employment at twenty-one. The working title I had was *Anecdotal Evidence*.

Perhaps you can tell which chapters I wrote first.

Very quickly, the book became something else. It's only as you begin writing an autobiographical story that you realise what you are writing. I told one friend what I was working on and they wondered if I'd included the story of how I shoplifted from the model shop I was ordering stock for, as he'd always thought that was surreal. I hadn't, but I said I'd consider it. Another asked if there would be something about how much trouble my haircuts had got me into on the streets of Paris. I replied that wasn't on the agenda, but I would chew it over . . .

Soon I realised I needed to go back to the beginning.

It's symbolic that the idea for the book came to me on Primrose Hill. When you're on that mound, looking out across London, the view hoodwinks you. Some distant parts of the capital appear much closer than you imagined, others feel as if they're in the wrong place. Near parts of Central London can barely be seen, other suburban areas are clearly defined. So it came to be with my memories.

I tried to be as reliable a narrator as possible. I did not bend the truth at any stage so as to appear a better, more honourable or decent person than I am (which is to say, not particularly). I did not want to hurt anybody, either, but I know there will probably be one or two who appear in the pages who may dispute their characterisation. I told my truth, is all I can say. In the case of one or two of the workplace dramas that I relate, I ran them by witnesses for verification. I believe I was fair in every instance. I own my behaviour. It's good to do that.

Besides, *Paper Cuts* is not a venue for score-settling. It's about me, an everyday idiot, trying to share my story so others can laugh and cry along, recognise their own idiocies and perhaps feel inspired to avoid some of my errors if able. I would include my children in this, yet they're not allowed to read the book until they are adults or, better still, I am dead.

I started the book at a time when I felt lost, devoid of direction, at an age when a new career seemed unlikely and my skill set made it an impossibility, those feelings intensified by the pandemic and lockdown. I end the book in a similar place, uncertain of what happens next.

In between these two miseries, as I wrote *Paper Cuts*, I felt alive, enthused, whole. Billy Childish once told me that he created his art as a 'conversation with God'. I came to understand that. All that we are is what we leave behind; creation is the highest state of being.

So, though I am today bereft, I know where relief lies ahead. I'll see you there.

Acknowledgements

Business time

All praise to Lee Brackstone at White Rabbit for signing and editing the book, and to special agent Becky Thomas of Lewinsohn Literary for wise counsel throughout.

Thanks to Ellie Freedman, Kasimiira Kontio, Tom Noble, Martha Sprackland and Clarissa Sutherland for know-how.

Steve Marking for the jacket.

Thanks, too, to Jenny Lord for always putting in a good word for me when required, and to anyone else at Orion whose work on this publication I do not currently know about. I appreciate it nonetheless.

Thanks for the memories

The inner-circle: Jean, Jagger, Joey forever. Maximum love and respect. (But do as I say, not as I did.)

Anne, Felix, Mark, Daniel, Gaby, Jair, Jim, Liv, Rose, Sasha, Florence, JB, Layla and all Kessler clan members, including each Bacall. Carole and the Coffeys, too.

The Strettells: Su, James, Jo, Polly, David.

Tei, Michelle, Phil, Tamsin, Louis-Marc, Omar, Charly, Olivier, Kate, Alain, Claire, Katie, Morgan, Sean, Tiffany, Kathryn, Chris and all other co-conspirators, 1980–85.

Jo and The Butlers.

Jake Cunningham, Barnaby Hall, Matt Aarons, Ben Rayner, Tim Altmann, David Tonge, Rupert May, Andrea, Oliver Lim, Myf Moore.

Britt and Patrick. Steve Lamacq.

Simon Williams, John Harris, Johnny 'Cigarettes' Sharp, Paul Moody, Keith Cameron, Iestyn George, John Mulvey, Sam Steele, Gina Morris, Sherman At The Controls, Stephen Dalton, Barbara Ellen, Angela Lewis, Angus Batey, Brendan Fitzgerald, Andy Fyfe, Kathy Ball, Ian McCann, Steve Sutherland, Stuart Baillie, Johnny Dee, Cate Jago, Gill Sutherland, Grainne Mooney, John Perry, Karen Walter, David Quantick, Roger Morton, Jody Thompson, Mark Sutherland.

James Oldham, Andy Capper, Neil Thomson, John Robinson.

Kevin Cummins, Roger Sargent, Derek Ridgers, Andy Willsher, Martyn Goodacre, Ed Sirrs, Kevin Westenberg, Steve Double, Steve Gullick, Tom Sheehan, Peter Walsh.

Acknowledgements

Kitty Empire, April Long, Victoria Segal, Paul McNamee, Siobhan Grogan, Alan Woodhouse, Kris Short, Martin Boon, Phil Savill, Lindsey McWhinnie, Matt Phare, Martin Horsfield, Conor McNicholas, Ben Knowles.

Jo McCaughey, Helen McLaughlin, Alex Needham, Marion Patterson. Nicky Deeley and Nicola Searle.

Paul Stokes, Jamie Woolgar.

Jeff Barrett, Robin Turner, James Endeacott, Carl Gosling, Danny Mitchell, Martin Kelly, Austen Harris, Grace and Mandy, Swank, Ivan, and anyone who has erased time with me in The Chris Penn Suite of The Social.

Niall Doherty and Chris Catchpole.

Gareth Grundy, Simon McEwen, Daniel Knight, Andrew Harrison, Rob Fearn, Paul Rees, Dave Everley, Sophie Watson-Smyth, Mark Blake, Rupert Howe, Matt Yates, Matt Mason, Joe Bishop, Eve Barlow, Paul Elliott, Cilla Warncke, Peter Kane, Salman Naqvi, Mark Taylor, Steve Peck, Ian Whent, Ian Stevens, Mic Wright, Steve Dobson, Russ O'Connell, Marguerite Peck, Helen Scott, Dave Brolan.

Dorian Lynskey, Sylvia Patterson, Tom Doyle, Laura Barton, Laura Snapes, Simon Goddard, Andy Perry, Matt Allen, Alex Lake, Andrew Cotterill, Andrew Whitton, Mick Hutson, Rachael Wright.

Anna Wood.

Matt Turner, Mark 'Wag' Wagstaff.

Phil Alexander, Danny Eccleston, Ian Harrison, Pat Gilbert, Jenny Bulley, Andrew Male, Geoff Brown, Russell Moorcraft, Ali Rees.

Terri White.

All musicians mentioned (and many I have not, especially those who I have interviewed), but thanks in particular for support with this book: Paul Weller, Florence Welch, Billy Childish, Liam Gallagher, Miki Berenyi, Jah Wobble, Emma Anderson, Baxter Dury, Felix White, Jason Williamson. Thanks, too, to Frank Cottrell-Boyce.

The ghosts of Regents Park Thursdays and Finsbury Sundays.

All music PRs, other than those I must avoid. Let's have a long lunch, please, Phoebe Sinclair, Laura Martin, Susie Ember, Louise Mayne, Ruth and Beth Drake, Amanda Freeman, Terri Hall, Polly Birkbeck, Andy Prevezer, Sophie Williams, Ted Cummings, Steve Philips, Stuart Kirkham, Barbara Charone, Carl Delahunty, Julie Bland, Natalie Quesnel, Gillian Porter, Morad Khokar, Mick Houghton, Sarah Pearson, Ben Ayers. Debbie and Katie Gwyther, of course.

Pour one out for:

John Brooker, David Cavanagh, George Dyer, Dele Fadele, Pat Long, Eugene Manzi, Gavin Martin, Marc Pechart, Steven Wells.

To anyone I have forgotten, I am sorry.

Thank you for reading.